HISTORY OF AMERICAN THOUGHT AND CULTURE

Paul S. Boyer, *General Editor*

T0164149

AMERICAN FICTION IN THE COLD WAR

Thomas Hill Schaub

The University of Wisconsin Press

The University of Wisconsin Press
1930 Monroe Street, 3rd floor
Madison, Wisconsin 53711-2059
uwpress.wisc.edu

3 Henrietta Street
London WC2E 8LU, England
eurospanbookstore.com

Printed in the United States of America

Library of Congress Cataloging-in-Publication Data
Schaub, Thomas H., 1947–
    American fiction in the Cold War / Thomas Hill Schaub.
    224 pp.   cm.—(History of American thought and culture)
    Includes bibliographical references (p. 195) and index.
    1. American fiction—20th century—History and criticism.
2. Political fiction, American—History and criticism.
3. Liberalism in literature.   4. Cold War in literature.   I. Title.
II. Series.
PS374.P6S3   1981
813' .5409358—dc20
ISBN 0-299-12840-7   90-50652
ISBN 0-299-12844-X   CIP

ISBN-13: 978-0-299-12844-9 (pbk: alk. paper)

Contents

Preface

To write history is so difficult that most historians are forced to make concessions to the technique of legend.

Erich Auerbach

And what I sought throughout this book were significant features. Is this a significance which *I* read into them? In other words, is there a mythology of the mythologist? No doubt, and the reader will easily see where I stand.

Roland Barthes

This book is about the discourse of revisionist liberalism—what was then called "the new liberalism"—as it appears within the discussion and practice of fiction in the United States during the forties and fifties. The origins of my study, however, were another time and place, in which I set out to defend the experimental writing of the sixties and seventies against the criticisms of it in such books as Gerald Graff's *Literature Against Itself*. I thought the way to do this involved knowing the history of recent experimentalism, and this quickly returned me to the decade of the forties when such writers as John Hawkes, Kurt Vonnegut, Norman Mailer, Flannery O'Connor, and Ralph Ellison first began publishing their work. Once there, I found that the arguments of the critics I meant to engage also had their origins in this time, when both writer and critic were in the process of renegotiating the relationship between politics and aesthetics.

I began to think that what I had been researching as a confrontation between forms of writing, or aesthetic values, was really an expression of political turmoil, in which the nature and obligations of writing were altered in response to the decline of the left, to the fact of Hiroshima, Nagasaki and the Holocaust, and to the anticommunism which dominated politics and culture for some years afterward. The "new liberalism" was born from the trials of this "crucible," in the metaphor Arthur Miller used to suggest, among other things, the inquisition then taking place in the House Committee on Un-American Activities.

The story of chastened liberalism which emerged in accounts of the transition from thirties radicalism to postwar "realism" I call the "liberal narrative." This book investigates how that narrative reappears within—helps to constitute and influence—literary discourse of American criticism and fiction in the fifteen years after the Second War. Not surprisingly, this narrative functions as a kind of subliminal or lesser-order cultural myth, not identical with the rhetoric of the "American Century," but posing that nationalism little threat. The first chapter describes this narrative and its wide dispersion among a number of influential cultural texts.

The next three chapters show that what are ostensibly a set of oppositional debates—between New Critics and New York intellectuals, and between both sets of critics and the new writers of the postwar—are nevertheless debates in which both sides accept a common set of assumptions. All are inhabited and constrained by terms of the new liberal discourse—all are soaked in its language and its representation of recent history and culture. The manner in which liberal discourse appears in the four writers I discuss in Part 2—Ellison, O'Connor, Mailer, and Barth—varies considerably, but one would expect the negotiation of discourses to alter with the cultural circumstances of each. With Ellison one is inevitably thrust into the relations between liberal discourse and the black community in the forties. O'Connor's work emerges from a southern view that positions itself in opposition to liberal sentiment. Mailer's essay "The White Negro" is particularly useful because it shows the undertow of liberalism operating within a text ostensibly devoted to its critique. When John Barth began to write, the relations of art and politics were of little interest to him, and his play with representation seems to evolve into the "metafiction" of the Vietnam years entirely within the aesthetic terms of literary tradition. In all these writers the liberal narrative may be shown operating within their work, sometimes allowing it to proceed with ease while at others disturbing the effort of writing to present itself whole.

To the degree that my project attempts to identify the sources for a new discourse, I have been interested in showing an "interpretive community" come into being, showing how this new community acquires its sense of what is natural and given, of what goes without saying, and how these givens, in turn, operate within a range of cultural narratives, for the most part literary and intellectual. Although four of the chapters are devoted to individual writers, the book is continuously about the way a revised explanatory paradigm operates within a variety of texts.

Much of this book was written during 1986–87 with a National Endowment for the Humanities Research Fellowship. I would like to thank the members of the fellowship committee for their interest and confidence in the project. The Graduate School of the University of Wisconsin also provided me with two summers of research support. These two granting agencies have been of immeasurable help by providing the time to immerse myself in my subject, temporarily free of other academic duties.

Even so, the writing of this book has occupied me for several years. During this period of what often seemed to be the never-ending story, I have had the advice and conversation of many people. Among those who read parts of the manuscript in various stages I want to thank Robert Bloom, James B. Breslin, Mitchell Breitwieser, Joel Drucker, Phil Gould, Gerald Graff, Eric Meyer, Nellie McKay, Masao Myoshi, Sherman Paul, Carolyn Porter, Michael Rogin, Eric J. Sandeen, Gilbert Sorrentino, Khachig Tölölyan, and Joseph Wiesenfarth.

The chapter on Ralph Ellison evolved from an essay I wrote for Robert O'Meally's *New Essays on Ellison's Invisible Man* (Cambridge University Press 1988). I would like to thank Cambridge University Press for permission to reprint brief passages from that essay. I also want to take this opportunity to thank Robert O'Meally, John Callahan, and Kimberly Benston for their help in preparing that first essay; writing that piece enabled me to write the second, which appears here. The careful and thoughtful critiques that Greg S. Jay and Leah Marcus gave this chapter helped me to see what I was trying to do.

I wish to note my special debt to Susan Friedman, Gordon Hutner, and Eric Rothstein, each of whom gave me detailed responses to the chapters on Mailer and Barth. To Gordon Hutner I owe special thanks, for his willingness, during a crucial period in my reassessment of this study, to engage me in discussion about subject and method. Howard Brick provided a thorough report that was invaluable to me in revising the manuscript.

I am grateful to Barbara Hanrahan of the University of Wisconsin Press for her assistance and good humor, and to Susan Tarcov for her skilled editing. For his encouragement and support of my project from its beginnings, I want to express my gratitude to Allen Fitchen, director of the Press, and finally to Paul Boyer, general editor of the History of American Thought and Culture series, who gave me detailed comments and advice at every stage of the writing.

The book is dedicated to Bonnie Munroe Schaub and to Jessica Ann, our daughter, who have, it might be said, insisted that there is a life beyond the book, if not the text.

Part 1

1

Introduction

The Liberal Narrative

> From now onwards the all-important fact for the creative writer is going
> to be that this is not a writer's world. That does not mean that he cannot
> help to bring the new society into being, but he can take no part in the
> process *as a writer*. For *as a writer* he is a liberal, and what is happening
> is the destruction of liberalism.
>
> George Orwell, 1940

> I got along fine with Marshal Stalin. . . . I would call him something like
> me, . . . a realist.
>
> Franklin Roosevelt, 1943

I

On August 22, 1939, Alfred Kazin was in New York at work on his
study of modern American literature, published three years later as *On
Native Grounds*. At this time, Hitler was already occupying Austria and
the Sudetenland, and had taken Czechoslovakia in March. The Spanish
Civil War was in its last year, and stories circulated about the GPU (Soviet
secret police) massacre of anti-Stalinist communists and anarchists, dividing the left and undermining its common cause against the fascist forces
of Franco and Hitler. Kazin was already disgusted by the Moscow trials,
begun in 1936, but still assumed the Soviet Union would keep the promise
of the Popular Front to maintain unity against fascism. English and French
military missions were then in Moscow, and Kazin expected to hear news
of some agreement among the nations against Germany. At noon on the
twenty-second of August, during a break from his writing, Kazin heard over
the radio that Ribbentrop, the German foreign minister, would be in Moscow the next day to sign a nonaggression pact with Stalin. "No!" he shouted

3

at the radio. "It's not true!" The treaty was signed on the twenty-third, and nine days later, on September 1, 1939, Hitler marched into Poland without declaring war.

What I am calling the "liberal narrative" has its origins in the experience of disillusionment—of betrayal—that I have retold from Kazin's memoir, *Starting Out in the Thirties* (137–41). In varying degree, Kazin's astonishment was repeated throughout the intellectual community which defined itself as left of center, from New Deal liberal to socialist to anti-Stalinist Trotskyite, to member of the Communist Party. In his book *Writers on the Left*, Daniel Aaron notes that for each writer the cause of final disenchantment with the party varied (309–13), but the collective accounts of this period suggest the purges of the Moscow show trials and Stalin's self-interest in making peace with Hitler were the principal events that exhausted the allegiance of liberals in the United States.[1] Asked why American intellectuals after World War II no longer seemed at odds with American culture, as they had been throughout the twenties and thirties, Philip Rahv, editor of *Partisan Review*, pointed to the record of Stalinist communism: "Among the factors entering into the change, the principal one, to my mind, is the exposure of the Soviet myth and the consequent resolve (shared by nearly all but the few remaining fellow travelers) to be done with Utopian illusions and heady expectations" ("Our Country," 304). Introducing *Homage to Catalonia*, George Orwell's account of the Spanish Civil War, Lionel Trilling summarized the experience of an entire generation: "We tried as hard as we could to believe that politics might be an idyll, only to discover that what we took to be a political pastoral was really a grim military campaign or a murderous betrayal of political allies. . . . The evidence of this is to be found in a whole literary genre with which we have become familiar in the last decade, the personal confession of involvement and then of disillusionment with Communism" ("Politics of Truth," 63).

1.   Alan Wald describes the Moscow trials as a "decisive event that simultaneously consolidated the anti-Stalinist left while setting the stage for its disintegration" (128); Norman Holmes Pearson identified the Nazi-Soviet Non-Aggression Pact as the "crisis" which "brought an end to the decade that had begun with the Depression, and joined enemy to apparent friend in a confusion of loyalties that shattered the confidence of many writers" (439).

   The relationship between politics and literature in the thirties and forties in the United States is the subject of a large number of studies and essays, many of which I refer to within the text. In addition, readers interested in this subject should consult Terry Cooney's *The Rise of the New York Intellectuals*, Murray Kempton's "The Literature of Crisis," collected in *Part of Our Time*, Christopher Lasch's *The Agony of the American Left*, Geraldine Murphy's "The Politics of Reading *Billy Budd*," and Walter Rideout's *The Radical Novel in the United States 1900–1954*. Mark Walhout's exploration of the "*interdiscursive* context" of the New Criticism, in "The New Criticism and the Crisis of American Liberalism," is especially relevant to my own project.

The liberal narrative isn't simply the fairly repetitive accounts of recent intellectual fellow traveling, but concerns instead the elemental assumptions and structures one finds within them. Several of these are present in Trilling's sweeping remarks above, in which the complex and varied involvement of a heterogeneous group of men and women is subordinated to a Blakean journey from innocence to experience, from the myopia of the utopian to the twenty-twenty vision of the realist. I identify this as a *liberal* narrative, rather than "radical" or "communist," because the term "liberalism" adequately encompasses the spectrum of those interested in social reform, and because the word denotes, as many have written, a "habit of mind" rather than a specific creed. The word "liberalism" refers not to a monolithic or univocal event, set of people, or doctrine, but to a moiré of usage, invoking an indeterminate array of connotations, each of which brings into play other terms and meanings. Dozens of books and essays have been written attempting to define the essence of liberalism, and to provide it with an origin, a history, and a tradition. My study attempts no such definition of liberalism; instead, I am interested in the accounts of liberalism produced in the wake of the thirties and forties and the recurrent story line one finds within them.[2] The discourse of "the new liberalism" is

2. As Stuart Hall notes, "Liberalism" as a proper noun refers to the "political creed, associated with the Liberal Party which dominated British politics in the nineteenth century," while the term "liberal" "denotes 'an attitude of mind rather than a political creed' " (34). By 1945, one might accurately point out that liberalism had been in crisis for over half a century. Perhaps the most famous articulation of liberal thought is L. T. Hobhouse, *Liberalism*, published in 1911, in which he sets forth the view that British liberalism of the nineteenth century was by then defunct and in need of a "new liberalism." As Hall notes, there seemed to be a perfect fit in the nineteenth century between "the commitment to radical individualism and the passionate belief in *laissez-faire*" (65).

Hobhouse wrote at a time when the conflict between these two commitments had become apparent, and published his book in part to reformulate liberalism as a doctrine or set of assumptions that would turn liberalism toward social reform, while still preserving individual freedoms. Hobhouse wanted to define a line between conservatives (whom he called Imperialists) and radicals (whom he called the Socialists), by describing a "Liberal Socialism" (90) that would provide the means of opportunity but not the actual sustenance: "It is for the State to take care that the economic conditions are such that the normal man who is not defective in mind or body can or will by useful labour feed, house, and clothe himself and his family," but "it is not for the State to feed, house, or clothe them" (83). Thus in almost all accounts "liberalism" was founded upon individual freedom and freedom of trade from state intervention, but evolved to the position that trade must be restricted in the interest of the individual and social welfare—what Harold Laski, citing Chamberlain, called the "gospel of ransom" by which the rich justify their wealth by paying off the poor with "the social service state" (275).

The relevance of British liberalism should be apparent. Not only is liberalism an attitude underlying political practice and theory common to both American and British traditions, but the shift of definition that Hobhouse advocated was in effect executed by the Roosevelt administration in the 1930s. The programs of that administration were the occasion of a renewed

concretely available to our study in these accounts. In them we find no hesitancy to define "liberalism" as an identifiable phenomenon, with a specific history and set of attributes, though these definitions should be understood less as neutral accounts of "liberalism" than as strategic maneuvers in a struggle of vested interests both political and personal.

Certainly by August of 1939 a great many liberals, social democrats, socialists, and communists had long ago separated themselves from Stalinist communism, developed loyalties to Trotsky or other communist and socialist alternatives, or had turned their backs on communism altogether. Their decisions were invariably accompanied by narratives of maturation and realism, of awakening to a more sober and skeptical perception of

---

concern with definition—of liberalism, of government's role, of the United States itself—as all the old issues by which the relations of state and individual were negotiated resurfaced under the economic conditions of the Depression and government efforts to ameliorate them.

John Dewey's essay *Liberalism and Social Action* (1935), for example, not only takes a view similar to the one Hobhouse advanced, but gives us some indication of the instability of the term "liberalism" within the political debate of the period. Dewey's thesis was that the "crisis in liberalism" arose from the fact that it was a philosophy that provided for the liberation of individuals but did not provide for their reorganization into groups and institutions that preserve and encourage the full development of their individualities: "The eclipse of liberalism is due to the fact that it has not faced the alternatives and adopted the means upon which realization of its professed aims depends . . . the notion that organized social control of economic forces lies outside the historic path of liberalism shows that liberalism is still impeded by remnants of its earlier *laissez-faire* phase, with its opposition of society and the individual. The thing which now dampens liberal ardor and paralyzes its efforts is the conception that liberty and the development of individuality as ends exclude the use of organized social effort as means. . . . We must reverse the perspective and see that socialized economy is the means of free individual development as the end" (90).

Dewey wrote his book not merely to energize the radical possibilities of liberalism—to encourage its move toward what Hobhouse called a "liberal socialism"—but to defend it against attacks from the radical left, "who want drastic social changes effected in a twinkling of an eye, and who believe that violent overthrow of existing institutions is the right method of effecting the required changes." Dewey wrote these lectures as a response to those who called liberalism a "mealy-mouthed, a milk-and-water doctrine and so on" (1–2).

This study is concerned with the evolution of "liberalism" in the postwar, when the discourse of "crisis" in liberalism becomes even more complex, or multivoiced: to the "crisis of liberalism" as defined by Dewey engaged with those further to the "left" than he, was added the intensified problem of being associated with radicalism at all. The discourse of the "new liberalism" that is my subject in this chapter was created in the midst of this atmosphere. To those essays I draw upon as evidence of this discourse should be added Robert Bendiner, "The Liberals' Political Road Back: The Days of Reform from Above Are Over," Arthur A. Ekirch, Jr., *The Decline of American Liberalism* (especially chap. 17), Louis Filler, "The Dilemma, So-Called, of the American Liberal," Harry K. Girvetz, *From Wealth to Welfare*, and Robert Warshow, "The Liberal Conscience in 'The Crucible.'" Richard H. Pells, *The Liberal Mind in a Conservative Age*, is especially useful.

political reality and human nature. Stalin's brutal "realism" played a large role in these reassessments, for though people like Kazin had little but scorn for apologists who defended Stalin's expedience as political "realism," that expedience and its impact upon world affairs could not be denied. Stalin's realism, whatever one thought ~~of it~~, had to be taken into account, had to be dealt with if one's own position were to be "realistic."

As the unwelcome realities of war and politics became unbearably present to such people as Kazin, Rahv, and Trilling, the narrative of chastened liberalism that emerged as a result of confronting them sought to redefine liberalism and liberal hope along more realistic lines. By the time the cold war was in full swing—Truman exacted the loyalty oath, Churchill declared the fact of an "iron curtain," and all of Eastern Europe seemed to be in the grip of an advancing communism—the basic elements of this narrative had become conventions informing a wide spectrum of cultural narratives, from those in which one would expect to find them, such as *The Vital Center* by historian Arthur Schlesinger, Jr., to those in which the relation to politics is less direct, such as Richard Chase's study of Herman Melville. In the preface to this book, Chase set forth the political reasons for his literary study:

> My second purpose is to contribute a book on Melville to a movement which may be described (once again) as the new liberalism—that newly invigorated secular thought at the dark center of the twentieth century which, whatever our cultural wreckage and disappointment, now begins to ransom liberalism from the ruinous sellouts, failures, and defeats of the thirties. The new liberalism must justify its claims to superiority over the old liberalism. It must present a vision of life capable, by a continuous act of imaginative criticism, of avoiding the old mistakes: the facile ideas of progress and "social realism," the disinclination to examine human motives, the indulgence of wish-fulfilling rhetoric, the belief that historical reality is merely a question of economic or ethical values, the idea that literature should participate directly in the economic liberation of the masses, the equivocal relationship to communist totalitarianism and power politics. (*Melville* v)

The list of charges that liberals brought against themselves is here in full: the "old" liberalism was unimaginative, it subscribed to "facile" ideas of progress and "history," it wavered in its rejection of totalitarian politics. Chase links the old liberalism with literary kinds—with the "social realism" and proletarian fiction promoted by the John Reed Clubs and the Writers' Congresses. The old liberalism was incorrect in thinking that literature should play a direct role in the "economic liberation of the masses." Chase's summary recapitulates the stages which follow: historical experience ("ruinous sellouts") embarrassed the "wish-fulfilling rhetoric" of radical liberalism, which in turn produced a new realism: the new liberalism must be unequivocally opposed to totalitarianism and take fuller account of human motives. Further, in this account the terms of the old liberalism are now held under suspicion: the new liberal will speak of "progress," "history," and the "liberation of the masses" only with the kind of irony that recognizes that these ideas can be realized, if at all, with only partial success.

Left implicit in Chase's summary are the specific shocks to radical conscience experienced in the thirties, but Chase's determination to distinguish a "new liberalism" from the failures of an earlier, prewar liberalism is also a response to the contemporary circumstances of liberalism under the Truman administration. The Congress of 1942 had already begun a "systematic assault" on New Deal programs, dismantling both the Works Progress Administration and the National Youth Administration. Harry Truman, thrust into the presidency by Roosevelt's sudden death, wavered in his commitment to the liberal vision of the Roosevelt administration and failed to support the program for full employment, higher minimum wage, and national housing, which he submitted to Congress in 1945 (Chafe 26, 80–82). In 1946 Republicans won control of both houses of Congress, and the new Congress passed the Taft-Hartley Act, reduced taxation on those with high income, and refused federal assistance for public housing, education, strong price controls, or extended social security (Goldman 56).

Throughout these years the fear of communist influence exerted such pressure on political and intellectual life in the United States that many liberal programs for social reform were attacked as subversive. At least since 1937, conservatives had interpreted New Deal thinkers and programs as part of a Red conspiracy, but Republicans in the elections of 1942 and 1946 showed real success in smearing their opponents as communist sympathizers (Chafe 98; McAuliffe 5). At the same time, this reactionary environment was reinforced by Truman's use of scare tactics to win congressional approval for the Marshall Plan, and by Stalin's purges of anticommunists in Hungary and Czechoslovakia. The victory of Chinese communism in 1949 and the discovery that the Soviet Union had exploded an atom bomb further contributed to the culture of anticommunism. "Ultimately," William Chafe concludes, "the most damaging effect of the politics of anticommunism was to define as perilous, unsafe, and out of bounds advocacy of substantial social reform" (66–71, 108).

The new liberalism sought to define an anticommunism that was still liberal, but this was a high-wire act difficult to perform at a time when such distinctions seemed overly subtle to most citizens. Chafe cites the remarks of an intelligence officer to a congressional subcommittee: "a liberal is only a hop, skip, and a jump from a Communist. A Communist starts as a liberal" (108; see Miller and Nowak 21–43). In *Prodigal Sons*, Alexander Bloom describes the efforts of the New York intellectuals to fashion a liberal anticommunism in the midst of this reactionary atmosphere: "Despite their early and vehement anti-Stalinism, many liberals and intellectuals found themselves actual or potential targets of reactionary 'witch-hunters.' Liberals believed that no one left of center was entirely safe from the inquisitors" (210).

The pressure of anticommunism directly caused the splintering and breakup of unity on the left in the United States, as liberals scrambled to retain political power without sacrificing their hopes for social reform. One result was the creation in 1947 of the ADA, Americans for Democratic Action, which attempted to certify its centrist liberalism by excluding communists from its membership rolls. The ADA's vision of what postwar liberalism should be differed considerably from that of the PCA, the "progressive" alternative that advocated a more understanding interpretation of Soviet action and attacked the rhetoric of a "cold war." The major voice of the PCA was Henry A. Wallace, vice-president under Roosevelt and third-party candidate running against Truman and Dewey in 1948. Mary Sperling McAuliffe summarizes her account of the differences on the left by concluding that the PCA wanted to unite "the entire political left" and saw itself as "left-of-center," while the ADA "viewed liberalism as properly a movement of the center, operating between 'totalitarian extremes'" (7; see Chafe 103–5).

Two of the most influential leaders of the ADA were Reinhold Niebuhr and Arthur Schlesinger, Jr., for it was their articulation of the "new liberalism" which defined the "center" for postwar liberalism. Their accounts of liberalism and recent history are the most explicit versions of "the liberal narrative." Schlesinger begins *The Vital Center: The Politics of Freedom* (1949) by describing his essay as a "report on the fundamental enterprise of re-examination and self-criticism which liberalism has undergone in the last decade" (vii). Like Chase, Schlesinger promotes the "new liberalism" by distinguishing it from the "old." He locates the historical necessity of that pivot, as Chase does, in the history of the 1930s:

> The degeneration of the Soviet Union taught us a useful lesson, however. It broke the bubble of the false optimism of the nineteenth century. Official liberalism had long been almost inextricably identified with a picture of man as perfectible, as endowed with sufficient wisdom and selflessness to endure power and to use it infallibly for the general good. The Soviet experience, on top of the rise of fascism, reminded my generation rather forcibly that man

was, indeed, imperfect, and that the corruptions of power could unleash great
evil in the world. (viii–ix)

Perhaps the most striking feature of this passage is the way in which
historical events are interpreted within ahistorical and moral categories.
These categories, implicit within Chase's brief summary, are spelled out
by Schlesinger: historical events have forced liberals to reexamine "human
motives" and find in them a mixture of "good" and "evil." In the view
of Schlesinger and others, this transcendental or religious interpretation of
human action cut across those political categories which had governed liberal thinking. In another instance, Leslie Fiedler wrote, "We who like to
think of ourselves as liberals must be willing to declare that mere liberal
principle is not in itself a guarantee against evil . . . ; that there is no magic
in the words 'left' or 'progressive' or 'socialist' that can prevent deceit and
the abuse of power" (Bloom 180–81). Schlesinger provides a genealogy
for what Chase termed "facile ideas of progress" in the "optimism" of
the nineteenth century, and he identifies the "degeneration of the Soviet
Union" as the underlying meaning of the phrase "ruinous sellouts, failures,
and defeats of the thirties."

Thus out of the complexities of recent history emerges a fairly simple
narrative, almost mythic in its dimensions and in the elemental service it
provides the intellectual culture. This story is told over and over again in
myriad variation for a period of at least twenty-five years, and continues
to play an important role in political and social discourse. It had its greatest necessity within the liberal-to-left culture, for the turmoil of modern
history seemed to confirm conservative dogma rather than refute it. Essay
after essay tees off on "liberal culture" by explaining recent history as a
lesson in innocence and naiveté.

Insofar as sources for a time's way of thinking may be identified at all,
one of the most influential in defining the liberal narrative's moral ahistoricism was Reinhold Niebuhr. Niebuhr was a Protestant theologian who
resigned from the Socialist Party in 1940 and in 1941 became chairman of
the Union for Democratic Action (UDA), the organization which preceded
the ADA. In *The Children of Light and the Children of Darkness* (1944),
Niebuhr argued that democracy "requires a more realistic vindication than
is given it by the liberal culture with which it has been associated in modern
history" (xii). Niebuhr's point of view, deeply committed to ideas of innate
human corruption and inherent limitation in the ability of men and women
to control history, was powerfully set forth in *The Irony of American History* (1952): "Our modern liberal culture, of which American civilization
is such an unalloyed exemplar, is involved in many ironic refutations of

its original pretensions of virtue, wisdom, and power. Insofar as communism has already elaborated some of these pretensions into noxious forms of tyranny, we are involved in the double irony of confronting evils which were distilled from illusions, not generically different from our own" (viii).

Several aspects of Niebuhr's viewpoint were central themes of the liberal narrative. The idea that American culture is an example of "unalloyed" liberalism was fundamental to the arguments of Lionel Trilling in *The Liberal Imagination* (1950) and Louis Hartz in *The Liberal Tradition in America* (1955). All three men advanced this thesis in support of their conviction that American cultural and political life is plagued by a habitual and dangerous innocence, insufficiently complicated and disciplined by an opposing conservatism. Men like Chase, Schlesinger, Niebuhr, Trilling, and Hartz—all of whom considered themselves liberals—were attempting to provide that conservative critique from within liberalism.

Niebuhr's view that both communism and democracy evolved from "illusions" generated by Enlightenment secularism, an optimistic rationalism which ignored the complex ambiguity of human behavior recognized by the Christian explanation of existence, also found currency among postwar liberals. "In the liberal world the evils in human nature and history were ascribed to social institutions or to ignorance or to some other manageable defect in human nature or environment," and this led to man's "confidence in his power over historical destiny" and a rejection of "the Christian idea of the ambiguity of human virtue" (*Irony* 4). Throughout *The Irony of American History*, Niebuhr's great foe appears to be a naive confidence that afflicts both Marxist and bourgeois culture. Indeed, the "grace" of American experience has been its comparative common sense, which has saved the United States from trying to "cut through the vast ambiguities of our historic situation and thereby bringing our destiny to a tragic conclusion by seeking to bring it to a neat and logical one" (*Irony* 75; see 3, 6, 92).

Though I mean to suggest that the discourse of revisionist liberalism was "dominant," the views to which Niebuhr gave powerful expression were not without opposition within liberal thought. John Dewey, philosopher of pragmatism, and Sidney Hook both deplored the inroads of irrationalism upon the secular turf of liberal thought. In *Liberalism and Social Action* (1935), Dewey had insisted that liberals must "see that socialized economy is the means of free individual development as the end." The unwillingness to do so, he argued, merely "shows that liberalism is still impeded by remnants of its earlier *laissez faire* phase" (90). Sidney Hook, a student of Dewey's at Columbia and philosopher in his own right, supported William Z. Foster, the communist candidate for president in 1932, wrote the platform for the American Workers Party, and later served on the Trotsky Defense Committee (Bloom 79, 48; Wald 3–16). Both men thought of themselves as liberals, but in the aftermath of disillusionment with Russia and the tensions of the Cold War they remained unapologetic for their insistence upon the virtues of naturalism and rationality, rejecting the association of these ideas and methods with totalitarianism. Both men felt the scientific "temper" of liberalism to be "everywhere on the defensive" (Hook 3). Hook's article "The New Failure of Nerve" and Dewey's companion piece, "Anti-Naturalism in Extremis," which appeared together in *Partisan Review*, both attacked the view that "the attempt to live by science has resulted in chaos, relativism, Hitler and war" (Hook 9). Hook charged that Niebuhr's theology was not only "irrelevant" but harmful, for it "breathes a defeatism more congenial to Toryism than to his own political progressivism" (17). Dewey also rejected the reductive association of naturalism and scientific method with a "dangerously romantic, optimistic, utopian view of human nature" (37) and reminded readers that naturalists "give equal weight to facts that point in the direction of both non-social behavior and that of amity and cooperation" (37). In contrast, the religious point of view assumes an "intrinsically sceptical, even cynical and pessimistic, view of human nature." On the other hand, because naturalists find the values of existence "founded in human nature itself" rather than in "some centre and authority entirely outside nature," they are able to focus upon social and political means of developing the possibilities of human relations (32).

Still, as Daniel Bell told Alexander Bloom, "Niebuhr's explanations became much more congenial to us" because they combined "a kind of tough-minded attitude about human nature, a complex view of society, a complex view of human motivation, and a willingness to talk about politics" (Bloom 188–89). Bell's memory is well supported by the preface of *The Vital Center*, where Schlesinger acknowledges the importance of Niebuhr's thought. "We discovered a new dimension of experience," he wrote, and added parenthetically, "Or it may be, as Reinhold Niebuhr has brilliantly suggested, that we were simply rediscovering ancient truths which we should never have forgotten" (ix). Niebuhr's imprint is everywhere in the book. When Schlesinger attacks the old liberalism represented by Henry Wallace in the 1948 campaign as "Doughface progressivism," he isolates the "sentimental belief in progress" as the central failing of liberalism: "The belief in progress was the product of the Enlightenment, cross-fertilized with allied growths, such as science, bourgeois complacency, Unitarianism and a faith in the goodness of man. It dispensed with the Christian myths of sin and atonement" (*Vital* 38).

Because Niebuhr opposed the realities of human corruption and an irrational history to the utopian illusions of science and secular humanism, elements of his Christian realism became essential components in the "end of ideology" rhetoric and in exhortations for a more modest and realistic foreign policy. Though Niebuhr took issue with the "egotism" of George Kennan's emphasis upon national self-interest, the discourse of the two men overlapped at several points. Kennan is widely credited with creating Truman's foreign policy in the years following World War II; his telegram to the State Department setting forth his view of Soviet assumptions and intentions was decisive in formulating the policy of "containment" and winning support for the Marshall Plan. George Kennan's effort to generate a *Realpolitik* in United States foreign policy shared with Niebuhr's position the recognition of limits to American power, the way in which violence emerges from good intentions, and the "irony" that the United States had never been more powerful than it was in 1950, yet neither had it felt so insecure. In *American Diplomacy, 1900–1950*, Kennan attacks what he calls the "legalistic-moralistic approach" of this century's foreign policy. This phrase may stand as the diplomatic version of "ideology," which Kennan would supplant with a more pragmatic, less "ambitious," and more consciously self-interested policy. The awkward double negative of the essay's last sentence expresses something of the difficulties involved in realigning liberalism with the new realism: "To many," he concludes, "it may seem to smack of cynicism and reaction. I cannot share these doubts. Whatever is realistic in concept, and founded in an endeavor to see both ourselves and others as we really are, cannot be illiberal" (82, 88–89). Like Schlesinger, Chase, and Niebuhr, Kennan assumed that liberalism had been unrealistic; his foreign policy is another example of the effort to redefine liberalism as the philosophy and political persuasion of the tough-minded realist.

A range of historians, whose political positions differ in many respects, all aligned themselves against the tendency toward ideological certainty or moral self-righteousness in foreign policy. The title of C. Vann Woodward's lecture "The Irony of Southern History" refers directly to Niebuhr's book, published the previous year, and propounds a similar message of human and national limitation, based not on Christian doctrine but upon the southern experience "of military defeat, occupation, and reconstruction." Like Niebuhr and George Kennan, Vann Woodward urged a foreign policy of the center, "between the perilous extremes of isolationism and world crusade" (186). Both Daniel Boorstin in *The Genius of American Politics* (1953), and Louis Hartz in *The Liberal Tradition in America* (1955), develop their discussions of American political culture upon the premise that America is without a conscious political ideology. For Boorstin, this means that the genius of American democracy lies in its having no philosophy, while for Hartz the uniform liberalism of American culture is so unconscious, left inarticulate by the absence of a conservative tradition, that the nation fails to recognize that it has an ideology. Like Vann Woodward, Hartz worried that a nation unaware of its own ideology might press its claims beyond its power or right to do so. Arguing along lines similar to Niebuhr's analysis in *The Irony of American History*, Hartz said that American political culture had avoided these extremes so far because "the alliance of Christian pessimism with liberal thought" saved Americans from the "unlimited humanism" of the European Enlightenment and produced an "unconquerable pragmatism" instead (39–43, 78–86).

Accounts like mine run the risk of seeming to collapse points of view which differed markedly, but this is because my focus is on the appearance within these different accounts of elements common to a narrative constituted outside of any particular one. I am interested in showing how writers during this period use those elements to help make their arguments, in order to show the liberal narrative operating within or inside other interpretive projects. The impact of revisionist liberalism is clear enough, for example, in Chase's study of Melville. Similarly, Vann Woodward, Hartz, and Boorstin were expressions of what historiographer John Higham termed "The Cult of the 'American Consensus,' " produced he argued by cold war dynamics that "swept aside the characteristically progressive approach to American intellectual history as a dialectic of warring ideologies" (96). Richard Hofstadter's *The Age of Reform: From Bryan to F.D.R.* (1955), another example of consensus history that Higham cited in his article, further illustrates the close fit between consensus analysis and elements of the liberal narrative. Hofstadter's introduction to *The Age of Reform* is a reprise of the assumptions and concerns that inform the work of Trilling, Schlesinger, Niebuhr, and Hartz. He announces his affiliation with "the old liberalism," but "chastened by adversity, tempered by time, and modulated by a growing sense of reality." From the vantage of this new liberalism, he "aims to reveal some of the limitations of [the populist-progressive tradition] and to help free it of its sentimentalities and complacencies." Liberals, he says, "find themselves far more conscious of those things they would like to preserve than they are of those things they would like to change." Like Kennan and Niebuhr he is wary of "moral crusading" and urges upon his readers a "sufficient sense of limits" that inhere within "the human condition." His aim is to show not that the "Populist and Progressive movements were foolish and destructive but only that they had, like so many things in life, an ambiguous character" (14–18).

In all of its variants, the new liberalism tended to attribute to the "old" qualities and aspirations—moral crusading, tyrannical idealism, absolutism, sentimentality, naive rationalism—that few would espouse at any time.

In part, this rhetoric developed from the need liberals felt to preserve their socialist ambitions from contamination by association with progressivism and communism on the left, and from a revived conservatism on the right that exploited any appearance of that relation. In the process, of course, liberalism itself became conservative, as it helped to form the "false consensus" of the fifties (Hodgson 17). At the same time there was little that was especially calculated in these rhetorical contrasts, for many liberals did feel "chastened," did feel the "growing sense of reality" that Hoftstadter claimed adequately expresses the transformation that took place in the very givens of their thought. Gene Wise, in *American Historical Explanations* has described such transformations as "paradigm revolutions" (223). We might also describe this rhetoric as part of the formation of a new, temporarily persuasive "interpretive community." Thus, when David Riesman wrote a new introduction to *The Lonely Crowd* in 1961, the characteristic assumptions of the liberal narrative continued to inform his recollection, not as constituting an alternate interpretive framework but as the ideologically neutral method of truth itself: *"The Lonely Crowd* was one of a number of books which in recent years have eschewed dogmatism and fanaticism and preferred openness, pluralism, and empiricism. Many intellectuals, influenced by Reinhold Niebuhr or George Kennan, have done battle against American tendencies to unrealistic moralizing with its implications of total engagement in war and politics" (xxxiii).

Another important element of the liberal discussion in this period was the discourse of "mass society," for the new realism that revisionist liberalism sought to establish for itself (and its reputation) involved a reassessment of the concept of the masses and the relationship of radical thought to mass culture. The use of "mass culture" and "mass society" as interpretive concepts for understanding the behavior of societies and nations has origins much earlier than the postwar period of the new liberalism, having arisen with the critique of capitalism in the late eighteenth and early nineteenth centuries and continuing to be a central element in cultural critique for conservatives and radicals alike.

The conservative reaction to mass culture gained greater currency among liberal thinkers during the thirties and forties as they tried to account for the apparent willingness of entire populations in Italy and Germany to submit to fascism. Invariably these accounts either displaced or modified the economic and class analysis characteristic of Marxist sociology with psychological theories, and in some measure they may be credited with initiating the predominance of cultural, psychological, and sociological studies after the war. One of the first to speculate on the sources and reasons for the success of National Socialism was Wilhelm Reich, the Austrian-born psychologist who published *The Mass Psychology of Fascism* in 1933. "*Why did the myriad masses of the freedom-loving and anti-imperialistic oriented workers allow themselves to be betrayed?*" Reich asked (22). He argued that the success of fascism resulted not from the unique powers of Mussolini or Hitler, but from the "*psychic structure*" (xx) of mass man, which is "embedded" early in childhood by the "authoritarian family" (18). From the internalized repression experienced in this family, Reich continued, the individual developed a conservative personality, "a fear of freedom" that prevented men and women from acting in their economic self-interest (24–33).

At the same time Reich was writing, members of the Frankfurt School also explored the relations between Marxism and psychoanalysis and produced studies of the "authoritarian character" (Bottomore 20–21). In 1941, Erich Fromm, one of the leading participants in this analysis, published *Escape from Freedom*, which established the terms by which many in the United States understood the success of fascism. Like Reich, Fromm set out to "analyze those dynamic factors in the character structure of modern man, which made him want to give up freedom in Fascist countries" (20), and, like Reich, Fromm argued that the "attraction" of fascism could be explained only by the "dynamics of the psychological processes operating within the individual." Fromm's thesis further included the view that the freedom which accompanied liberation from "pre-individualistic society" brought with it great anxiety and powerlessness. In sharp contrast, fascism offered order and certainty, the comforts of authority that modern freedom couldn't provide (viii). The authoritarian personality, Theodor Adorno argued, possessed an "intolerance of ambiguity," which "characterizes all hierarchic systems of art and society" (290).

Though the thinking of Reich, Fromm, and Adorno was originally motivated by the rise of National Socialism, liberal discourse in the United States throughout the 1940s tended to conflate fascism and communism as similar totalitarian systems, that took root in the anxious passivity of the masses. Schlesinger devoted a chapter of *The Vital Center* to describing their similarities. Schlesinger's analysis throughout recapitulates Fromm's thesis: "the 'escape from freedom,' as Erich Fromm has called it, is a characteristic pattern of our age," both fascism and communism have "displaced the 'anxious man' by the 'totalitarian man,' " and "in both the masses are plunged in a profound and trancelike political apathy" (52, 59). Similarly, Hannah Arendt's powerful analysis of the forces arrayed against freedom, *The Origins of Totalitarianism* (1951), gave virtually no attention to the differences between fascism and communism that had been insisted upon with such vehemence fifteen years earlier.

Accordingly, the "serious threat" to the United States, as John Dewey wrote in *Freedom and Culture*, "is not the existence of foreign totalitarian states. It is the existence within our own personal attitudes and within our own institutions of conditions similar to those which have given a victory to external authority, discipline, uniformity and dependence upon The Leader in foreign countries" (49). When Fromm cited this passage from Dewey in *Escape from Freedom*, he made explicit Dewey's correlation between the dangers of "external authority" and the habit of "uniformity": "the principal social avenues of escape in our time are the submission to a leader, as had happened in Fascist countries, and the compulsive conforming as is prevalent in our own democracy" (155).

This line of reasoning continued to shift the focus away from purely social and economic sources of historical change and emphasized instead psychological and behavioral categories like "anxiety" and "conformity," which cut across class divisions and became dominant analytical terms in the fifties. David Riesman remembered that "Fromm's *Escape From Freedom* and *Man For Himself* were decisively influential models in the application of a socially oriented psychoanalytic characterology to problems of historical change" (xiv). Class conflict, as John Higham noted of the consensus historians, tended to be transformed into the subjective stresses in American life. "A psychological approach to conflict enables historians to substitute a schism in the soul for a schism in society" ("Cult," 95). In fact, within the binary assumptions of cold war thought, global confrontation and psychoanalysis tended to blur into a psychopolitics that affirmed anxiety and conflict as realistic and inevitable consequences of sustaining freedom. "So long as society stays free," Schlesinger wrote in the conclusion to *The Vital Center*, "so long will it continue in its state of tension, breeding contradiction, breeding strife. . . . You cannot expel conflict from society any more than you can from the human mind. When you attempt it, the psychic costs in schizophrenia or torpor are the same" (255).

The changed relationship of radical thought to the masses or the working class appears most conservatively in postwar liberalism as the need to preserve high culture from the degradations of mass culture. In this discourse mass culture was associated with totalitarian control, both as evidence of passive susceptibility to propaganda and as an instrument of it. This was also a central preoccupation of the Frankfurt philosophers and sociologists who saw firsthand Hitler's success at using film and radio to influence the opinions of the German people. After they took up residence in the United States in 1933, they continued to theorize about the relationship between state power and popular culture. For example, in "The Culture Industry: Enlightenment as Mass Deception" (1944), Adorno and Max Horkheimer argued that "films, radio and magazines make up a system which is uni-form as a whole and in every part," and which contributes always to the "absolute power" of monopoly capitalism (120).

A similar critique had emerged in the United States in such essays as Clement Greenberg's "Avant-Garde and Kitsch" (1939), and Dwight Mac-donald's series of essays on mass culture. Because "kitsch is the culture of the masses," Greenberg wrote, the "encouragement of kitsch is merely another of the inexpensive ways in which totalitarian regimes seek to in-gratiate themselves with their subjects" (390). Macdonald saw the relation of power to the operations of mass culture more aggressively: "The Lords of *kitsch*, in short, exploit the cultural needs of the masses in order to make a profit and/or to maintain their class rule" ("A Theory," 2).

The content of this critique is less important here than what it registers about the changed nature of political criticism in postwar liberalism. This critique was invariably a prelude to self-estrangement, since it didn't iden-tify a simple target or provide the structure for political action. For example, one of Macdonald's images for mass culture, "the spreading ooze," sug-gests that this culture has a life of its own, producing the conditions in which totalitarianism thrives. Though the upper classes might have used popu-lar culture to make money and dominate the masses, Macdonald argued, they "end by finding their own culture attacked and even threatened with destruction by the instrument they have thoughtlessly employed." For Mac-donald the political parallel was unmistakable: "thus Nazism began as a tool of the big bourgeoisie and the army *Junkers* but ended by using *them* as *its* tools" ("A Theory," 4–5). Because this analysis reverses the direction of exploitation, suggesting that pandering to the tastes of the lower classes un-intentionally empowers them, Macdonald's position begins to merge with the point of view advanced by such conservatives as Ortega and Eliot, to whom he was ostensibly opposed. Thus one of the persistent charges lodged against mass culture was its erosion of class distinctions, the way it "mixes and scrambles everything together" in a "homogenization process" that "destroys all values" (5). Indeed, the liberal critique of mass culture exposed its own class bias and implicit elitism, for the only solution that Greenberg and Macdonald offered to the debasements of mass culture was to remain above it. "If under present conditions," Philip Rahv wrote, using language intended to acquire force by evoking the cold war image of com-munism, "we cannot stop the ruthless expansion of mass-culture, the least we can do is to keep apart and refuse its favors" ("Our Country," 310).

The liberal critique stopped short of confusing the masses with those forces of media manipulation which exploited them, but in any case the likelihood that the most radical element within the masses—American workers—would be the instrument of social change seemed to disappear with the collapse of the labor movement after the war. After all, in radical terms, the workers were Marx's proletariat and the engine of revolutionary change, once they developed class consciousness. In the United States, the strongest manifestation of such a force had been the impressive growth and success of the labor unions. National union membership rose from a low of 2.5 million at the beginning of the thirties to 10 million by 1940, and under the favorable conditions established by the War Labor Board it increased sharply to 15 million by 1945. According to Chafe, "liberals envisioned organized labor as the phalanx of a movement that would transform America economically and politically," but these hopes evaporated under the heat of concern with inflation, conservative victories in congressional elections, and the politics of anticommunism (Chafe 9, 92–108). In his account of Daniel Bell's deradicalization, Howard Brick describes the "political absorption of labor" that took place when the unions rejected the Progressive Party under Wallace and supported Truman in the 1948 election. The following year, in an article for *Modern Review* titled "American Socialists: What Now?" Bell argued that the workers had shown their willingness to work within the social order of capitalist society, rather than trying to change it (Brick 187, 142–92).

As elements of the liberal narrative, the compelling specters of totalitarianism and mass society remained troubling interpretations of political and social reality well into the fifties. In his essay "Liberal Values in the Modern World" (1952), C. Wright Mills, who spoke from a position to the left of consensus liberals, nonetheless shared with them the view that "any 'democratic' or 'liberal'—even humanist—ideals . . . are in fact statements of hope or demands or preferences of an intellectual elite psychologically capable of individually fulfilling them, but they are projected for a population which in the twentieth century is not at present capable of fulfilling them." The new kinds of social and political organization which have arisen have left liberal values without any footing: "the ideals of liberalism have been divorced from any realities of modern social structure that might serve as the means of their realization" (194, 189).

Studies of the intellectual left in the United States, by Daniel Aaron as well as Alexander Bloom, Howard Brick, Richard Pells, and Alan Wald, have amply shown that within the expansive term "liberal" there was considerable room for disagreement among many of the writers on whom I have drawn for this excavation of the "liberal narrative." Certainly among liberal intellectuals there was a variety of responses to the events of the thirties and forties, and varying reactions to the pressures of anticommunism. At the same time, none of these accounts deny the emergence of a more conservative liberalism, chastened or cornered depending upon one's point of view, or the shift in the underlying assumptions—the rhetoric of realism, inherent limitation of the good and evil in human nature, the intractable complexity of social history and mass behavior—upon which that conservatism was justified or explained. The relative stability of these elements in the liberal narrative speaks at once to their importance in liberalism's effort to revise itself from within, and to their intertextual power as an informing myth affecting cultural interpretation and imagination.

II

In reading the specifically literary history of the forties and early fifties, one cannot fail to notice how fully these reassessments of history, politics, human nature, and destiny also inform or mediate the literary community, in its critical and imaginative production. Subsequent chapters focus explicitly upon the way revisionist liberalism operated within narrative fiction and its criticism, but here we may note more generally that literary discourse not only was another locale of liberal revisionism, as in the instance of Richard Chase, but also produced some of its most powerful expressions, in such books as Lionel Trilling's *The Liberal Imagination*.

There is widespread agreement among recent critics that Trilling's collection of essays represented, in Gene Wise's words, "one of those threshold moments marking the transition from Progressive explanations to counter-Progressive ones" (223–24). In Russell Reising's view, the ideas Trilling set forth in *The Liberal Imagination* emerged as "the dominant interpretation of American culture and literature" (93). Alexander Bloom argues that this book, more than any other, "marks the emergence of the New York Intellectuals into the postwar" (190).

Like Chase and Schlesinger, Trilling framed his essays as a critique of liberalism from within liberalism itself, with the aim of recalling "liberalism to its first essential imagination of variousness and possibility, which implies the awareness of complexity and difficulty" (xv). They were, Trilling noted twenty-four years later, written "with a polemical purpose and with reference to a particular political-cultural situation" (vii). Trilling charged those American liberals who had given their commitment to the Soviet Union with a naive politics, a form of utopian impatience with "what politics entails of contingency, vigilance, and effort." This "large segment of the intelligentsia," in Trilling's view, had tried to escape the obligations of mind and will as they confront the "social and political contradictions" of history, hoping to find in the "monolithic" government of Stalin "rest" from the "often clashing requirements of democratic society" (viii).

As in the discourse of Chase, Schlesinger, and Niebuhr, the cold war confrontation between Stalinist Russia and American democracy works to produce or require within Trilling's thought a new definition of reality —complex, difficult, intractable—and its underlying assumptions. Here democracy is the more artful of the two systems because it is a more adequate political representation (or response) to the inherent nature of reality itself. This both reproduces and extends the typical polarities of new liberal discourse between totalitarianism and democracy, utopianism and politics, certitude and ambiguity, resolution and conflict or contradiction. In Trilling especially these polarities become indistinguishable from aesthetic categories, as both politics and art must subscribe to or recognize the complexities and difficulties of life.

The new liberalism must thus recognize and conform itself to this complexity, which is to say, the new liberalism must take greater account of conservative ideas, in which tragedy and moral ambiguity have long been uncontested assumptions. In setting forth what "conservatism" meant to Trilling we note at once that the fundamental assumptions informing his charge reproduce the central elements of the liberal narrative and give to it the added momentum of his voice. The world, for example, "is a complex and unexpected and terrible place which is not always to be understood by the mind as we use it in our everyday tasks" (xiv). Trilling's views in these essays thus help constitute that element of irrationalism which was characteristic of Niebuhr's and Schlesinger's revised understanding of historical process. In his essay on Freud, for example, Trilling affirms Freud's view that man "is not simply good" but has "a kind of hell within him from which rise everlastingly the impulses which threaten his civilization" (57). Accordingly, conflict—as in "consensus history"—becomes a "natural" element of psychic and social existence. Indeed, reality is finally at base a psychological reality, an experience of complexity that has its generative roots in the ineradicable conflicts of the private self. Ideation and rational action have their troubled source in subterranean emotions. Similarly, as Bloom reports, Schlesinger "scorned 'official' (traditional) liberalism for rejecting the 'dark and subterranean forces in human nature.' 'There are moody and destructive impulses in man of which official liberalism has taken no serious account' " (Bloom 189–90).

This point of view is developed by Trilling in the conclusion to "Manners, Morals, and the Novel," originally given as a talk at Kenyon College in 1947. Trilling asserts a connection between an undisciplined or unrealistic liberalism and the inevitable abuses of power which follow from that naiveté:

> Some paradox of our natures leads us, when once we have made our fellow men the objects of our enlightened interest, to go on to make them the objects of our pity, then of our wisdom, ultimately of our coercion. It is to prevent this corruption, the most ironic and tragic that man knows, that we stand in need of the moral realism which is the product of the free play of the moral imagination. (*Liberal* 221–22).

Here, as in so many versions of the liberal narrative, the moral ambiguity of human nature—its intractable alloy of good and evil—and its susceptibility to the corruptions of power serve as truths which rebut the simplifications of the old liberalism. Art, on the other hand—and the novel in particular—can do what a "rational" politics cannot: it is the perfect vehicle for the ironies and paradoxes of the moral life and the social history it produces.

As with the corrections insisted upon by Niebuhr, Schlesinger, and others, Trilling's are based upon ideas or assumptions about human nature that transcend historical circumstance. Trilling's characteristically elliptical style fails to specify the historical instances to which words like "paradox" and "corruption" might refer, but his audience must have had in mind the failure of Russia to fulfill the liberal aspirations of the 1917 revolution, and the complicity of fellow-traveling liberals in being so late to recognize that failure. Typically, Trilling's focus wasn't the historical particular, but the universal and "everlasting" truths which recent history had called to the attention of liberals. But the effect of this perception, as Dewey and Hook objected, was to lift the possibilities for change out of the realm of material cause and situate them within the workings of a mystical human nature. If reform is possible, it is only a moral reform produced by "moral realism"—essentially a reform of the expectations for reform.

As Carolyn Porter, Russell Reising, and others have pointed out, this ahistoricism was the typical mode of American criticism during this period, and one which deeply influenced United States literature and culture for at least two decades. But as should be clear by now, this ahistoricism can be situated within the historical assumptions and pressures operating upon and through the critics. Writers such as Chase, Trilling, and R. W. B. Lewis, all of whom had a great deal to do with the way we think about American fiction, didn't imagine they were being ahistorical. It is only our contemporary understanding of myth and symbol criticism that sees their work as failing to address history. Our current impatience with the antimaterialism of postwar criticism derives from the fact that our present literary criticism is committed to the view that all representation is always already ideologically marked, with the result that much of contemporary critical practice—seeing no other recourse—is unabashedly partisan. Thus we are quick to point out that the postwar derogation of ideology—condemned as a simplification of social and political reality—was itself an ideology that served to reinforce the dominant cold war polarities which privileged American democracy, imagined as a fruitful tension of conflicting groups in contrast with the monolithic repressiveness of the Soviet Union.

Richard Chase, for example, didn't think he was being indifferent to history when he wrote his study of Melville. "I once advanced the opinion," Chase wrote in the *Kenyon Review*, "that if one had read and understood Melville one would not vote for Henry Wallace. I still believe this to be true, . . . because Melville presents his reader with a vision of life so complexly true that it exposes the ideas of Henry Wallace as hopelessly childish and superficial. Literature tells us that life is diverse, paradoxical, and complicated, a fateful medley of lights and darks. . . . It warns us that the tendency of modern liberal politics has been to bleed political ideas white, to deny them their roots in natural reality, to deny them their extension over the possible range of human experience" (590–91). Thus literature doesn't merely tell us what reality is like; as a "mode of knowing" (590) it reminds us of what reality really is, and gives us both access to it and instruction in it. Chase stops short of insisting that political programs should be derived from literature, but he argues that political ideas could gain from literature—"supposing, furthermore, that it is not to literature we wish finally to expose political reality but to reality itself" (591).

R. W. B. Lewis maintained a less direct or sympathetic relation to the discourse of the new liberalism, but *The American Adam* (1955) was written in dialogue with that discourse, and his arguments, like those of Chase about Ishmael and Ahab, should be understood in part as a response to it. Lewis directly linked the activity of fiction with the foreign policy of George Kennan by concluding his study with an epilogue titled "Adam as Hero in the Age of Containment":

> The hopeful attitudes [of the nineteenth-century party of Hope] are phenomena, indeed, about which we are today somewhat embarrassed. . . . We have had to get beyond such simple-minded adolescent confidence, we suppose; . . . and we sometimes congratulate ourselves austerely for having settled, like adults or Europeans, upon a course of prolonged but tolerable hopelessness. We call that state of hopelessness the human condition: something we study to realize in our literature and reflect in our behavior. (195)

Despite the wry irony evident in Lewis' description of the "contemporary philosophies," he admits they contain "many remarkable and even irreversible psychological, sociological, and political insights." His own study meant to engage these insights "dialectically," by countering the environment of "the new hopelessness" with the image of the "innocent" Adam, but on that account Lewis should not be charged with having cast in his lot with the proponents of facile optimism. His argument, after all, is that the image of innocence has been used throughout American cultural production with irony, because writers who used that image recognized the New World's "historic, sinful, inheritance" (197). This irony, he tells us, has been lost, for "the new hopelessness" is as "simple-minded as innocence." Here the local target of Lewis' epilogue begins to clarify: "something which began as a valuable corrective to the claims of innocence in America and which has declined into a cult of original sin" (196).

References, such as this one, to the pessimism of revisionist liberalism are nearly lost to us, or are not resonant or meaningful to those unfamiliar with the discursive history I have sketched here. On the other hand, to note this isn't to recover the vitality of the Adamic interpretation of American culture, but to situate it within the social and political discourse of the early fifties. If nothing else, we understand Lewis' view as an effort to redress a perceived imbalance, originating not in disagreement with the foreign policy admonitions of Kennan, Hartz, and Vann Woodward, but in an impatience with the gloomy Augustinianism of Reinhold Niebuhr.

At the same time Lewis' insistence upon the dynamic of innocence and sin in the evolution of American thought marks his book's essential congeniality with the central elements of postwar liberalism, for the conflict here is ironic, rather than economic, and it figures American culture and history within the ahistorical oppositions which structure so many other cultural narratives written in the postwar period. The closing sentences of Lewis' study may be a bit more upbeat than many of the expressions of revisionist liberalism published only a few years earlier, but in the emphasis Lewis gives to the "special complexities" and the "encircling doubt of the still unfolding American scene" may be heard the characteristic accents of the liberal narrative.

2

The Politics of Realism

Novelistic Discourse in the Postwar Period

> The fact is that Hawthorne was dealing beautifully with realities, with substantial things. The man who could raise those brilliant and serious doubts about the nature and possibility of moral perfection, the man who could keep himself aloof from the "Yankee reality" and who could dissent from the orthodoxies of dissent and tell us so much about the nature of moral zeal, is of course dealing exactly with reality.
>
> Lionel Trilling, "Reality in America," 1940

> "Other people die on Fridays just the same as any other day," Della observed. "Why should murderers be exempt?"
> Mason lowered his eyes from the window to look at her. "Della, you are fast becoming a realist."
>
> Erle Stanley Gardner, *The Case of the Crooked Candle*, 1944

I

The novel's relationship to social history—to "reality"—was the central preoccupation of the critics who wrote about narrative fiction in the years after World War II, and this relation inevitably turned upon the redefinition of "reality" and "realism" that cut across so much social thought in this period. The importance of the novel to intellectuals and critics of the New York milieu was directly linked to the function of the novel as social history and to their participation in the redefinition of liberal thought and action. At the same time, contributors to the *Kenyon Review* and *Sewanee Review* also developed a new interest in the novel form. Although the two groups of critics differed sharply, both used discussions of the novel to promote conservative ideas of subject and form; their differing assumptions about the novel's social function were an expression of a long-standing conservatism

25

persisting on the right (with roots in southern culture and religion), and of a new conservatism characterizing postwar liberalism's politics of the center. These assumptions quickly became the prescriptive orthodoxy with which young writers after World War II had to contend.

The contributions of the New Critics or formalists—in Grant Webster's useful designation—to the discourse on fiction should be included with the New York criticism because together they comprise the most visible and influential commentators of the postwar text. The New Critics help demonstrate the degree of conservatism that liberal criticism embraced, and also—from the other direction—help us see how the postwar dominance of the New Criticism owed a great deal to transformations within liberalism, that is, to those northern liberals with whom they were in ostensible conflict. Together they produced, unintentionally, a discursive formation or "interpretive community" in which "consensus" seemed to most anti-ideological, natural, and democratic.

From our present vantage, in fact, it is surprising to remember that "the novel" as an object of critical attention hadn't generated much interest before the Second War. In 1949, Wellek and Warren acknowledged this fact in *Theory of Literature*: "Literary theory and criticism concerned with the novel are much inferior in both quantity and quality to theory and criticism of poetry" (212). By that year the New Criticism was already established as the central force in the reading of poetry, and slowly but surely the New Critics began turning to the novel. R. P. Blackmur asked for a "second look" at the novel: "The novel needs precisely the kind of attention . . . that in the last twenty years or so we have been giving poetry" ("Second Look," 9). The previous year, Mark Schorer had done just that in his influential essay "Technique as Discovery," where the interest seemed to be the aggrandizement of critical application rather than the novel itself: "the case for fiction is not yet established" (67). "So far as criticism of the novel is concerned," Arthur Mizener wrote in 1950, "we are—with *The Craft of Fiction* [1921] and *Aspects of the Novel* [1927] and the rest—still living in the age of Sir Arthur Quiller-Couch and A. C. Bradley—which, in fact, we are not" (1–2).

Although during the fifties this new attention produced some of the early classics of novel study, in 1959 Daniel Howard still began his review of three new books on the novel with the statement that "the criticism of the novel just before World War II still consisted mainly of the suggestions of the novelists themselves—James, Flaubert, Gide, Forster—and further comments of Percy Lubbock and Joseph Warren Beach. Indeed, the critical vacuum can be measured by the importance accorded such a slight book as Forster's *Aspects of the Novel*" (309). The vacuum was not so complete as

Howard thought, of course, for one of the books under his review was Ian Watt's *The Rise of the Novel*, and the new critical focus of the late forties and fifties had also produced Feidelson's *Symbolism and American Literature* (1953), Edel's *The Psychological Novel* (1955), Chase's *The American Novel and Its Tradition* (1957), and Van Ghent's *The English Novel* (1959). In 1960, Leslie Fiedler began *Love and Death in the American Novel* with the virtual coronation of the genre: "We are living not only in the Age of America but also in the Age of the Novel. . . . our endemic fantasy of writing 'the Great American Novel' is only a local instance of a more general obsession. The notions of greatness once associated with the heroic poem have been transferred to the novel" (23).

Because of the novel's association with popular culture and social history, many of those critics we now associate with the formalist analysis of New Criticism approached the novel with evident distaste. The novel "is our drunken, disreputable cousin, never mentioned when the subject can be avoided," Arthur Mizener wrote in the *Kenyon Review* (1–2). Reviewing Philip Rahv's *Image and Idea* in an article titled "The Understanding of Fiction" (1950), John Crowe Ransom seemed eager to admit his ignorance of the genre: "I have had next to no experience in the criticism of this art." Still, he bravely perseveres, "citing a few passages that come to [his] mind from *reputable* fictions" and analyzing them "like fictional analogues of lyrical moments" in poetry (emphasis mine, 193).

In their discussions of the novel, New Critics always distinguished the formal qualities of fiction from its popular and more political association with social history. In "The Present Function of Criticism," Allen Tate acknowledged that "the novel is very close to history," but added, "indeed, in all but the great novelists, it is not clearly set off from history" (*Reason* 14). In the section of his essay from which this remark comes, Tate was attacking the "Doctrine of Relevance" which judges literature by its correlations with the "observation of the world that it represents." Similarly, for Schorer a novelist's subject is not in the world, but is created or "discovered" by the techniques of art. When the writer lacks "adequate resources of technique," as Schorer wrote of Defoe, "his contribution is not to fiction but to the history of fiction, and to social history" ("Technique," 70). Tate's specific targets help to remind us of the historical dialogue which these universalist propositions are meant to engage: "the late Marxists and the sociological and historical scholars . . . would not study literature at all if it were not so handy in libraries; they don't really like it; or they are at any rate ashamed of it—because it is 'unreal' " (*Reason* 18).

Further, Tate's insistence upon the separation of history and politics (in the "great novelists") served an idea of culture which it was the duty of literature to preserve. In an article he wrote for the *Southern Review* in 1936, Tate candidly asserted that the editor of a literary quarterly "owes his first duty to his critical principles, his sense of the moral and intellectual order upon which society ought to rest" (*Reason* 195). Similarly, in Wellek and Warren's *Theory of Literature*, the advice that readers attend to the "intrinsic" properties of the aesthetic illusion helped distinguish the novel "in its high form" from novels of "entertainment, amusement, and escape"—"manufactures made with a narrow aim at the market" (212). This formulation reproduces the characteristic dichotomy of New Critical discourse between art as the medium of ahistorical universals and art as a commercial product designed for the masses. That this effort to keep art and history apart was itself political, now engaged in an act of preservation, is also apparent in Arthur Mizener's reason for taking up the novel: "the novel is the last of the verbal forms to retain a wide popularity. . . . It is about all we any longer share with the common reader, and whatever the reasons for his interest may be, they are very probably not the kind which concerned Henry James so much of the time in his prefaces and still concern those for whom the mechanical techniques of the novel are its main interest" (2). At the same time, Mizener implies, the novel exists as the last medium within which, conceivably, the literary critic might exert some effect upon the "common reader."

From a point of view apparently opposite to New Critical practice, Lionel Trilling and other New York intellectuals also used discussion of the novel as a vehicle for their political and cultural values. This was a natural transition for them to make, for they had just survived a decade in which the novel was to have been the principal aesthetic vehicle of proletarian expression in this country. As Grant Webster points out in *The Republic of Letters*, such critics as Rahv, Kazin, Rosenfeld, and Macdonald rarely discussed any genre but the novel (232). Webster might well have added Irving Howe's name to his list, for the main ideas in Howe's literary essays are almost always presented in discussions of novels; all his studies of individual authors are studies of novelists; and his single book about a particular genre is *Politics and the Novel* (1957). Trilling, too, belongs here. Though his critical range extended beyond the novel, his most influential collection of literary essays in the postwar period was *The Liberal Imagination* (1950), most of which concerns novelists and novels; and Trilling developed his ideas about social reality in America most tellingly in those essays.

In contrast to the New Critics, the novel's social and historical relevance—its "realism"—was precisely its interest to the New York intellectuals. Insofar as their interest in the novel was politically motivated, it manifested itself in a discourse remarkably empiricist or verisimilar, despite disclaimers to the contrary. Trilling said that the novel has taught us "most of what we know about modern society, about class and its strange rituals, about power and influence and about money, the hard fluent fact in which modern society has its being" (*Liberal* 63). Philip Rahv also insisted upon the novel's educative function: in his essay on Hawthorne, "The Dark Lady of Salem," he wrote that "the intention of the novel as we have come to know it . . . is to portray life as it is actually lived" (*Image* 22). The way they defined it, novelistic realism was a powerful tool of social analysis, for it "taught literature how to take in, how to grasp and encompass, the ordinary facts of human existence." The "medium" of the novelist "knows of no other principle of coherence" (*Image* 138). Of all the forms of verbal art, the novel is the one which works most through "experiential particulars— the particulars of scene, figures and action." The novel "is the most empirical of all literary genres; existence is its original and inalienable datum" (*Myth* 38–39). Irving Howe's criticism of fifties' novelists is based upon a related set of assumptions and interests: "they do not represent directly the postwar American experience. . . . They tell us rather little about the surface tone, the manners, the social patterns of recent American life, yet are constantly projecting moral criticisms of its essential quality" (*A World* 92–93).

Though we must understand Trilling, Rahv, and Howe as very different figures, who represent various positions within the New York milieu, all three used discussion of the novel as a common medium through which a relation between art (novel as aesthetic form) and politics (novel as social history) might be sustained. What they once had to say about culture and politics was now deflected into their criticism of the novel, as the cultural product most relevant to their skills and interests. "It is the wide sense of the word [politics] that is nowadays forced upon us," Trilling wrote in the preface to *The Liberal Imagination*, "for clearly it is no longer possible to think of politics except as the politics of culture, the organization of human life toward some end or other, toward the modification of sentiments, which is to say, the quality of human life" (xi).[1] Trilling's lecture "Morals, Manners, and the Novel" provides an explicit example of this deflection and its political and historical origin. In its conclusion, already cited above, Trilling made oblique reference to the disillusionments of recent political experience, characterized by Niebuhr as the "irony of American history." When

1. In *Political Man* (1960), Seymour Lipset wrote, "Since domestic politics can no longer serve as the arena for serious criticism from the left, many intellectuals have turned from a basic concern with the political and economic systems to criticism of other sections of the basic culture of American society" (quoted in Pells *Liberal Mind* 185). For the literary intellectual, the "novel" was one of these other sections.

Trilling reminded his audience of the "paradox" that liberal intentions may lead to a tragic "corruption," he was merely revoicing an interpretation of his time so widely dispersed that specific reference to communist betrayal and fellow traveling was unnecessary, and indeed would have undercut the universal force which Trilling saw operating in the particulars of recent history. Somewhat implausibly, Trilling told the gathering that only the "moral realism" produced by the "free play of the moral imagination" could "prevent this corruption" and that "the most effective agent" of that imagination "has been the novel of the last two hundred years" (*Liberal* 221–22).

Both Rahv and Howe shared an interest in the fiction writer's participation in the "modification of the sentiments"—that literature may help produce historical changes in sensibility and perception. Rahv often stated this as the "coherence" which novelistic realism can provide. "The genuine innovator," he wrote in 1942, is one who "*at the very same time that he takes the world apart . . .* puts it back together again. For to proceed otherwise is to dissipate rather than alter our sense of reality" (*Image* 130). Irving Howe admired the political novel precisely because he saw within it the conditions of social change, for here "the *idea* of society, as distinct from the mere unquestioned workings of society, has penetrated the consciousness of the characters in all of its profoundly problematic aspects, so that there is to be observed in their behavior, and they are themselves often aware of, some coherent political loyalty or ideological identification" (*Politics* 19).

When the two groups of critics consciously debated each other in their respective journals and quarterlies, the nature and aims of fiction were often the main issues, though their underlying cultural politics were the motive of these discussions. To the degree that Trilling, Rahv, and Howe insisted upon defining the novel as a picture of the social world because they themselves wished to sustain a relation that might modify that world, their position was indeed irreconcilable with the stated views of the southern writers. Their criticism was meant to be *active,* if not revolutionary, whereas the New Critics consistently described their critical activity in terms of style and form, "*standards of judgment*" and "critical principles" (Tate, *Reason* 186, 195). Trilling, Rahv, and Howe objected to the New Critics' ostensible exclusion of art's social and political milieu and the effects that art might have upon it. Rahv declared that the new fascination with technique had less to do with literature than with a "distaste toward the actuality of experience." In "Fiction and the Criticism of Fiction," he responded directly to the "recent infection of the prose sense by poetics" and singled out Mark Schorer's "Technique as Discovery" as an "extreme version of the formalist tendency." Rahv read the New Criticism as a form of spiritualism: "it is as if critics were saying that the representation of experience, which is the primary asset of the novel, is a mere appearance; the really and truly real is to be discovered somewhere else, at some higher level beyond appearance" (*Myth* 38–39, 44, 45). On the other hand, John Crowe Ransom objected to Rahv's emphasis on content and asked, with Mark Schorer, "Can we not say that fiction, in being literature, will have style for its essential activity?" Ransom distinguished his own preferences from Rahv's: "the novels which [Rahv most desires], but least finds, are to turn upon 'ideas,' which would oppose themselves to my sentiments" ("Understanding," 197, 204).

We do not obtain an adequate understanding of these critics, or their discourse on fiction, if we allow their terms to exist at the opposite poles they suggest. "Style" and "ideas," on closer examination, were not so far apart in either the practice or the theory of criticism, for the New Critics, as Mark Krupnick has noted, were "greatly interested in general questions of society and culture" (10)—a fact apparent enough to anyone who has read the Agrarians' manifesto, *I'll Take My Stand*. On the other hand, the conservative narrative underlying liberal revision of such concepts as "politics," "realism," and "reality" brought the New York critics into closer proximity with the assumptions of the New Critical agenda, so that the striking consistency of their terms during this period is perfectly understandable. After all, since so many of those critics whose work constitutes the revision of liberalism actively sought or courted conservative ideas, it is hardly an accident that they ended up speaking a common language. Indeed, as we shall see, there were cultural and political grounds shared by the two groups, and these are brought into sharp focus by the attention which each gave to fiction.

This convergence is clearest in the semiotic play constituting the terms "realism" and "reality" in the novel discourse of the New York critics. The term "realism," which had connected art and politics in the thirties, remained in play but was now redefined in ways meant to distinguish it sharply from either "naturalism" or "social realism," and this transformation of "realism" was at once part of and inseparable from the liberal revision of reality. At the same time, this new sense of reality conflicted with a residual or perplexed commitment to art's social and political function, with the result that a positivist (mimetic) expectation of external and social detail seems to interfere with a more dominant focus on psychological and formal characteristics—dramatic tension, conflict, complexity— that directly overlapped with the formalist terminology of the New Critics.

The most visible or explicit redefinition of reality within literary discourse was Trilling's attack on Parrington and Dreiser, in "Reality in America." Trilling's charges are familiar enough: Parrington and the liberal culture he represents believe in "a thing called *reality;* it is one and immutable, it is wholly external, it is irreducible"; his mind has "but a limited sense of what constitutes a difficulty" (*Liberal* 4); Parrington "expresses the chronic American belief that there exists an opposition between reality and mind and that one must enlist in the party of reality" (10). All of his "errors of understanding," Trilling argues, "arise from his assumptions about the nature of reality" (4). Against the backdrop of contemporary Stalinism, Parrington is too sure of himself, too settled in liberal self-congratulation, or too self-assured of the liberal, progressive virtues he saw as the "main currents in American thought."

Still, Trilling's own politics make him far from willing to forfeit the idea of an external and implacable reality, with the result that his ideas of reality in this essay and in "Manners, Morals, and the Novel," published seven years later, do not always seem to square. In "Reality in America" (1940), Trilling disdains the correspondent, "transparent" relation between art and reality, and declares resolutely on behalf of "imagination and creativeness" (5), but in "Manners, Morals, and the Novel," Trilling takes American writers to task who "have not turned their minds to society" (*Liberal* 212). Their failure to touch "significantly on society, on manners," is evidence that Americans have committed themselves to an idea of reality which remains "abstract" because it doesn't evolve from and remain rooted in the facts of the social world—for example, though Americans may believe in the reality of "social class," they are unwilling to admit that social class "is indeed so real that it produces actual differences of personality" (216). Here Trilling doesn't really dismiss what he takes to be Parrington's position, but complicates the "external and hard" by insisting—in orthodox Marxist terms—upon the psychological determinance produced by that externality.

Trilling transferred the quality of "hardness" from the material world to the emotional complexity of a psychological world engaged in tension with the outer: "we want [our literature] to have . . . the completeness, the brilliance, the *hardness* of systematic thought" (Trilling's emphasis, 290). The "hardness" of literary ideas is their reality, but this is not simply the ability to discern the external facts of social existence—though it includes that—but also the capacity to remain in tension with them: "ideas may also be generated in the opposition of ideals," Trilling wrote in "The Meaning of a Literary Idea," "and in the felt awareness of the impact of new circumstances upon old forms of feeling and estimation, in the response to the conflict between new exigencies and old pieties" (*Liberal* 298). In such passages and definitions as these there is as much autobiography as there is theory, for Trilling is not only again stating here the central thesis of *The Liberal Imagination*—that liberalism must engage conservative ideas that complicate its own positions—but also abstracting from the dilemma of his own recent history.

The general target of Trilling's attack is the tendency of ideas in liberal culture "to deteriorate into ideology" (286), but, as much recent scholarship has pointed out, Trilling's vehemence had more specific sources, not only Parrington's influence but also Dreiser's "role in left-wing literary polemics" (Krupnick 67; see Cain 120–23). Parrington and Dreiser stood for those simplifications of reality which had produced the left's naive fascination with Stalinism, and Trilling had committed himself, as Krupnick notes, "to redefine 'reality' so as to wrest it from the Stalinists"—what Reising calls "a semantic war" (Krupnick 64; Reising 93). Thus the full meaning of Trilling's insistence upon "ideas" makes sense only when that term is paired with "ideology," the term signifying liberal failure. "Ideas" still carries within it the residual recognition of the political mind and its powers, though these became, in "The Meaning of a Literary Idea," the product of conflicting emotions.

Paradoxically, in valorizing the literary idea the New York critics effectively endorsed the stylistic priorities of the New Critics. It was here in the "literary idea" that Trilling, Rahv, and Howe tried to retain a political stance at the same time that they drew upon the conservative—often reactionary—modernism of European writing for their models of literary form. The "literary idea" didn't so much resolve this contradiction as make a virtue of it. The New Critics would object—and did—to the view that literature should have some political and social "relevance" (to recall a term from Tate's argument), but the New York critics were more in accord with them than either group was willing to admit, for their view of how literature achieved this relevance relied, as it did for Blackmur, Schorer, Ransom, and Tate, on form.

Trilling attempted to distinguish his position from the New Criticism at the beginning of "The Meaning of a Literary Idea"—the last essay of *The Liberal Imagination*—but the effect of his argument is to close rather than clarify the distance between himself and Wellek and Warren's *Theory of Literature*. Trilling describes two different kinds of ideas: the first, which the New Critics are most likely to reject, are those which appear in drama as "explicit exposition and debate"; but the second, on which Trilling places the greater stress and burden of his essay, are those which arise "whenever we put two emotions into juxtaposition" (283). Here we have a sense of the idea as emotion rather than thought, a sense closer to the "primitive" and "intuitive" for which Ransom argues in his review of Rahv ("The Understanding," 201–4) than to rational conceptualization. Indeed, Trilling affirmed the "primitive" throughout his essay on the literary idea, as the countervailing force to civilization, the necessary contradiction which produces ideas and great art (293, 301).

The contemporaneity or historical specificity of Trilling's formulation may be gauged by the transformation it enacts upon the two authorities supporting his thesis. Early in his essay, Trilling cites from Wordsworth's preface to *Lyrical Ballads*: "A poet's simple statement of a psychological fact recalls us to a proper simplicity about the nature of ideas. 'Our continued influxes of feeling,' said Wordsworth, 'are modified and directed by our thoughts, which are indeed the representatives of all our past feelings' " (287). In "Art and Fortune," an essay written the year before, Trilling had drawn upon Plato as his warrant against Eliot's rejection of ideas: "I think Plato was right when in *The Symposium* he represented ideas as continuous with emotions, both springing from the appetites" (*Liberal* 273). To this understanding Trilling brings the lived experience of contradiction felt by his generation, reincarnated throughout *The Liberal Imagination* in Trilling's dialectical view of "reality" in America, in the "indifference" which the best modern writers have shown to "liberal ideology" (98), in the "paradox of our natures" (221), and here, in the element of "juxtaposition" by which "the two emotions . . . are brought to confront each other" (283).

This formulation is as complex as it is useful: on the one hand it grounds the literary idea in the emotions produced by history; on the other it establishes the aesthetic, or formal, standard of contradiction and paradox as the central quality of great art. Nevertheless, insofar as Trilling's theory of the literary idea was modeled on the tragic paradoxes of history, and the moral ambiguity of human action, it reinforced the view of reality underlying New Critical thought, for writers like Cleanth Brooks established the same equation between "reality" and literary form. "Indeed, almost any insight important enough to warrant a great poem," Brooks wrote in "The Language of Paradox," "apparently has to be stated in such terms. Deprived of the character of paradox with its twin concomitants of irony and wonder, the matter of Donne's poem unravels into 'facts,' biological, sociological, and economic" (17–18). Trilling's kinship with New Critical technique is even more evident in his attending to "the way the confrontation" of emotions is "contrived." Finally, "the very form of a literary work, considered apart from its content, so far as that is possible, is in itself an idea" (283).

Certainly Trilling is trying to make room for direct statements of ideas in literature by emphasizing the role of dramatic form in maintaining the oppositions of those ideas (and emotions). This distinction between ideas and ideology served as a strategic maneuver used by Trilling, Rahv, and Howe to defend their ideas of literature against the charge of propaganda, but their appeal to dramatic form was nevertheless an appeal to one of the central elements in the New Critical aesthetic. Not only was "tension" the "central achievement in poetry" for Allen Tate (*Reason* 72), but the genealogy of that value reached back to Eliot's essays "Tradition and the Individual Talent" and "The Metaphysical Poets" and his ideas of "material compelled into unity," of "fusion" and the "concentration" of elements to "form a new compound." The emotion of poetry, Eliot argued, results from "the proper combination" of elements, remaining latent in them and not in the poet. Thus when Trilling suggested that "dialectic"—a word which carried within its history the injunction to revolutionary change—"is just another word for form," he wasn't very far from Brooks's discussion, in "The Heresy of Paraphrase," of drama's usefulness for describing poetry: "for the very nature of drama is that of something 'acted out'—something which arrives at its conclusion through conflict—something which builds conflict into its very being" (204). Both these passages are part of a parallel argument in which Trilling and Brooks try to distinguish literary discourse from mere statement, though Trilling attacked such statement as "ideology" and Brooks called it "a formula for action" (204).

Like Brooks, Trilling understood that dialectic form "has for its purpose . . . the leading of the mind to some conclusion" (283), but nothing in the remainder of his essay offers any other result from dramatic juxtaposition than uneasy equilibrium. Indeed, he praises Tolstoi and Dostoevski for rejecting "the attempt at formulated solution" and for their ability to "rest content with the 'negative capability,' " for "this willingness to remain in uncertainties, mysteries, and doubts, is not, as one tendency of modern feeling would suppose, an abdication of intellectual activity" but "is precisely an aspect of their intelligence, of their seeing the full force and complexity of their subject matter" (*Liberal* 299).

Thus the literary idea is not only an aesthetic dynamic, but also a psychological and a social one all at once. Krupnick has called this position Trilling's "enabling myth, of the self-divided man as cultural hero" (69), but this myth was widely dispersed, not only among liberals in conservative retreat, but also among the southern critics as well. For nearly all of them, the virtue of self-division was always double: on the one hand it was a guarantee against ideology; on the other, this guarantee was the mark of its adequacy to the form of "reality" itself. Trilling made this doubling explicit in the most often cited passage from "Reality in America": "in any culture there are likely to be certain artists who contain a large part of the dialectic within themselves, their meaning and power lying in their contradictions; they contain within themselves, it may be said, the very essence of the culture, and the sign of this is that they do not submit to serve the ends of any one ideological group or tendency" (*Liberal* 9). Rahv's understanding of the artist is strikingly similar, for he identifies "the depth and quality of the contradictions that a writer unites within himself" as "the truest measure of his achievement." Like Trilling, Rahv pointedly distinguished the artist from the ideologue, for "this is not primarily a matter of solutions, if any, provided by the writer . . . but of his force and integrity in reproducing these contradictions as felt experience" (*Image* 68).

In New Critical discourse, this opposition between "ideology" and "reality" is often presented in more formalist vocabulary as one between "paradox" and "paraphrase," but these binaries are constitutive of an identical point of view. In *The Well-Wrought Urn*, for example, Brooks argues that the "structure" of a poem does not unite "various elements into homogenous groupings," but joins "like with the unlike." Nor does this structure "reduce the contradictory attitudes to harmony by a process of abstraction." The "heresy of paraphrase" is precisely that it tends to "treat" this poetic structure "as propaganda" (195–200).

Further examples may be found almost at will in the literary discourse of the forties and fifties. Austin Warren, for instance, told his reader that the title of his book *Rage for Order* (1948) "couples together two contraries"; that art is successful when "there is an equilibrium which is also a tension"; that the artist must confront "disorder in one's self and in the world" (v). Just as Trilling affirmed this tension as the hallmark of Hawthorne's "cold realism," Warren valorized Hawthorne's fiction for its triplicate nesting of art, artist, and world: "The philosopher must decide between alternatives or reduce his thesis and antithesis to some underlying or overlying synthesis. But the novelist of a speculative turn need not push his positions to a stand. He can divide his conflicting insights between his characters, as Hawthorne does . . ." (89). As in Trilling's criticism, the language of "thesis," "antithesis," and "synthesis" is always an explicit but subdued reference to Marxist Hegelianism which supplies the differential politics of "equilibrium."

Trilling's language continued to employ a vestigial Marxism, stressing the importance of class, the material of manners, and the perception of contradiction; but his anti-Stalinism tended to convert historical, Marxist terms into romantic, ahistorical categories—what Gregory Jay has termed a "psychological Hegelianism" (567). In Krupnick's estimate, Trilling's mind worked "dialectically, not as the Marxists understand the dialectic— to bring about historical change—but to keep the culture on a steady course and maintain an always threatened equilibrium" (58). Trilling helped initiate the dematerialization of literary thinking and production by associating "realism" not with external facts but with the dialectic form of literary ideas produced by conflicting emotions. This was moral realism, in which literature became politics recollected in anguish.

The dominance of this position, as David Hirsch and Nicolaus Mills have argued, was decisive for the development of Americanist criticism in the fifties (Hirsch 420; Mills 4–6, 11–14). The literary idea reappeared in *The American Novel and Its Tradition*, where Chase identifies "contradiction" as the "form" of "many of the best American novels" (1, 6–7). It was the "unresolved contradictions" (244) that helped make American writing "romantic," and which distinguished it from the English novel (1–28). Properly situated in the fallout of postwar liberalism, the terms of *The American Novel* take their place in the cultural politics that constitute the literary idea and its transformation of "realism" and "reality." Chase meant to define American fiction on the basis of those very qualities for which it had been criticized: its "freedom" from "the conditions of actuality," its "obscurantism," its "willingness to abandon moral questions or to ignore the spectacle of man in society or to consider these things only indirectly or abstractly." To the ahistorical reader, Chase's argument might appear to distinguish American "romance" from European "realism" in fairly conventional terms, but in fact Chase revalued those terms by arguing the virtues of romanticism in the language of the "new realism": the "abstractness and profundity of romance allow it to formulate moral truths of universal validity"; romance can "express dark and complex truths unavailable to realism"; the "inner facts of political life have been better grasped by romance-melodramas . . . than by strictly realistic fiction" (ix–xi). Though Chase meant to identify qualities that are recurrent and essential to the American novel—"I do suggest," he wrote, "that the romance-novel *is*" (xi)—the way he reconstituted them merely reproduced the structures of postwar liberal discourse as a description of national genre.

Like Trilling, Philip Rahv and Irving Howe both thought that recent American writing suffered from a lack of literary ideas. In "Paleface and Redskin," Rahv declared that "literary life in America has seldom been so deficient in intellectual power," and saw the origin of this deficiency, as Trilling did, in "a dichotomy between experience and consciousness" (*Image* 4, 1). In "The Cult of Experience in American Writing," he noted the absence of any fictional character "who transforms ideas into actual dramatic motives instead of merely using them as ideological conventions" (9). In Howe's view, recent American fiction remained "oblique" and "indirect" precisely because the ideas necessary to "realistic portraiture" were missing: because it is a "mass society," "once familiar social categories and place-marks have now become . . . uncertain and elusive" (*World* 93, 88–89, 84).

Both men insisted that the best writing emerged from a system of relations—among the "coherence" of a literary work, its "realism," and its
informing "idea"—that suggests a parallel with Lukácsian "critical realism." In "Idea and Form in Literature," Lukács wrote that "without a
philosophy of life there can be no composition" (124) and cited Flaubert
to support his thesis: "I see no possibility today either of finding a new
principle or of paying any attention to the old principles. And so I am in
search of that idea upon which everything else depends, and cannot find
it" (letter to George Sand, in Lukács 125). For Rahv, Flaubert's dilemma
as Lukács framed it was his own; for the failure of the left had not been
redeemed by a "root-idea of a different order" and literary life seemed
detached "from principle" and fragmented ("Our Country," 309). Similarly, the "principle of realism" is the basis of the novel's "coherence,"
without which the writer cannot "alter our sense of reality" (*Image* 138,
130). Howe focused more specifically upon the writer's need for an "*idea*
of society" which penetrates "the consciousness of the characters in all of
its profoundly problematic aspects" (*Politics*, 19). Unable to "make eco-
nomical assumptions" that have their basis in "ideas," the postwar novelist
in "mass society" has a difficult time comprehending the social world and
giving "coherence to his perceptions" (*World* 84, 90).

Certainly Howe must be distinguished from the mainstream of postwar liberalism represented by Trilling and Niebuhr and Schlesinger. Part
of his controversial attack on Baldwin and Ellison, for example, emerged
from an impatience with "criticism" notable for its "Freudian corrosion of
motives," its "dialectical agility," and its "weary skepticism" with respect
to "ideal claims, especially those made by radical and naturalist writers"
("Black Boys," 359). Howe continued to think of Marxism as "the best
available method for understanding and making history. Even at its most
dogmatic, it proposes a more realistic theory of society than the currently
popular liberalism" ("Our Country," 577; see Wald 275). The stability of
Howe's commitment shows here in his resistance to the psychological and
formalist redefinition of realism, and in his requirement that a writer make
"the connection between subject and setting" (*World* 93). Accordingly, he
admired Richard Wright's understanding of "society as an enclosing force"
and rejected (what he read as) Ellison's "unqualified assertion of self-
liberation," which "violates the reality of social life, the interplay between
external conditions and personal will" ("Black Boys," 103, 115).

Still, both Rahv and Howe affirmed the pervasive distinction of the postwar period between art and ideology—without question the central nega-
tion which unified the entire spectrum of critics. Analyzing Rahv's 1939
essay "Proletarian Literature: An Autopsy," Alan Wald has shown that

Rahv came to believe in art as a form of "experience" inherently resistant to the simplifications of propaganda or ideology. Wald further identifies the source of this distinction in Dewey's *Art as Experience* (1934): "great literature, inasmuch as it captures and expresses experience, simply cannot be 'ideological' " (Wald 226–30). In "The Cult of Experience in American Writing," Rahv explicitly situates his affirmation of "experience" in a dialogue with discredited Marxism: "The part experience plays in the aesthetic sphere might well be compared to the part that the materialist conception of history assigns to economy. Experience, in the sense of this analogy, is the substructure of literature above which there rises a superstructure of values, ideas, and judgments—in a word, of the multiple forms of consciousness" (*Image* 18). Howe also argued that "unique forms of imaginative literature create a space free of political ideology" and defended an early story by Trilling on that basis (Wald 318, 237). What Trilling called "active" literature is work that "happily exists beyond our powers of explanation" (*Liberal* 292).

As Wald rightly notes, this was a naive view of the relations between experience and ideology, for today we are more apt to think of ideology as that which constitutes our experience, rather than as mere propaganda. The status they gave "experience" was another element of the consensus discourse which the New York writers shared with the New Critics; for both groups, the highest forms of literature, as Tate said of poetry, make use of "the rich connotation with which language has been informed by experience" (*Reason* 71). While it would be mistaken to collapse these very different critics into a homogenous unity, the social and political meanings embodied in their use of words like "drama," "contradiction," "ideology," and "experience" give us access to a set of discursive boundaries, as it were, which all of them observed.

One must recall that the New York writers understood the dynamics of tension and dramatic form to originate in their own social and political history, which they now distinguished from any utopian notions of History. From Trilling, Hook, Niebuhr, and other "intellectual Nestors," Daniel Bell wrote in 1957, "we have inherited the key terms which dominate discourse today: irony, paradox, ambiguity, and complexity" (*End* 300). Bell located these terms in the disillusionments of the thirties, but Cleanth Brooks listed the identical set of terms—" 'ambiguity,' 'paradox,' 'complex of attitudes,' and . . . 'irony' "—as those necessary to describe poetic structure (195). Seen in the context of revisionist liberal discourse, this otherwise accidental parallel shows itself as a plausible consequence of an underlying agreement about the homologous structures of reality and art.

II

Not surprisingly, this confluence produced a variety of agreements on a spectrum of subjects involving literary history and postwar culture. Indeed, a review of the collected essays published by the New Critics and the New York intellectuals reveals a rather startling similarity of interest in such writers as Yeats, Keats, Hawthorne, Kafka, James, Dickinson, and Forster, and these writers tended to play similar roles in the various arguments of the critics. Hawthorne is a case in point, valorized by Trilling for his "cold realism," useful to Yvor Winters for rejecting the "simplified conceptions of his Puritan ancestors" (174), affirmed by Austin Warren for his "conflicting insights" (89), and recovered by Arthur Schlesinger, Jr., as a "tough-minded Jacksonian" (*Vital* 161).

The liberal discourse on "reality" must also be credited with the pervasive attention given the work of Henry James. During the forties, discussions of James appeared in the books and articles of New Critic and New York intellectual alike, where his work is nearly always viewed as an example of what the novelist should emulate. This is the era of the James "revival," so noticeable that one of the questions in a *Partisan Review* symposium ("The State of American Writing, 1948") asked its respondents to speculate on the reasons for this renewed interest. F. O. Matthiessen alone edited three editions of James's fictions and notebooks, and published *Henry James: The Major Phase* (1944), an analysis of the later novels. Alexander Cowie's *The Rise of the American Novel* (1948) surveyed the development of narrative in this country from the standpoint of Jamesian artistic form; the penultimate chapter of his study is devoted to James, while the last fifty years (1890–1940) are treated in a chapter titled "New Directions." Austin Warren placed his essay on James at the end of *Rage for Order*. Trilling, Rahv, and Howe all wrote essays on James; Trilling and Howe showed special interest in *The Princess Casamassima*, the book in which James ventured furthest into political and historical ideas. "Since the centenary of James's birth in 1943," Edmund Wilson wrote in 1948, "he has been celebrated, interpreted, reprinted, on a scale which, I believe, is unprecedented for a classical American writer" (*Triple* 130).

Wilson offered his own ideas about the reasons for this celebration: "A novelist whose typical hero invariably decides not to act, who remains merely an intelligent onlooker, appeals for obvious reasons to a period when many intellectuals, formerly romantic egoists or partisans for the political Left, have been resigning themselves to the role of observer or of passive participant in activities which cannot command their whole allegiance. The stock of Henry James has gone up in the same market as that of Kafka" (130). Certainly, Trilling admired James for dramatizing, in Hyacinth Robinson, the "equilibrium of awareness" (*Liberal* 85; see Krupnick 69–75), and for elucidating in his criticism the "essential moral nature of the novel" (268). Rahv invokes James as the one American example of a writer capable of "apprehending the vitally new principle of realism by virtue of which the art of fiction in Europe was . . . rapidly evolving toward an hitherto inconceivable condition of objectivity and familiarity with existence" (*Idea* 13).

Predictably, the New Critics admired James's fiction for its technical contributions to the novel which have earned it the status of "art." In his seminal essay "Technique as Discovery," the only American writer Schorer mentions in the company of Conrad, Ford, and Joyce is James. These are the writers who have taught us "that technique *contains* intellectual and moral implications . . . it *discovers* them" (74). Characteristically, New Critics argued that the "moral implications" of literature were a consequence of technique, but that literature could refine and express morals was an idea they held in common with the New York critics. In 1934, near the height of interest in proletarian fiction in the United States, R. P. Blackmur wrote of Henry James: "There is in any day of agonized doubt and exaggerated certainty as to the relation of the artist to society, an unusual attractive force in the image of a man whose doubts are conscientious and whose certainties are all serene." For Blackmur the source of that conscientious serenity was James's loyalty to "the form of the imagination": "everything must be sacrificed to the exigence of that form, it must never be loose or overflowing but always tight and contained. There was the 'coercive charm' of Form, so conceived, which would achieve, dramatise or enact, the moral intent of the theme by making it finely intelligible, better than anything else" (*Art* xxxvii–xxxviii).

This New Critical marriage of human morality and aesthetic form is hardly distinguishable from Trilling's "moral realism." Both points of view are bound up in the search for a form in which a moral culture might be preserved (which is to say, in which a more complex idea of "reality" might be embodied and called to our attention). When Schorer concludes his article on the "technique of modern fiction," his claims and exhortations are not unlike those which Trilling is making at the same time. Technique, Schorer wrote, "discovers the complexity of the modern spirit, the difficulty of personal morality, and the fact of evil" (86). As we have seen, a similar sense of the times and of the obligations of the novel informs Trilling's plea for "moral realism" at the end of "Manners, Morals, and the Novel."

The most dramatic and consequential agreement among these critics was their uniform dismissal of most recent and contemporary American fiction.

At the end of his essay on the "literary idea," when Trilling gives an assessment of contemporary American literature, he finds it to be "essentially passive"—without the "activity" and tension of a mind grappling with contraries. Rahv thought recent fiction expressed the "disunity of the American creative mind": producing works "deficient in intellectual power" or marked by an "excess of refinement" (*Idea* 4–5). It is true, as I noted above, that Howe preferred the protest fiction of Richard Wright to the oblique moralism he saw in fifties writing, and he had greater patience with "abstract ideas" than either Trilling or Rahv; still, Howe felt that American writers had failed "to see politics as a distinctive mode of social existence, with values and manners of its own" and that the few attempts to do so failed to "sustain the theme" or develop it as effectively as did European novels (*Politics* 20, 161–63). The terms of the formalist estimates were different, but the judgment was the same: "In the United States during the last twenty-five years," Schorer declared, "we have had many big novels but few good ones" ("Technique," 80); and Ransom criticized Dreiser and Farrell as "American naturalists," whose "heroes and situations are always about to collapse into cases" ("Understanding," 200).

As may be apparent from Ransom's comments, these judgments were part of that more underlying agreement on a redefined reality, here working itself out as an attack on "naturalism." The relegation of earlier American narrative fiction to a second-order status was a characteristic corollary of the effort to dissociate one's position from the naiveté of literary politics in the thirties. Such writers as Dos Passos, O'Neill, and Wolfe, Trilling thought, were too dependent (or "passive") upon ideas which had hardened into ideology, too reliant upon a conception of ideas as "pellets of intellection or crystallizations of thought" (*Liberal* 302). As noted above, naturalistic thought became associated—mistakenly, Dewey and Hook argued—with a naive rationalism, a dangerous optimism and certainty in human affairs. This superficial construction of "naturalism" was the mirror image of the renewed authority given to psychological reality by the "new realism": the tragic sense of life, the moral imagination, the murky interiority of complex emotions and unconscious motivations.

The New Critics' critiques of literary naturalism were based upon its formal limitations for both reader and writer. Donne's poem "The Canonization," Brooks points out, "will scarcely prove to the hard-boiled naturalist that [its] lovers, by giving up the world, actually attain a better world" (211–12). In his essay "Technique as Discovery" Schorer attacks specific writers like James T. Farrell for their "endless redundancy in the description of the surface of American life" and argues that the naturalistic method prevents writers "from exploring through all the resources of technique the full amplifications of their subjects" (80, 82). During this time, "naturalistic" methods seemed to provide too little access to how things really are or might be. In its materialism, its assumption of determinate behavior, and its documentary methods literary naturalism relied too much for its truths upon surface detail and failed to provide an adequate portrait of the inner life. Schorer noted that "naturalism had a sociological and disciplinary value in the nineteenth century" because "it enabled the novel to grasp materials and make analyses which had eluded it in the past," but it did not "provide the means to the maximum of reality coherently contained."

> Even the Flaubertian ideal of objectivity seems, today, an unnecessarily limited view of objectivity, for as almost every good writer of this century shows us, it is quite as possible to be objective about subjective states as it is to be objective about the circumstantial surfaces of life. Dublin, in *Ulysses*, is a moral setting: not only a city portrayed in the naturalistic fashion of Dickens' London, but also a map of the modern psyche with its oblique and baffled purposes. (82)

Schorer is worth citing at some length because his analysis foregrounds so clearly the oppositions which structure aesthetic discourse at this time among both liberal and conservative critics. Remaining within the terms of "technique," Schorer isn't as explicit as he might have been about the political resonance of words like "circumstantial," with its implications of determinance and social reform (of circumstance).

Certainly for such critics as Tate, Ransom, and Brooks, the antipathy for naturalism was a position of long standing, so that what they had to say about naturalism in writing was always connected in their minds with the modern world's surrender to various forms of "positivism"—in politics as well as science and technology. Thus Ransom suggests that we "go a long way towards defining the fiction which we call 'naturalistic' by calling it the fiction of the author who has no style," for the "labor [that style] requires of us is paradoxical. . . . It does not furnish us the kind of language to use in business or science, and we do not seem to be quite honest if we claim that its language is calculated to serve our ideological designs" ("Understanding," 200–201). Here Ransom not only argues the very same thesis propounded by Trilling, Rahv, and Howe, that true art cannot be ideological, but provides a measure of the new conservatism in the liberal position.

For the liberal critic, the rejection of naturalism was a more difficult matter, for it involved a reorientation of outlook, in both philosophy and politics. "It becomes easier and easier to *say* these days (we have known it for a long time)," Leslie Fiedler responded to a *Partisan Review* inquiry, "that the writer in the forties is essentially concerned with establishing alternatives to naturalism. This involves the reinstatement in his vocabulary of such words as 'freedom,' 'responsibility' and 'guilt,' words which a little while ago he regarded as obscenities, and which even yet he cannot manage without uneasiness" ("State of American Writing," 870).

In 1942, Philip Rahv noted the "decline of naturalism" with some displeasure, because naturalism had been an important component of the novel's ability to promote social change—to "alter our sense of reality." Naturalism, Rahv reminded his readers,

> also enlivened and, in fact, revolutionized writing by liquidating the last assets of "romance" in fiction and by purging it once and for all of the idealism of the "beautiful lie"—of the long-standing inhibition against dealing with the underside of life, with those inescapable day-by-day actualities traditionally regarded as too "sordid" and "ugly" for inclusion within an aesthetic framework.

This passage is a striking exposure of contrary emotions and ideas, for Rahv's figurative language associates the virtues of naturalism with Stalin's liquidations and purges, actions that had embarrassed the left a few years earlier and were a major force in subverting radical liberalism. There is perhaps an intended correlation between naturalism and Marxism: both had helped to expose Capital ("the last assets"), and both were now in decline, for both had "lost the power to cope with the ever-growing element of the problematical in modern life" (*Image* 136). It is no small irony that Rahv's judgment is based on the same assumptions made by Schorer, six years later, in the article which Rahv attacked for its formalism.

Like Schorer and Trilling, Rahv looked to Europe's fiction for examples of what American narrative should become. As James Gilbert notes in his description of literary radicalism in America, Rahv's internationalism was no sudden preference, but had existed from the beginning of *Partisan Review* in uneasy alliance with the program for revolutionary literature in the thirties. Rahv's experience during this period confirmed his view of American anti-intellectualism and convinced him, as Gilbert writes, that "only the Europeanization of American literature offered a resolution to the contradiction between the artist's revolutionary consciousness and the stagnation of American art" (185).

As Trilling understood, however, their admiration for the aesthetic complexity of the modern Europeans put liberal readers in the difficult position of rejecting writers produced by "the liberal democratic tradition" they espoused, while they preferred the work of writers who "do not seem to confirm in us the social and political ideals which we hold." Such writers as Yeats and Eliot, Proust and Joyce, Lawrence and Gide appealed to Trilling because of their "literary qualities"—that is, because their work expresses the primitive tensions of conflicting emotions that define the "literary idea"—and because these literary qualities "demand of us a great agility and ingenuity in coping with their antagonism to our social and political ideals." From the tension of confronting and entertaining conservative ideas, the democratic liberal tradition will develop a more complex view of reality and produce a more powerful literature: "then we shall stand in a relation to ideas which makes an active literature possible" (*Liberal* 301, 303).

To the degree that these critics held in common a suspicion of naturalist thought and an admiration for European literature, they were united in the effort to preserve "art" from contamination with mass culture.[2] Surely this was nothing new for many of the formalists. After all, the virtue of "tension," for Tate, was its usefulness in distinguishing "good poetry" from "the poetry of the mass language," from merely didactic poetry or propaganda (*Reason* 62–63). Such a distinction was always implicit in the assumption that art could not be ideological. Nevertheless, it further defines how conservative the politics of culture became in the discourse of the new liberalism.

For the liberal critic, the identification of high art was often set against the proletarian aesthetics of the thirties, which Rahv thought had encouraged the "worst tendencies" of the writer. For the "popular political creeds of our time," he wrote, have had the effect of "sanctioning the relaxation of standards and justifying the urge to come to terms with semi-literate audiences" (*Image* 4). Furthermore, reconceiving the function of art in terms of its "essential morality," as Fiedler did, allowed the liberal critic and writer to retain a sense of public mission ("the *necessity* of the practice of his art"), but in the defense of art: "Our awakening was gradual, though a little faster than our political disenchantment, toward a realization of the enormous *contempt* for art just below the culture-vulturish surface of the John Reed Clubs" ("State of American Writing," 871).

The "mass society" trope that was a key interpretive figure in discussion of culture during the forties and fifties was at once fully implicated

---

2. Grant Webster has defined the New York intellectuals as "a group of men and women whose intellectual life is defined in terms of a dialectic or tension between social reality and avant-garde tastes. On the one hand they acknowledge the reality of society" in a way that makes them "essentially bourgeois and realistic," while on the other hand, their intellectual life "is marked by its antagonism toward bourgeois culture, its compulsive desire to make cultural fashion, and its defense of the avant-garde, 'modernist' tradition in literature and art" (212).

in and denied by the discourse of irony and ambiguity, for mass culture became the object of critique by those no longer compelled by revolutionary urgency but not entirely happy with the alternative either. Here is the origin of the beleaguered determination in such remarks as Rahv's: "If under present conditions we cannot stop the ruthless expansion of mass-culture, the least we can do is to keep apart and refuse its favors" ("Our Country," 310). Richard Chase employs rhetoric that has come to be associated with Norman Mailer: "heresy and an idea of culture are the modern critic's best weapons against the smothering uniformity of public opinion and the totalitarian mind, the monstrous offspring of contemporary history" ("Art, Nature, Politics," 593). The field of politics, as Trilling said, was transformed or limited to "culture," but in practice what this meant was a displacement of their former interest in social reform by a new concern with the specter of Stalinism at home, "public opinion and the totaliarian mind."

In the defense of art, the critics themselves were willing to admit they shared a common enemy. John Crowe Ransom found a "modest comfort" in his "impression that . . . the *Sewanee* and *Kenyon Reviews* are as much opposed to the 'middlebrow' critics as is the *Partisan*" ("State of American Writing," 883). Their common opposition to middlebrow critics (Ransom names Van Wyck Brooks, H. M. Jones, Donald Adams, and Bernard De Voto) and middlebrow culture is another expression of their sense of powerlessness before the onslaught of the mass, and in their effort to define and segregate a "highbrow" culture we see again that thinking about the novel was always thinking about the preservation of an idea of culture. The novel—as the art form most habitually related to history and contemporary society—was to preserve an elite culture from one which it could not change.

For the Old Left, the defense of highbrow culture was begun early by Rahv and Clement Greenberg to rescue avant-garde art (once disparaged by American socialists as the decadent creation of bourgeois culture) as inherently revolutionary (opposed to bourgeois, mass culture) and to distinguish it from "kitsch." The most dangerous threat to high art, in their view, came from hybrid "middlebrow" culture, an idea given its fullest exposition by Dwight Macdonald: "Masscult is at best a vulgarized reflection of High Culture," and competition between the two "leads at best to that middlebrow compromise called Midcult." The primary threat comes from the fact that even these distinctions are difficult to recognize and maintain: "High Culture could formerly address itself only to the *cognoscenti*," whereas "in this country . . . class lines are especially weak" and the boundaries between high and low culture tend to blur (*Against* 34). Here, as in the thinking of Trilling and Rahv, one is faced with the paradox that critics who had in one degree or another associated with the "radical vanguard" (Bloom 43–67) were using Marxist analytical tools to defend class distinctions as the basis of high art and legitimate culture.

One of the more interesting examples of the uprooted Marxism haunting the discourse of liberal critics was the conclusion they reached that the novel was dying. Trilling began his "Art and Fortune" by rebutting Ortega's argument that the novel's death had evolved naturally from a technical exhaustion, insisting instead that the deterioration of society was the cause of the novel's decline (*Liberal* 257). This is a characteristic Marxist reluctance to attribute to art an autonomous, technical evolution, distinct from the conditions of society in which art is produced; but the subtext seems to be that the obituary on the novel is a kind of allegory for the end or impossibility of socialism in the United States. Because the novel, in their thinking, was the product of class conflict, it must decline along with revolutionary socialism if the dynamic of social contradiction is absorbed by the new shapelessness of "mass society."

Trilling hadn't always held this position. As recently as 1939, Trilling wrote that Hawthorne's complaint about the comparative dearth of novelistic materials in the United States could no longer be advanced: "There is a superb 'thickness' about the feel of American life"—which is to say, the life here offers sufficient materials for the novel ("Situation in American Writing," 625). But nine years later, in "Art and Fortune," Trilling argues that the "diminution of the reality of class, however socially desirable in many respects," has contributed to "the falling-off in the energy of ideas that once animated fiction." In the United States, "the real basis of the novel has never existed" (*Liberal* 262, 260). Such people as Martin Luther King, Daniel Bell, and Michael Harrington make clear in subsequent years the inaccuracy of the "mass society" concept, but it was instrumental in producing the evident circularity and denial of Trilling's argument. The belief in the existence of a mass society, blurring all the distinctions upon which the novel depends, necessarily entails the death of the novel (so defined).

Trilling's logic persisted in some quarters throughout the fifties. In *After the Lost Generation* (1951), one of the first books on postwar fiction to appear, John Aldridge followed a similar line: when a "stable order of values . . . breaks down and disappears altogether from a society not only must the society itself but literature, as we normally think of it, cease to exist" (232). The most influential restatement of Trilling's position was Irving Howe's assessment of fifties fiction in "Mass Society and Post-Modern Fiction": instead of the familiar terms of conflict between classes, the writer was now faced with representing a "prosperous malaise" that was at once "vague and without shape." One can represent shapelessness,

Howe avers, but "to do it one needs to be Chekhov; and that is hard" (*World* 89). Leslie Fiedler's contributed to this analysis as well: he had no sooner announced the "Age of the Novel" than he declared that "it has already destroyed itself" (*End* 170).

Their perception of the novel's decline was really an obituary for a time in which radical politics and revolutionary aesthetics had seemed compatible: "the old connection between literature and politics has been dissolved," Trilling wrote in 1963 (*Beyond* 10). The New York intellectuals preserved their political spirit (by being realistic) at the same time as they defended highbrow aesthetics against the incursions of mass culture (by defending European modernist formalism). At bottom this was a conflict between their aesthetic sensibilities and their political energies. The important fact about this conflict in the anti-Stalinist era of the forties and early fifties was that modernist aesthetics seemed to offer a more adequate refuge for the ironic complexities of their imperiled political spirit than the conventions of realism. Thus their injunctions for narrative fiction became entangled in self-canceling prescriptions for novels of manners on the one hand (to keep their "clear and effective relations with reality") and on the other for novels which provide the "opportunity to identify ourselves with a mind that willingly admits it is a mind and does not pretend that it is History or Events or the World but only a mind thinking and planning—possibly planning our escape" (Trilling, *Liberal* 270). This was a delicate operation for the New York critics because they wished to preserve the feeling—as Joseph Frank wrote in 1956—that "they were actively engaged in the political life, while in fact they were tacitly rejecting it from the standpoint of art that the New Critics defended with less tact and more belligerancy" (256).

Together, the two groups established a dominant literary discourse. On the one hand, New Critics discussed fiction as a "pure" form, attending in unprecedented fashion to the "technique" of fiction; on the other, the New York intellectuals despaired of finding the kind of novelistic realism they agreed could not be written in a mass culture. Both valued form, coherence, and forms of dramatic presentation—complex, ironic, ambiguous. As Grant Webster has shown, the interweaving of the positions these two groups embodied was to some degree institutionalized in the *Kenyon Review*: "during its great days, the *Kenyon Review* was edited by both ex-Fugitives and New York Intellectuals and thereby united the two most active and often hostile groups of critics under one benevolent aegis" (104, 102–7); at the same time *Partisan Review* also printed the work of "both persuasions" (221). "Relations have improved between the 'social' and the 'aesthetic' camps of criticism," Ransom declared. "The disillusionment with revolutionism in this country has not knocked out the social camp, far from it, and it makes that kind of critic all the more impressive. I incline to think that we shall come, presently, to a felt need for breadth of view" ("Understanding," 208). Indeed, such writers as Ransom and Rahv, Schorer and Trilling, were helping to constitute that view, though to the postwar writer it might seem more constraining than broad.

This confluence of critical thought was made possible largely by the redefinition of reality and realism produced by the decline of the left and the revision of liberal discourse. Though the real benefactor of all this jockeying would appear to have been "art," it should be clear by now that "art" was in one sense a spectral image projected, as it were, by this discourse, almost necessary to it, as it came into uneasy alliance with formalist vocabulary. In noting this and elaborating upon the unifying elements of their dialogue, we observe the intimidating spectrum of orthodoxy which evolved in novelistic discourse, within which the imagination of the postwar writer was equally immersed.

3

Form and Authority

The Writer's Point of View

> The New Criticism seems to have triumphed pretty generally, PR's view
> of American life is indeed partisan, and a large proportion of writers,
> intellectuals, critics—whatever we may care to include in the omnibus—
> have moved their economic luggage from the WPA to the Luce chain as
> a writer for *Time* or *Life* once remarked. Among the major novelists, Dos
> Passos, Farrell, Faulkner, Steinbeck, and Hemingway have traveled from
> alienation to varying degrees of acceptance, if not outright proselytizing,
> for the American Century.
>
> Norman Mailer, 1952

> The "realistic" story as a container and expression of this life has be-
> come a mockery, a form that is unable to speak to us any longer in a
> pertinent way.
>
> Seymour Krim, 1952

In the late forties the voices of the formalists—speaking largely from the
academy—and the New York intellectuals alike exerted a paralyzing effect
upon American narrative fiction. Their seemingly opposed demands for
social relevance and formal technique actually endorsed a view of reality—
both elitist and politically debilitated—which writers either did not share,
or could not afford to share, since such a view defined only what seemed
no longer possible (politically relevant art) or defined a formal "container"
into which a fiction writer must pour his or her content. At the same time,
the writer was in essential agreement with the underlying assumptions that
marked the conservative retreat of the "new liberalism" and formed the
basis of the discourse the writer found so prescriptive. The broad effect of
this prescriptive atmosphere was to erode further the authority of the writer,
already weakened by the literary history of the thirties and early forties,

when the ideological impulse behind naturalism and social realism was both discredited and displaced by ideas of art and culture thought to be ideologically neutral. That loss of confidence had amounted to the removal of an entire and habitual point of view, as well as a subject, and in this vacuum the postwar emphasis upon formal craft acted as a tourniquet, inhibiting the circulation of those sources of feeling and consciousness to which the new writer inevitably turned in the search for a vantage of unembarrassed authority.

For the most part, the postwar writers saw themselves in direct opposition to both their critics and their popular audience, rather than engaged with them in a dialogue structured by shared assumptions. From writers as different as Flannery O'Connor, Robert Creeley, Ralph Ellison, Norman Mailer, Jack Kerouac, Mary McCarthy, Saul Bellow, Gilbert Sorrentino, and Thomas Pynchon, one gathers at least a uniform impression of constriction, of being expected to write fiction according to a standard at odds with their own points of view. Robert Creeley described the late forties as a time when "the colleges and universities were dominant in their insistence upon an *idea* of form extrinsic to the given instance. . . . [It] was this assumption of a *mold*, of a means that could be gained beyond the literal fact of the writing *here and now*, that had authority" (42).

As Grant Webster has shown, the formalists had pretty much taken over the university by 1950, part of what Edmund Wilson called "the inevitable gravitation toward teaching jobs of able young literary men who can find no decent work outside them" (111–29, 238–43; Wilson, *Classics* 116). In *The Literary Situation* (1954), Malcolm Cowley argued that this development was both direct and debilitating: "All the novelists have a double audience in mind: first there is the broader public they would like to reach without really trying, and second there are the critics they must be sure to please— the distinguished critics for the quarterlies, who write with such an air of certainty about the faults to be shunned and the virtues to be praised in American fiction" (62). Speaking of Kerouac's difficulty in finding a publisher, Gilbert Sorrentino directed his criticism at the New York literary establishment rather than the academy: "in the fifties there was quite literally no place to publish if you did not either know those people or write the way they thought you should write" (Barone 237).

This sense of constraint was so widely felt that narrative form in those years was influenced by an explicit determination to break free of it. Even John Updike, perhaps the virtuoso craftsman of the last thirty years, recognized the need for a prose fiction more open to existence, and praised Salinger for making "new room for shapelessness, for life as it is lived" (*Writers*, 4th ser., 451). Saul Bellow, who would increasingly speak on behalf of form and restraint in culture, nevertheless remembers the need to escape them at the beginning of his career:

> My first two books are well made. I wrote the first quickly but took great pains with it. I labored with the second and tried to make it letter-perfect. In writing *The Victim* I accepted a Flaubertian standard. Not a bad standard, to be sure, but one which, in the end, I found repressive—repressive because of the circumstances of my life and because of my upbringing in Chicago as the son of immigrants.

Eventually, he decided "I was afraid to let myself go." From that recognition, Bellow produced *The Adventures of Augie March*, in which he "took off many of these restraints" (*Writers*, 3d ser., 182).

Bellow himself later criticized the looseness and intimacy of *Augie*, saying, "I took off too many [restraints], went too far, but I was feeling the excitement of discovery" (26). Thus Bellow's early development is a persuasive index of that period, for even Bellow's conservative temperament shared to some degree the conviction that opposed craft and feeling, and sought a new authority in the immediacy of feeling. One measure of Bellow's success is the freedom his third novel made possible for a younger generation. Beginning to write short fiction in the last years of the fifties, Pynchon was encouraged by such models as "Kerouac and the Beat writers," and "the diction of Saul Bellow in *The Adventures of Augie March*," which showed him how "at least two very distinct kinds of English could be allowed in fiction to coexist. . . . The effect was exciting, liberating" (*Slow* 6–7).

The arbiters of form were identified explicitly with the schools and the literary journals they supported. When Sorrentino got out of the army in 1953 and began a "massive, hopeless novel," he remembers there was "an enormously conscious drive among many lost young writers at that time to make the prose look different from the prose in the *Partisan Review* of the day and the *Hudson Review* of the day, and, oh God, *Commentary*" (Alpert 17–18). In 1958, Kenneth Koch imagined that if "one goes to the *Hudson Review* / With a package of matches and sets fire to the building," he might well "end up in prison with trial subscriptions / To the *Partisan, Sewanee*, and *Kenyon Review*." The speaker in this poem ("Fresh Air") quotes another disgruntled voice: "You make me sick with all your talk about restraint and mature talent!" (233, 229). Thomas Pynchon came back to Cornell from his hitch in the navy and "found academic people deeply alarmed over the *cover* of the *Evergreen Review* then current, not to mention what was inside" (*Slow* 8).

The pressure of those New York intellectuals who proclaimed "the death of the novel" was strong enough to provoke, in 1957, a collection of essays entitled *The Living Novel*. "We are told by critics that the novel is dead," Bellow contributed, in "Distractions of a Fiction Writer." "These people can't know what the imagination is nor what its powers are. I wish I could believe in their good-natured objectivity. But I can't. I should like to disregard them, but that is a little difficult because they have a great deal of power. Not real power, perhaps, but power of a sort. And they can be very distracting" (Hicks 6–7). In the same collection, Ralph Ellison showed that he too had been listening: "They tell us again and again of the Lost Generation [who], we are told, did that which we cannot hope to do, and if this fails to discourage us the nineteenth century novel of manners is held before us as final evidence of our futility and the novel's point of highest glory and swift decline" (75).

In such reactions, Henry James is often the explicit object of resistance, not only because he is the model which many critics held up, but also because the formal order these critics valued in James seemed alien to the contemporary experience of the postwar writer. In the preface to *Roderick Hudson*, written for the New York edition of his novels, James had confidently remarked that although "relations stop nowhere," the "exquisite problem of the artist is eternally but to draw, by a geometry of his own, the circle within which they shall happily *appear* to do so." The novelist is like the painter who "wishes both to treat his chosen subject and to confine his necessary picture" (Blackmur, *Art* 5, 14).

Ellison objected to such geometry because it resulted in a form "too restricted to contain the experience [he] knew" (*Shadow* 103). By itself, this sense of James's art would not bear much scrutiny, but it was James's attention to form, to the social details and moral discriminations of specific class realities, that chiefly recommended him as a model to postwar critics, and it was to this model that the young writers objected. For Ellison, such an idea or model of narrative art didn't allow room for a "society hot in the process of defining itself," for a reality—psychological or social—always in the making. It was this perception of realism as a kind of formal "container" or "mold" that Krim referred to in his book review of 1952: "Our fiction is now addressing a fiction of ourselves—not what is actually going on." Significantly, Krim found it necessary to append a comment to his article after reading *Invisible Man*, which he described as "the only recent U.S. novel trying to pioneer in the direction we've been discussing" (353).

The most outspoken opponent of "craft" at the time was Jack Kerouac, whose *On the Road* and later experiments in "spontaneous prose" provoked such contempt from the critics and academic press. "I spent my entire youth writing slowly with revisions and endless re-hashing speculation and deleting and got so I was writing one sentence a day," he told one interviewer, "and the sentence had no FEELING. Goddamit, FEELING is what I like in art, not CRAFTINESS and the hiding of feelings." In Kerouac's caricature of what he was rejecting—"all that dreary analysis and things like 'James entered the room, and lit a cigarette. He thought Jane might have thought this too vague a gesture' "—the figure of Henry James appears twice (once as Jane) in the room of Kerouac's imagination. Kerouac's parody was certainly inadequate to the accomplishments and difficulties of traditional fiction, but his dismissal shows that when a writer becomes conscious of certain narrative devices and specific kinds of sentences, they become unusable and lose their authority. To employ them feels like parody, or fraud, or both (*Jack* 541, 555).

For Kerouac, the contemporary emphasis upon technique meant subordinating experience to form, instead of allowing experience to develop its own form. Craft was thus a form of dishonesty which Kerouac associated with the novel-as-picture—James's repeated analogy, as well as one that recurs in the writing of Trilling, Howe, and Rahv. This view underlies a passage late in *On the Road*, in which Sal recounts the time Dean Moriarty showed him a photograph of his girlfriend Camille and their new baby.

> these were all snapshots which our children would look at someday with wonder, thinking their parents had lived smooth, well-ordered, stabilized-within-the-photo lives and got up in the morning to walk proudly on the sidewalks of life, never dreaming the raggedy madness and riot of our actual lives. (208)

Sal's objection to the stable confinement of the picture serves not only as a critique of photographic realism and the naturalist's reliance upon pictorial documentation. This objection, of course, he shared with the current critical opinion of naturalism, but Kerouac objected to form itself as an aesthetic goal. The fiction writer for whom form was a prior value would have a tendency to freeze life and miss the motion; like Ellison, Kerouac wanted a prose that expressed the fluid present, "hot in the process."

Mary McCarthy also found James's requirements too limiting: "you find that if you obey this Jamesian injunction of 'Dramatize, dramatize,' . . . there is so much you can't say because you're limited by [the] mentalities [of the characters]." McCarthy discusses this limitation as if it were simply part of the "technical difficulties" facing a novelist, but her underlying objection to James, similar to Kerouac's, is not to the stringency of his rules, but to the idea of art as illusion: "in feigning an alien consciousness, . . . too much energy gets lost, I think, in the masquerade" (*Writers*, 2d ser., 311, 312).

James had devoted himself to the creation of realistic illusions, but in the context of postwar criticism and publishing that devotion now seemed to be a sterile charade, and the reaction against it appears as the old antinomy between form and feeling posed by the romantics a century and a half earlier, but specific to the decline of the left and the aesthetic discourse it fostered. "One is trying, after all, to capture reality," Mailer reminded an interviewer, and craft is too often a way of avoiding "a reality which might open into more and more anxiety and so present a deeper and deeper view of the abyss" (*Writers*, 3d ser., 273). As we have seen, even Bellow was a temporary party to this dichotomy, though *The Adventures of Augie March* was a far cry from *Howl* or *On the Road*.

Writers were not always confident in their dismissal of the dominant aesthetics. Mailer, for example, remembered wanting "to be respected the way someone like Katherine Anne Porter used to be respected. . . . As a master of the craft." In partial corroboration of Mailer's memory, we may note that Edmund Wilson wrote admiringly of her work in 1944, and Mark Schorer, in "Technique as Discovery" (1948), cited Porter as one of the very few contemporary American writers exhibiting such technique. Although Mailer told his interviewer that he was now more "cynical about craft," that Porter's example and the idea of technique had once intimidated so bellicose a personality as Mailer's helps confirm the sense of inhibition experienced by many writers (*Writers*, 3d ser., 272–73).

Mailer identifies craft not as an enabling discipline that might help a writer "discover" reality, but as a disposition toward the world—mechanical, ordering—which by its very nature cannot explore the mysterious complexities of feeling and consciousness. This argument is not unlike those made by Schorer and Rahv about literary naturalism, but the theoretical issues which underlie such conviction—What do we mean by "reality"? Is formal, referential representation inadequate to the portrayal of actual "reality"?—are less noteworthy here than the widespread belief that form and craft, and the idea of an objective reality one could represent, were incapable of presenting contemporary lived experience.

Yet to state the case in this way is to accept too easily the oppositional point of view assumed by many of the writers in the postwar years, for the interaction between the serious young writers and the literary intellectuals who were their main audience was guided and shaped by the same discourses which informed the thinking and assumptions of the critical community. For example, the young writer's rejection of naive realism and naturalism often implied that these were modes the critics were urging upon them, when in fact both writer and critic were seeking forms that embodied a new psychological idea of "reality." Further, there was considerable agreement among them that any active relation between literature and politics was now exhausted; most writers and critics made unquestioning use of the "mass society" trope as an analytical category and acknowledged a general level of affluence among the masses; both groups generated an image of the artist as a conflicted, morally ambiguous self, at once alienated from society and expressive of its innermost contradictions.

Situated within these common givens, Mailer's opposition between "craft" and inner "reality" expressed not only a defensive reaction to New Critical expectations but one shaped by or intermixed with the rejection of naturalism (and naive realism) shared nearly universally by all parties. That is, the shortcomings that Mailer attributes to "technique" are the same as those both Schorer and Trilling ascribe to the naturalist fiction of the thirties. Further, the writers' desire to represent interior, lived experience wasn't very different from the privileging of subjectivity in both Schorer and Trilling. At the same time, the rejection of naive realism was of course a cornerstone of new liberal aesthetics—as in Trilling's attack on Parrington and Dreiser—in which modernist complexity came to define the "new" realism. The writers' was essentially a modernist sensibility, restless within the culture both critic and writer defined as a "mass society."

To a degree, the rejection of realism was itself a conventional modernist activity, here mediated through the conservative politics and culture of the postwar years. One curious result of this dynamic is that modernism re-emerges from the ashes of naturalism as a resurrected "realism" of the sort described in Schorer's "Technique as Discovery" and Trilling's "Manners, Morals, and the Novel." For example, when Bellow reviewed Ellison's *Invisible Man*, he praised the depiction of a character who overcomes the mass society and its institutions: "what a great thing it is when a brilliant individual victory occurs, like Mr. Ellison's, proving that a truly heroic quality can exist among our contemporaries. People too thoroughly determined— and our institutions by their size and force too thoroughly determine—can't approach this quality" ("Man," 28). In the terminology of this passage Bellow was speaking within the discourses of antinaturalism and "mass" culture, but he also used the occasion of this review to reassert the power of nineteenth-century realism: "There is something terribly impressive," Bellow noted ironically, "about the boredom of a man like Valéry who could no longer bear to read that the carriage had come for the duchess at four in the afternoon" (29). Bellow meant to suggest that Ellison had proven Valéry wrong, that his novel had shown the superiority of "realism" to an exhausted modernism and an inept naturalism; but this invocation of "realism"—with his emphasis upon individualism and freedom—was an expression more of liberal cold war realism than of the nineteenth-century novel Valéry could no longer bear to read.

In the continuing debate over the future and obligations of the novel, Valéry's remark serves as a kind of synecdoche for what critics and writers took to be "realistic fiction." Even those who admired the fiction of Tolstoi and Flaubert—what Mary McCarthy called "real novels"—used this remark of Valéry's to describe the difficulties of the contemporary writer. Having told her audience how the changing world has made writing novels seemingly impossible, Mary McCarthy decided to end her talk on a more positive note: "Someone, somewhere, even now may be dictating into a dictaphone: 'At five o'clock in the afternoon, in the capital of the Province of Y., a tall man with an umbrella was knocking at the door of the governor's residence' " (458).

"The Marquise went out at 5 o'clock" may be a reductive "epitome" of realism, serving, as Fredric Jameson has argued, merely as "that with which modernism has had to break" (206); but it stands for what many writers and most readers have meant by the term and certainly is no more reductive than Trilling's caricature of Parrington in "Reality in America." Modern and contemporary writing exposed the illusionist character of documentary, reflective realism and made the reader attend to the linguistic reality or medium of the fiction itself. This modernist shift in emphasis continued after the Second War in the work of such writers as Ralph Ellison, William Burroughs, and John Hawkes. Hawkes, who published his first novel, *The Cannibal*, in 1949, once told an audience: "There are certain fictions that are transparent. . . . you see through them, you read through them. You're interested not in the fiction but in the 'life' the fiction seems to be about. Such writers think they are reflecting or reproducing reality. They must think they know what reality is; they must think that 'out there' is reality, which I don't think at all" (LeClair and McCaffery 18). This point of view is essentially a modernist viewpoint, and one with which Trilling wouldn't have had too much to quarrel.

At the same time, writers and critics of the postwar period who made the modernist argument against "nineteenth-century" realism were displacing more immediate historical motives onto an earlier debate, and, wittingly or not, helping to consolidate the modernist aesthetic and epistemology at a time when it served conservative ends.

If the writer's dispute with realist discourse often reinforced the new realism of postwar liberalism, the demands of the popular reader confused the issue further: not only did some of the powerful critics, such as Trilling, Rahv, and Schorer, define novelistic standards in language that sometimes affirmed the conventional tropes of "realist" discourse—language as a mirror or painting—but the writers for *Time* and *Life* also expected conventional narratives and ones that painted a specific picture. Though William

Styron's first novel, *Lie Down in Darkness* (1951), met with a degree of critical success, *Time* dismissed the book as belonging to the "dread-and-decay camp of U.S. letters" ("Unbeautiful," 106).

Writers, as Cowley pointed out, didn't have the comfort of attacking the mass culture as wholeheartedly as critics did, for they wanted to write for the readers of *Life* as well as the *Hudson* and *Partisan* reviews. The pervasive pressure for a new tone of acceptance and affirmation of American culture—an aspect of the postwar euphoria as well as a consequence or requirement of the cold war—was exerted by the academic and popular audience alike, but the popular audience especially, as the *Time* review suggests, had little patience with novelists who didn't confirm their idea of the American reality.

In 1955, *Life* ran an editorial titled "WANTED: AN AMERICAN NOVEL," which attacked novelists who "are still writing as if we were back in the Depression years." The editorial suggested that American writers aspire to the "redeeming quality" of Edmund Hillary's recent *The Conquest of Everest*. "In every healthy man," the editorial informed its audience, "there is a wisdom deeper than his conscious mind, reaching beyond memory to the primeval rivers, a yea-saying to the goodness and joy of life" (48). In these sentiments may be detected a desire for an origin outside of social history not entirely contrary to the searches then being conducted by the contemporary writers *Life* disdained; but *Life* wished to employ these sources of energy in the affirmation of that social history, whereas such writers as Ralph Ellison and Jack Kerouac hoped this new vitality—could they express it—might expose and renew American society.

We gain some appreciation of the catch-22 the writer must have felt by setting *Life*'s exhortation beside the aspirations of Sal Paradise. Kerouac's character has no more respect for despair than *Life* does ("all my New York friends were in the negative, nightmare position of putting down society and giving their tired bookish or political or psychoanalytical reasons"), and Moriarty interests him because he appears to be a Whitmanian alternative, a "wild yea-saying overburst of American joy." Ironically, *Life*'s demands repeat Kerouac's phrase, and Kerouac had even begun his first novel, *The Town and the City*, with a description of the Merrimac as a "primeval" river. But Sal's search for origin and paradise is a subterranean journey, and the wisdom he finds is more melancholy than joyful: "I could hear a new call and see a new horizon," Sal remembers at the start of *On the Road*, but adds, "and believe it at my age" (11). Typically, *Life*'s editorial imagined an ascending redemption (the higher the mountain, the better), and expressed no interest in realities that might have been lost in the move to suburbia. For *Life* and its audience, the descent never beckons.

In 1957, Flannery O'Connor was sufficiently irritated by this same editorial to make it the starting point of her essay "The Fiction Writer and His Country." First of all O'Connor questioned the optimistic assumptions of the editorial: would "these screams for joy," she wondered, "be quite so piercing if joy were really more abundant in our prosperous society." But the artist, she pointed out, doesn't make judgments about her country or perceive it "in the light of statistics," and any artist who did would only "produce a soggy, formless, and sentimental literature" (*Mystery* 30–31). She concluded her reaction to the *Life* editorial with the conviction that "where the artist is still trusted, he will not be looked to for assurance" (33–34, 46). Similarly, Mailer answered the *Partisan Review* symposium "Our Country and Our Culture": "It is worth something to remind ourselves that the great artists—certainly the moderns—are almost always in opposition to their society, and that integration, acceptance, non-alienation, etc. etc., have been more conducive to propaganda than art" (*Advertisements* 177).

Though postwar liberalism drew essentially pessimistic lessons from recent history, within popular discourse the moral and economic victory of the United States seemed to make continued attack on American culture during the cold war stubborn and pointless. "Although activists and liberals may have been disappointed at the slow pace of social reform after World War II, the attention of most Americans was so riveted on the astonishing new world of consumerism and prosperity that social issues—for the moment at least—seemed relatively unimportant" (Chafe 111). "Between 1947 and 1960," Chafe notes, "the average real income for American workers increased by as much as it had in the previous half-century" and "the gross national product soared 250 percent between 1945 and 1960" (111–12).

The prosperity of the fifties seemed indisputable. Even critics of culture so resolute as Paul and Percival Goodman took the material superfluity of the American future as a given in their book on social design, *Communitas* (1947): "for the first time in history we have, spectacularly in the United States, a surplus technology, a technology of free choice, that allows for the most widely various community-arrangements and ways of life" (11). John Kenneth Galbraith argued in *The Affluent Society* (1958) that the science of economics must overhaul its assumptions of scarcity and poverty.[1] Amid so much plenty, taken for granted by social sentinels as well as by the general public, especially among a population that accepted the communist threat,

---

1. Galbraith's book begins with the assertion that the ideas by which Western Europeans and Americans understand their world "were actually products of a world in which poverty had always been man's normal lot" (13).

political criticism—even when it took the form of cultural critique—was not only unacceptable but dangerous.

This atmosphere created a peculiarly stringent form of alienation for the artist, the central feature of which was the unacceptability of alienation itself. The writer lived among "norms," Paul Goodman wrote in 1951, that were "extraordinarily senseless and unnatural—a routine technology geared to war, a muffled and guilty science, a standard of living measured by commodities, a commercial art, a moral 'freedom' without personal contact." Among such norms, "there could be no audience recognition of any product of inward daring, if anyone could dare to produce it. . . . What an artist would say spontaneously would now seem hopelessly irrelevant, likely even to himself" (204). The continued massive government support of the military industry during the cold war was a particular target for many writers. Richard Hofstadter called this "military Keynesianism" (Chafe 113), and Mailer noted in the pages of the *Partisan Review* that "the prosperity of America depends upon the production of means of destruction" (*Advertisements* 176–77).

For those writers who did not share the new mood, this pervasive pro-Americanism made the dissenting artist's position all the more isolated. Though the majority of respondents to the *Partisan Review*'s "Our Country and Our Culture" were far from "unequivocal" in their support of democratic culture, Mailer was one of the few to reject outright the symposium's suggestion of rapprochement: "the artist feels most alienated when he loses the sharp sense of what he is alienated from. In this contest, I wonder if there has been a time in the last fifty years when the American artist felt more alienated" (*Advertisements* 175).

In Mailer's remarks may be read the contradiction he and other writers felt between their modern sense—inherited from Flaubert and Joyce—that an artist's vocation requires estrangement and difference, and their contemporary recognition of America's powerful comfort. Mailer didn't want the proffered acceptance of his culture, for he knew that reconciliation could cost him his artistic authority. At the same time, he knew this authority did not yet count for much, in "the warmed-over sentimentality of the war years" (176). By 1964, the situation of the writer, in Paul Goodman's view, had not changed much:

> The present crisis in which an American writes is a peculiar one. He confronts in his audience the attitude that things are well enough, there is nothing to be grievous or angry about, and anyway our situation is inevitable. This attitude is the audience's technological and organizational helplessness mollified by the famously high standard of living. It puts writers in the position of, as we Jews say, banging a teakettle, when his readers couldn't care less. (xvi)

The new liberalism thus was complicitous in producing this perception and the discursive assumptions within which both criticism and fiction emerged.

But this apparent material wealth made only more dissonant and inexpressible the alienation which the writer felt. Sometimes one may note the two discourses woven together, as in the dialogue below from Walker Percy's *The Moviegoer*. In writing the dialogue between Binx Bolling and Nell Lovell (love-all) of *The Moviegoer* (1961), Walker Percy was as interested in isolating the peculiar malaise of his disaffected protagonist as he was in parodying the sentiments of *Life*:

> I can talk to Nell as long as I don't look at her. Looking into her eyes is an embarrassment.
> "—we gave the television to the kids and last night we turned on the hi-fi and sat by the fire and read *The Prophet* aloud. I don't find life gloomy!" she cries. "To me, books and people and things are endlessly fascinating. Don't you think so?"

Binx tactfully agrees, but a "rumble has commenced in [his] descending bowel, heralding a tremendous defecation" (84). A bit of the contrary impulses at work is evident here in the oscillation between the critique of mass society's superficiality and the isolation of the self within it. The eventual object of Percy's satire is not Nell, but Binx's absurd alienation.

Thus for the writer as well as for the critic, politics became the politics of culture, though this was a more difficult transition for the writer to make than it was for the critic. Writers' reactions to popular culture were essentially in accord with the critical consensus, and, as was the case with the critics, for the most part took the place of the idea of a political art. Mailer's objections to the *Partisan Review* symposium, for example, reinforced the postwar critical position that art is inherently anti-ideological. Mailer felt empowered to make political statements about the country's military-industrial policies, but he sharply distinguished art from ideological critique. All that was left was culture, and the frustrated exertions of the alienated intellectual caught within its straitjacket. Further, the reactions of the writers show them conflating two separate audiences—the popular and the academic/critical—while the terms of their rejection and hostility are clearly drawn from the same vocabulary as those of the new liberal critic.

Assuming so many of the conditions that informed the critical discourse, many writers found it nearly impossible to remain political, in spite of their intentions, and the focus—as it was in books like *The Lonely Crowd*—tended to be instead upon the self alienated within or from this prosperity. Their agreement on this score provides one of the most explicit examples of the way the narrative of a "disabled liberalism" emerges within the discourse of the postwar fiction writer. The intellectual and writer in the thirties had felt some possibility of playing a role in the politics of the United States, as James Gilbert has demonstrated in *Writers and Partisans* (see also Wald 75–97), but after the war this possibility seemed a chimera. "The insurgent movement in this country which defended 'modernism'—that is, the aesthetic experimentalism and social protest of the period between 1912 and 1950—has expired of its own success," Richard Chase wrote in "The Fate of the Avant-Garde." The role of the critic is "to keep the avant-garde attitude alive during periods which have no immediate task for its polemical mission" (149, 156) "The old connection between literature and politics has been dissolved," Trilling wrote in 1963 (*Beyond* 83).

That connection had been irreparably damaged by the embarrassment of the literary left, but in the years after World War II it resurfaced in the "end of ideology" rhetoric which served to confirm the idea an "American Century." The writers' point of view reveals how the assumptions of the new liberalism inform their own perceptions as they applied to the task of fiction writing. "The work seems done," Mailer wrote in response to the *Partisan Review* symposium "Our Country and Our Culture," for the artist "does not have the naiveté of the twenties with its sure pleasure of *épater le bourgeois*," nor can he still "believe in the social art of the depression; he is left only with the warmed-over sentimentality of the war years" (*Advertisements* 176). When William Styron, then author of a single novel, *Lie Down In Darkness*, wrote the preface to the first issue of the *Paris Review*, he attacked the "literary magazines" which seem "on the verge of doing away with literature," but he nevertheless repeated the central insistence of the new liberal discourse and New Critic alike that there is now no place for politics in art: "if we have no axes to grind, no drums to beat, it's because it seems to us—for the moment, at least—that the axes have all been ground, the drumheads burst with beating. . . . It's not so much a matter of protest now, but of waiting" (10, 12).

Though critic and writer alike widely accepted the trope of "mass society" and read in this a form of domestic totalitarianism, the new writer nevertheless shared the misgivings critics often had about their new positions in academia and within society. Bloom, Wald, Gilbert, and Webster have all described what Philip Rahv labeled the "*embourgeoisement* of the American intelligentsia" as writers and critics found acceptance and security within the university and government, but as the "Our Country and Our Culture" responses show, they didn't give an "unequivocal" (284) endorsement of the culture that welcomed them, and remained somewhat jealous of their claims to the continued radicalism of their alienation.

This discomfort may well account for the insistence of the New York critics that the new writers were not genuinely radical at all, but instead expressions of the very society they should be exposing. Although writers remained critical of culture, they were challenged by it and sought to represent it; while the Old Left critics, whose politics had also become the politics of culture, denied the cultural politics of the new writing because it wasn't "political" in the terms they retained from their experiences in the thirties—vestiges of which appear in their criticism as a lingering attachment to empirical realist representation. At the same time, the primary threat posed to the new liberals was the persistence of naive radicalism, yet they abhorred their own inactivity and impotence, which they also attributed to the younger writers.

The most vivid example of this conflicted dynamic appears in Diana Trilling's essay on Allen Ginsberg's poetry reading, published in *Partisan Review* as "The Other Night at Columbia." Trilling's essay shows these contending forces or competing unintegrated elements at work in her critique of Ginsberg and the Beats, for she denies the authority of the new generation's cultural critique, measuring them against her own radicalism in the decade prior to the war: "How different it might have been for Ginsberg and his friends if they had come of age ten or fifteen years sooner was one of the particular sadnesses of the other evening." Her inability to credit Ginsberg's emotion derived explicitly from a nostalgia for the days of her "very strong feeling," when the intellectual thought she was participating on the stage of History—"surely a time of quicker, truer feeling than is now conjured up with marijuana or the infantile camaraderie of *On the Road*."

A great deal of the patronizing that others have noted here (Bloom 301–5) is really peripheral to the motivational conflicts that emerge at the center of Trilling's essay. There it becomes clear that her disregard for Ginsberg, Corso, and Kerouac has less to do with a personal knowledge of Ginsberg's family problems than with her own thwarted radicalism. In her memory of radical youth, an intellectual might be dedicated to "historical or economic determinism," but "personally he had a unique sense of free will," and it is the absence of that active confidence Trilling misses most—not just in the poetry she heard at Columbia that night, but in postwar liberal life generally. Two pages at the essay's middle are devoted to asserting a connection between Beat protest—"the wholly non-political form of a bunch of panic-stricken kids"—and "the liberal intellectual" who is "convinced he has no power to control the political future." She accuses both of denying free will and conceiving of themselves "as incapable of exerting any substantial influence against the forces that condition" them (221).

Trilling here enunciates not only the tough-minded "realism" of new liberal discourse and its contempt for those who failed to make the transition to the realpolitik of the cold war, but also the frustration of the radical figure who believes in action and wants to act, but can find no means of doing so. Her subordination of the Beats to liberal passivity is in some measure, then, a displacement of that frustration, for although she describes herself as one who departs from "dominant liberal opinion," and insists "upon what I call political responsibility" (222), she herself notes at the beginning of the essay that her radicalism—anti-Stalinist or otherwise—has been "reduced to such marginal causes as the Metropolitan Museum, after-dinner coffee cups, and the expectation that visitors would go home by 2 A.M." (215).

At some level Trilling must have been perfectly aware that her own politics were as suspended as those of Mailer or Styron, and this fact made her even more critical than she might have been of Beat writing about the United States. As Irving Howe recalled about the foundation of *Dissent* in 1954, "We were saying, in effect, that socialism in America had to be seen mostly as an intellectual problem before it could even hope to become a viable movement. Simply to publish a magazine might not be enough, but there are moments when patience is all—and stubborness, too" (*Margin* 236). The cultural politics of the postwar years constituted a holding pattern that pleased no one, and few were willing to acknowledge any substantial critique in the cultural politics of the new writing. This was especially the case with the Old Left: they claimed a continued commitment to radical politics on the one hand, while denying either the political or literary importance of the new generation on the other.

Because Trilling's effete dismay was something of a company line, in which Lionel Trilling, Daniel Bell, Norman Podhoretz, and Irving Howe all concurred, it is a splendid example of the way in which the political experience of the Old Left froze their capacity to greet the new work after World War II. Lionel Trilling had little to say of the Beats, except his reference in *The Opposing Self* (1955) to "a group of my students" who "have come to feel that could they but break the iambic shackles, the whole of modern culture could find a true expression. The value of form must never be denigrated" (96). Other members of the New York group were more explicit. In Bell's *The End of Ideology*, Kerouac and the Beats evince, "like Peter Pan, the denial of growing up. It is, of course, an apolitical movement" (301). This point of view not only insisted, implicitly, that Bell's group themselves had grown up, but defined "politics" in a way peculiar to their own experience. They had no sense of Kerouac's work as having an implicit political impact (though their own reaction betrayed it). Irving Howe argued that "the beats manifest the very malaise they seek to escape," for in "their contempt for mind, they are at one with the middle class suburbia they think they scorn" (*World* 95). The value of the writing the Beats produced is less relevant here than the dialogue which engaged both critic and writer, because these evaluations help clarify the terms of discussion which characterized literary discourse in the postwar.

The writer who took "mass society" as a given was to some extent buying into the difficulties of having to represent new "realities" different from those which had been the typical material of the novel described by Trilling, Rahv, Howe, and Aldridge. For these critics the interpretive paradigm of the mass society—the absence of defined classes, the disappearance of agreed-upon moral codes, the distancing of power sources from private initiative—had put the writer at a disadvantage. "Our society no longer lent itself to assured definition, one could no longer assume as quickly as in the recent past that a spiritual or moral difficulty could find a precise embodiment in a social conflict," Howe wrote in "Mass Society and Post-Modern Fiction," and asked rhetorically, "How give shape to a world increasingly shapeless and an experience increasingly fluid?" (*World* 86–87).

Though this was an interpretation of society used by critics to explain what they felt were the failures of post–World War II narrative rather than one which enabled them to understand and appreciate this fiction, their point of view had considerable credence among the writers themselves. Some writers, like Ellison and Kerouac, were determined to convey the riot and madness they saw existing within or beyond the deceptive discourse of postwar "conformity." Ellison saw a "whole chaotic world existing within the ordered social pattern" of the mass society ("What's Wrong with the American Novel," 470).

This point of view was part of the general thesis that the new "facts" of postwar reality were no longer the "ordinary facts" that realism—as Rahv argued early in the forties—had taught us to "grasp and encompass." Instead, the mass of social phenomena seemed to multiply into a variety and scale that defied comprehension. Chief among these were the revelations of the Holocaust, the sociopathology of everyday life in mass society, and the atom bomb. Mary McCarthy told an audience in 1960 that the improbability of recent history renders "our daily life . . . incredible." She remembered reading of the Hiroshima bombing while shopping for groceries on Cape Cod, and asking herself, " 'What am I doing buying a loaf of bread?' The coexistence of the great world and us, when contemplated, appears impossible" (455). The A-bomb (and then the hydrogen bomb), in particular, entered the imaginations of writers, and made even more implausible the role of writer-as-liberal. For liberal thought requires a future in which the amelioration of the human condition may occur, and the specter of atomic devastation made even the idea of a future doubtful.

In the thinking of the *Partisan Review* crowd, these new facts helped confirm the death of the novel. "The world of today has become inaccessible to common sense," McCarthy declared, and the novel, "with its common sense, is of all forms the least adapted to encompass the modern world, whose leading characteristic is irreality" (455–56). This thesis is really a variant of Trilling's thesis in "Art and Fortune" and directly opposed such views of the novel as may be found in the essays of D. H. Lawrence, or M. M. Bakhtin, for whom the novel is "plasticity itself . . . the only possibility open to a genre that structures itself in a zone of direct contact with developing reality" (39). Philip Roth was far from throwing in the towel, but he, too, worried that "the actuality is continually outdoing our talents. . . . the American writer in the middle of the twentieth century has his hands full in trying to understand, describe, and then make *credible* much of the American reality" (120).

Other writers understood that this dilemma and the dire prophecies it spawned were partly a consequence of continuing to operate within used-up forms, atrophied conceptions of "realism." Mailer made this connection between the implausibility of reality and narrative form explicit in the story "The Man Who Studied Yoga," in which the central character, Sam Slovoda, exclaims, "It's all schizoid. Modern life is schizoid." Slovoda, a failed writer, is looking for a "form" appropriate to postwar life, and in the dialogue between him and his companion Mailer locates the loss of authority which realistic form had suffered in the embarrassment of the literary left. "Doesn't the Party seem a horror now?" Slovoda's friend asks, and shortly thereafter, in what would otherwise seem to be a non sequitur, Slovoda excuses his inability to write a "realistic novel" on the grounds that "reality is no longer realistic" (*Advertisements* 167). The Party had provided a narrative explanation of social and political reality that no longer seemed to apply.

In one way or another, Slovoda's logic was the principal structure within which postwar writers understood their situation. In searching for forms that had authority, they were understandably wary of inherited forms which acted as a veneer for the mass society they sought to represent. The individual man, Ellison told a group of writers and publishers in 1955, "is more apt to get a sense of wonder, a sense of self-awareness and a sharper reflection of his world from a comic book than from most novels" ("What's Wrong with the American Novel," 472). Several years after McCarthy's lectures were published, Donald Barthelme, in an article titled "After Joyce," isolated the fundamental weakness in her analysis: "The facts of contemporary life are not 'real' facts, like the facts available to Tolstoi; therefore either my enterprise [novel-writing] is impossible or I must return to the kind of material it can accommodate, that is, to the substance of the 19th century novel. . . . Anxiety about the Bomb is translated into an abomination of literary innovation. In any case, Miss McCarthy's conservative manifesto adequately expresses a real dilemma—that of the writer betrayed by outmoded forms" (15).

The kind of social details which interested Howe and Trilling, Rahv and McCarthy continued to assume a world of discrete, atomistic individuals interacting socially through rumor, dialogue, physical action, and dress. Novelists were to portray reality through these manners, to "penetrate" to the "intention which the manner and manners stand for" (Trilling, *Gathering* 61); but though such details may accurately record the reality or truth (some would say illusions) by which people continue to live, the postwar reality seemed to be far more in evidence in the new organizational capacities inherited from the war and the centralization of power that resulted, in the impersonality of these systems, in the lurid advertising of the mass media, or in the possibility "that the world might be preparing to destroy itself." Norman Mailer agreed with Trilling that it is the novelist's business to "capture reality," but he thought tracking the new reality might require "insane insight" (*Advertisements* 87).

These contrasting views of narrative realism—how to define "reality"—help emphasize how the conventional understanding of the realistic novel requires not only that there be an objective world held in common (which provides the measure by which we judge the "realism" of portrayal), but also, somewhat circularly, that this common world be "realistic." By this reasoning "reality" is virtually indistinguishable from ideas of plausibility which have been developed, implicitly, on a scale accessible not only to the physical senses, but to conventional morality as well. Because the irrationality of modern events, though real, seemed "irreal," many writers were convinced that a true "realism" would seek to convey this rupture; but this rupture is a quality not of objective reality, but of its apprehension by consciousness and conscience. The inherited realism which so many critics and readers alike rejected surveyed only a small quadrant of the "mass society" and did not address at all the new agility being demanded of the mind.

Postwar writers produced fiction within this discourse, and though their dialogue with and position within it diversify and complicate representation in this period, their work often reproduced variations on its central elements. This is especially true of the new psychologism of postwar fiction. A politics of culture is precisely what the postwar critic got in the new fiction, but it was a critique that accepted a set of significations already established by the dominant tropes of postwar liberalism—especially those of "mass society" and the alienated self within it.

4

The Unhappy Consciousness

In going underground, I whipped it all except the mind, the *mind*. And the mind that has conceived of a plan of living must never lose sight of the chaos against which that pattern was conceived. That goes for societies as well as for individuals.

Ralph Ellison, *Invisible Man*, 1952

The sour truth is that I am imprisoned with a perception which will settle for nothing less than making a revolution in the consciousness of our time.

Norman Mailer, *Advertisements for Myself*, 1959

For those writers to whom the option of joining in the general euphoric Americanism was no more tenable than persisting in "social realism," the logical strategy of choice was a way of telling stories which both reflected their rupture with society and established at the same time a legitimate source of authority for describing a redefined "reality." Here, as throughout the literary community, political interest remained but reemerged within the psychological terms of the new liberalism. For a surprising number of these writers, this strategy amounted to the invention of first person voices, often autobiographical, a point of view which embodied in one degree or another the isolation of the speaker, while at the same time issuing from the unimpeachable authority of his consciousness and perception.

The "first person point of view" may seem to be an ineffectual category with which to snare anything unique about the writing that appeared after World War II, for in many ways the first person is a peculiarly American stance, from Emerson, Douglass, and Thoreau to Huck Finn, from Jake Barnes and Nick Carroway to Holden Caulfield and Invisible Man. But the distinct movement I am attempting to isolate isn't simply a mechanical one of "person," but involves the specific reasons for adopting such a point of view at that time in our literary history. Within the narrower scope of the years I am investigating, the move to the first person was simply an effect of the shift from economy to mind so visible throughout the intellectual community of that time.

Seen more narrowly within formal terms, the shift to the first person represented a decisive break with the immediately prior literature and the creation of narrators whose consciousnesses are strikingly similar to the divided self as culture hero that we have seen in Warren, Rahv, and Trilling. The new literature seemed designed to embody the "literary idea." In contrast, the work produced by Farrell, Wright, Steinbeck, and Dos Passos had been driven by a radical certitude about the nature of the social (economic and political) world, revealed in part by the writers' use of the third person to manipulate and gain access to all areas of the reality they sought to expose and dramatize. Notably, those authors from the recent past—Thomas Wolfe, William Faulkner, Nathanael West—who often served as models for the new generation of writers after World War II, commonly made use of the first person as a mode of immediacy or a way of dramatizing the dilemmas of the estranged self. Their work, along with that of such Europeans as Kierkegaard, Dostoevski, Kafka, and Céline, was recovered as a more fitting lineage for the postwar world. Within the postwar discourse of "mass society," "conformity," and "totalitarianism," which governed thinking about society for writer and critic alike in the forties and fifties, the first person voice of the alienated hero developed a subversive aura.

One of the most compelling qualities of the "first person" category turns out to be its bland catch-all ability: during this period writers as different in personality, vision, and style as McCarthy and Mailer, Barth and Burroughs, Bellow and Kerouac all favored first person modes of narrative fiction. Not only did writers who began to publish in these years elect the first person; many writers who had already begun their careers switched from the third person perspective of their first work to the first person invented voice. For all of them, during that time, the first person appeared to be a form of resistance to general pressures, both popular and critical, for political conformity and controlled, crafted form. The discourse of resistance and reform was no longer dominated by the language of social and economic forces, giving way, instead, to explanatory models based in psychology—to a renewed focus upon the mind.

The significance of the first person was consciously debated by writers, and is especially apparent in the remarks of those writers who nurtured a commitment to some form of socialism. For them, the first person point of view was involved in a complex set of preoccupations and biases— political, aesthetic, and personal—which contended with each other. "The whole question of the point of view," Mary McCarthy told an interviewer, "tortures everybody." In particular, like many of her contemporaries, she was haunted by the specters of Flaubert, James, and Joyce, each of whom she characterized as encouraging "a kind of ventriloquism, disappearing in and completely limited by the voices of his characters." In contrast, McCarthy wished to write in her own voice: "I would like to restore the author! I haven't tried yet, but I'd like to try after this book [she was working on *The Group*], which is as far as I can go in ventriloquism" (*Writers*, 2d ser., 311).

Thought of as the voice of another, distinct from the author, the first person point of view may require a good deal more ventriloquism than third person omniscience; but McCarthy objected explicitly to the dramatic restrictions James had placed on that omniscience. The dramatic method of the novel, she argued, is not only "painstaking," but "limits" the author's presence to "*style indirect libre.*" Of course, in his depiction of Strether, James wanted to impose just such limits in order to "encage" Strether and "forbid the terrible *fluidity* of self-revelation"—all of which was in keeping with the "proprieties" James wished Strether to observe (311). Transferred to the literary dilemmas of the forties and fifties, James's concern for "precious discrimination" nicely identified the kind of sensibility the New Critics and Old Left tried to advance, with their emphasis upon "dramatic form," "difficulties," "ambiguities," and "irony," but James's interest in confining his character was precisely what so many writers were fighting against. Such narrators as Holden Caulfield, Augie March, and Invisible Man were meant to be a kind of Strether Unbound, liberated from both social convention and aesthetic orthodoxy. Accordingly, the first person voice of these years is most often very close to the author's, and was intended as a more direct and immediate medium, whose authority in fact depended upon that proximity.

At the same time, McCarthy betrays a reluctance to repudiate the heritage which restricts her, for she is still influenced by an idea of the novel she shared with other members of the *Partisan Review* community: "I'm not sure any of my books are novels. . . . Something happens in my writing— I don't mean it to—a sort of distortion, a sort of writing on the bias, seeing things with a sort of swerve and swoop" (310). Her view of the novel conformed to the definition of the novel as an outmoded form repeated in the influential essays of Richard Chase, Ian Watt, Lionel Trilling, Philip Rahv, Irving Howe, and José Ortega y Gasset—which, as we have seen, was bound up in an idea of social reality which it is the novel's obligation to "mirror."

McCarthy's political background and continued commitment to socialism play a part in her inner conflict, for the restoration of the author's voice is at once tantamount to the demise of the novel, and a reflection of her lack of confidence in the ability of the socialist point of view to prevail: "I still believe in a kind of libertarian socialism, a decentralized socialism," she said, "but I don't see any possibility of achieving it." Even in her own analysis, the socialist explanation of reality has lost its footing and is replaced by sociological terms: "it really seems to me sometimes that the only hope is space. That is to say, perhaps the most energetic—in the bad sense—elements will move on to a new world in space. The problems of mass society will be transported into space, leaving behind this world as a kind of Europe, which then eventually tourists will visit. The Old World" (300).

This fantasy is a wonderful reprise of the conservative reaction executed by so many writers and intellectuals of that time, in which the latent biases of the self—then being explored by so many others in more positive and forward-looking ways—were denied on behalf of the "Old World," both in politics and the novel. Though she thought James's admonitions had "become absolutely killing to the novel," her disappointment in the possibilities of socialism and her contempt for "mass society" outweigh her inclination to redefine the direction of narrative fiction. Instead, as she argues in "The Fact in the Fiction," she declares the novel moribund and reserves this honorific title ("the novel") for the very kind of narrative she found constricting.

McCarthy's dilemmas are magnified and clarified by the example of Norman Mailer. Even as a young man in his early twenties, Mailer was influenced by the social and political issues of his time and the changes which occurred in the political consciousness of intellectuals during the forties. One might even say he became a prisoner of these developments, absorbing too completely the ideas of the disenchanted left. For Mailer the connection between narrative point of view and a collapsed socialism is explicit: "I was a socialist after all," he told an interviewer. "I believed in large literary works which were filled with characters, and were programmatic, and had large theses, and were developed, let's say, like the Tolstoyan novel." His models for this project were "Farrell to begin with. Dos Passos, Steinbeck (I am trying to do it chronologically), Hemingway, and later Fitzgerald—much, much later. And Thomas Wolfe, of course" (*Writers*, 3d ser., 260, 265).

Mailer consciously sought to be the "public artist"—an idea Paul Goodman had suggested setting aside—and attempted to write what Flannery O'Connor described as a "realism of fact": "long fiction" made up of the "movement of social forces" (*Utopian* 211; *Mystery* 39). The result of his ambition and the models he kept in mind was *The Naked and the Dead* (1948), a book which won him immediate acclaim, in part because it matched precisely everyone's expectation of the novels that World War II ought to produce, and because its methods—so obviously patterned after Dos Passos and Steinbeck—had been introduced already to the reading public.

But after his first novel's success, Mailer found himself, like McCarthy, being pulled in two directions at once, for the socialist explanation of history, which had nurtured his youthful ambitions, was neither privately compelling nor publicly feasible, even to him, and this meant at the same time a diminution in the usefulness of the literary models he had admired. That is, in Mailer too we see the way in which a comprehensible history and a form of telling stories were inextricably associated. I have already cited the dialogue from "The Man Who Studied Yoga," in which Mailer juxtaposed the embarrassment of the American left ("Doesn't the Party seem a horror now?") and his character's search for aesthetic coherence: Slovoda can't write a "realistic novel, because reality is no longer realistic" (*Advertisements* 167); but this problem is already implicit in Mailer's development from *The Naked and the Dead* to his second novel, *Barbary Shore* (1951). His first book begins with an omniscient confidence ("All over the ship, all through the convoy, there was a knowledge that in a few hours some of them were going to be dead"), but *Barbary Shore* begins much more uncertainly and has already acquired the characteristic first person, often disturbed, voice of the fifties: "Probably I was in the war." Reflecting upon those years, Mailer said: "I must have felt at that time as if I would never be able to write in the third person until I developed a coherent view of life. I don't know that I've been able to altogether" (*Barbary* 5; *Writers*, 3d ser., 265).

In writing *Barbary Shore*, Mailer was feeling the contradictory tugs of wanting to write social history on the one hand, and to vent his sense of a more private anguish on the other. He has described writing *The Naked and the Dead* "mechanically," but in creating *Barbary Shore* he struggled between twin obsessions: "*Barbary Shore* was built on the division which existed then in my mind. My conscious intelligence, as I've indicated, became obsessed by the Russian Revolution. But my unconscious was much more interested in other matters: murder, suicide, orgy, psychosis, all the themes I discuss in *Advertisements*" (*Writers*, 3d ser., 261, 263).

Both McCarthy and Mailer substantiate the close relation between the decline of socialist thought and the use of the first person. The narrative "line"—the implicit story of so much fiction and essay writing—had dropped out, as it were, leaving only a battery of undigested (and intolerable) facts. Because certain narrative "containers"—to recall Krim's book review—no longer provided the "effect of the real," the new popularity of the first person was part of a strategy to regain this effect, since "reality" seemed to have devolved upon the relations of consciousness to the world. Moreover, if the world were shapeless, a "mass society" without traditional class structures on which novelists could depend (as Trilling and Howe insisted they had), the first person mode of presentation was less troubled than the third, for "consciousness"—as James knew—is a kind of form for formlessness, just as "mass society" was a label which sociologists gave to a society they couldn't identify.

Writers continued to see American culture in need of remedy—if not overthrow—and continued to inhabit an adversarial attitude, but they needed a vision of what such an attitude might mean, and a new form that would give traction to this adversarial stance. Thus the move from the third to the first person was neither without political importance nor entirely private. The psychological point of view was itself an ideology, best exploited by writers who conceived of themselves as minorities and outsiders, people who embodied in one way or another the repressions felt even (or especially) by those on the "inside." This accounts in some measure for the fact that much of the most interesting writing of the forties, fifties, and sixties was written by blacks, Jews, women, members of the drug world, and disaffected youth. For these writers, the "age of conformity" was a middle-class illusion, smugly indifferent not only to Michael Harrington's *The Other America*, but to its own desires and potentialities.

For them, the first person voice was the natural point of view to adopt in a politics of culture, because it gave voice to the communal impulses underlying the experience of alienation, and it was the idea by which many writers, like the critics with whom they quarreled, managed to retain a political relation to their society. Like Trilling, Mailer made the move from socialism to self-expression, from politics to psychology, without thinking he had sold out either his politics or his ambitions as a novelist. From *Advertisements for Myself* to *The Presidential Papers* to *Armies of the Night*, Mailer has refused to accept the idea that a literature which moves within, and beneath, to the unconscious psychology of character and society has at the same time forfeited any political territory. On the contrary, this move within was Mailer's way of remaining political, of continuing in an adversarial relation to his culture at a time when the public, third person voice and vocabulary of "the big social novel" was no longer tenable. Writing in *Esquire* on behalf of Kennedy's presidential candidacy, Mailer argued that "Americans have been leading a double life, and our history has moved on two rivers, one visible, the other underground; there has been the history of politics which is concrete, factual, practical and unbelievably dull if not for the consequences of the actions of some of these men; and there is a subterranean river of untapped, ferocious, lonely and romantic desires, that concentration of ecstasy and violence which is the dream life of the nation" (*Presidential* 38).

This formulation appears to oppose politics and psychology, but in fact Mailer was attempting to maintain both interests in just the way that Trilling insisted upon as the politics of culture, as emotions in conflict played out within a representative self. Mailer has always tried to maintain this polarity as a fusion: the two struggled with one another in the writing of *Barbary Shore*; they determined his hopes for Kennedy's presidency (and correspondingly, for the political impact of his subterranean views on the White House); and Mailer at last blended them successfully in *Armies of the Night* (1968), in which he interprets the march on the Pentagon as an existential event filtered through the schizophrenic consciousness of a fictionalized Self, wavering between private obsessions and political morality.

The instances of Mary McCarthy and Norman Mailer give explicit evidence of how closely intertwined with each other both writer and intellectual were in the paralyzing logic of this era. Both writer and intellectual shared the conviction of a thwarted socialism and what seemed then to have been a naive liberalism. The critic and intellectual essayist could capitalize on this enervated socialism and did: their group therapy occupies volumes of *Partisan Review*, *Commentary*, *Dissent*, and *Kenyon Review* during the forties and fifties; but the novelist—often a member of this same intellectual community—had to struggle with these dilemmas by supplying narrative line, and a striking number of writers filled in the blank with the voice of a distraught consciousness.

Lionel Trilling's novel *In the Middle of the Journey* (1947) provided one of the early models for this consciousness in the Christ-like figure of John Laskell. As Mark Krupnick has noted, Laskell along with the Crooms—a couple he is visiting—and Gifford Maxim, an ex-Party member Trilling patterned after Whittaker Chambers, "represent, in a fairly schematic way, the major possibilities of belief for intellectuals in midcentury America who had been affected by the experience of communism" (94). Aged thirty-three, Laskell arrives at the Crooms' country home recovering from an emotional and mental breakdown, whose origins are never quite specified, but we understand by the end of the novel that Laskell's experience stands for the fate of the liberal mind, caught between a sentimental left and a radical right. Maxim tells him that the times no longer permit "that flexibility of mind" on which Laskell prides himself and taunts Laskell as exemplifying "the supreme act of humanistic critical intelligence—it perceives the cogency of the argument and acquiesces in the fact of its own extinction" (338–39).

Laskell's position is really a literary version of what Arthur Schlesinger insisted a few years later was "the vital center." Schlesinger was trying to define a new liberalism that would be as compelling as the doctrines on the right and left, but Trilling's character can respond only that he does not "acquiesce," though by and large he admits the accuracy of Maxim's social analysis. In the last dialogue of the novel, Nancy Croom asks Laskell, about to board the train home, why they argued so much:

> He wanted very much to be able to answer her. He was on the point of saying, "Because we are parts of history, elements in the dialectic." But it would have been a wry joke. He said, "I don't know." (342)

Culture for Trilling, we should recall, is "nothing if not a dialectic" (*Liberal* 9), but the activity of the liberal mind within that dialectic is reduced in this ending to the silence of Christ before Pilate. Laskell does not acquiesce to his extinction, but neither does he act to avoid it.

Trilling may be said to have substituted for the vocabulary of socialism—collective language and action—the vocabulary of consciousness and conscience; but the varying degrees of mental and emotional disquiet that are related so explicitly to the troubles of the Old Left in the postwar in McCarthy, Mailer, and Trilling appear far less directly in much of the narrative fiction produced by a wide range of younger writers. In work by many of the writers who came of age after this politico-philosophical trauma, the political significance of Laskell's "disquiet" becomes obscured within types of character and voice we have come to think of as being merely "typical" of fifties fiction. In plot and theme too there is a falling away of explicit connection with liberal dilemmas, but this was itself symptomatic of them, now operating as givens—very often reappearing as a split between idea and experience, a failure to achieve coherence of vision, or in the insistence upon immediacy and spontaneity.

These developments are thus part of and help us to understand the cultural politics involved in the writers' use of the first person narrator. In Trilling's novel, John Laskell was but one character in the social world he described, but, in the new fiction that followed, Laskell's position often became the narrative frame, so that the third person perspective, which Trilling maintained, was inverted in order to give the reality and authority of the unhappy consciousness the central expression. Thus one of the characteristic voices of this period is the voice of a narrator just getting over an unspecified mental illness. Holden Caulfield promises to tell us "about this madman stuff that happened to me around Christmas just before I got pretty rundown," but after an account of the events of Christmas, concludes: "I could probably tell you what I did after I went home, and how I got sick and all . . . but I don't feel like it." Similarly, in *On the Road* Sal Paradise begins his memory with the statement "I had just gotten over a serious illness that I won't bother to talk about, except that it had something to do with the miserably weary split-up and my feeling that everything was dead." Invisible Man concludes his story of racism and misguided ambition with the realization that "at least half [the sickness] lay within."

An odd but related version of this tendency may be seen in the early experiments of John Hawkes. His first novel, *The Cannibal* (1949), was originally written in the third person, but in revision Hawkes says, "I found myself (perversely or not) wishing to project myself into the fiction and to become identified with its most criminal and, in a conventional sense, least sympathetic spokesman." To effect this transformation, Hawkes merely "went through the manuscript and changed the pronouns from third to first person" (Enck 150).

This pattern of self-recrimination and mental illness, through which the speaker works his way over the course of the novel, typifies American narrators during this period, on into the sixties, from Bill Lee in *Naked Lunch* (suffering from drug addiction), to Binx Bolling in *The Moviegoer* (who has Kierkegaard's "sickness unto death"), and Moses Herzog (who suffers the impotence of his thoughts). In such a lineage may be read the antecedents of such figures as Sylvia Plath's Esther Greenwood (*The Bell Jar*) and Ken Kesey's Chief Bromden (*The Cuckoo's Nest*).

John Barth chose to exploit the problems of authority and narrative form in the consciousness of his first invented voice, Todd Andrews of *The Floating Opera* (1956): "How does one write a novel? I mean, how can anybody possibly stick to the story, if he's at all sensitive to the significance of things?" (8–9). Barth capitalized on the difficulties of his narrators, their problems not very distant from his own, but the absence of explanatory assumptions about postwar reality appears in his work as an existential fact and the dilemmas of the liberal self which helped make existentialism appealing appear only indirectly.

For example, the absence of ultimate "reason" that paralyzes both Andrews and Jacob Horner, narrator of Barth's second novel, *The End of the Road* (1958), is perfectly compatible with the terms by which postwar liberalism rejected naturalism. The characteristic struggle of Barth's narrators remains an interior dialectic between a mind that doubts itself (remains skeptical of its own articulations) and a heart which has no reason for continuing to beat (although it continues to do so). The divorce between politics and literature appears here most forcefully as a divorce of idea and action, language and experience. Jacob Horner takes great pleasure in "articulation," even though he is convinced that "to classify, to categorize, to conceptualize, to grammarize, to syntactify it—is always a betrayal of experience"—though "only so betrayed can it be dealt with at all" (112–13).

The early novels of William Burroughs—though not a young writer when he first began to publish—provide the most extreme instance of the politics of form, of how the wariness about form and technique was at bottom the residue of a submerged or displaced politics. Burroughs' rejection of "technique" emerged from an agreement about the underlying paradigms of liberal sickness and the threat of totalitarianism, in its domestic incarnation as conformity and state repression.

In all of his books save the most recent, Burroughs is struggling with an idea of consciousness and freedom which is violated by any coherent or formal expression of that idea. Even his catchy aphorism "To speak is to lie. To live is to collaborate" is a logical contradiction, and the result is a body of work continually at war with the tendencies within itself to achieve form. On the one hand *Naked Lunch* is predicated upon an aesthetics of presentation—"The word cannot be expressed direct" (116)— which rejects any coherent re-presentation as a species of thought control or totalitarian form; while on the other, *Naked Lunch* is a didactic satire, in which the Parties of Interzone are allegories for the various human tendencies: to preach (The Senders), to reduce to conformity (the Divisionists), or to eliminate difference (the Liquefactionists). Burroughs himself explicitly favors the Factualists.

Like so many of his contemporaries, Burroughs was searching for some means of achieving "nakedness" or immediacy without succumbing to the atrophy or imposition of form. Like them, he first evolved a language of consciousness by trying to move the words closer to the source and quality of perceived experience within the voice of a first person narrator. The authority of his works depends in part upon the claims of such immediacy: "I am a recording instrument," he insists in the "Atrophied Preface" to *Naked Lunch*. "I do not presume to impose 'story' 'plot' 'continuity' " (221). Furthermore, the few accounts we have of Burroughs' composition of *Naked Lunch* would lead us to believe that little of a writer's characteristic control and objective distance was included in his chaotic methods. Brion Gysin, living with Burroughs in London during his composition of *Naked Lunch*, remembers "the raw material of *Naked Lunch* overwhelmed us," so that they resorted to papering the walls of their room with it: "Stick it on the wall along with the photographs and see what it looks like. Here, just stick these two pages together and cut down the middle. Stick it all together, end to end, and send it back like a big roll of music for a pianola. It's just material, after all. There is nothing sacred about words" (Burroughs and Gysin 43).

Repeated readings of *Naked Lunch* reveal that the book depends upon a number of typical structures. Burroughs has supplied his "mosaic of juxtaposition" (116) with considerable narrative continuity in the consciousness of Bill Lee, the figures of Doctor Benway and "A. J." Further, the sequence of the novel may be described as the picaresque progress of an isolated figure in a hallucinatory landscape. Finally, the book is an inversion of narrative, its structure loosely paralleling the sickness of withdrawal from addiction, in which the body of the book is presented as a "nightmare interlude of cellular panic," where life is "suspended between two ways of being" (57). Late in the novel, both sickness and nightmare structure emerge into sense as the story of a recovery from drug addiction—"I had been occluded from space-time like an eel's ass occludes when he stops eating" (217)—at which point Burroughs supplies an "Atrophied Preface" and his quite coherent, formal letter to the *British Journal of Addiction* that serves as a documentary epilogue.

Nevertheless, as a revision of his first novel *Junkie* (1953), *Naked Lunch* shows Burroughs transforming his text so that it expressed a more intimate representation of consciousness. Evidence of a critical, revising intelligence in the book is especially clear in the novel's forceful opening: "I can feel the heat closing in, feel them out there making their moves, setting up their devil doll stool pigeons, crooning over my spoon and dropper I throw away at Washington Square station, vault a turnstile and two flights down the iron stairs, catch an uptown A train" (1). This opening is a revised scene Burroughs first described in *Junkie*. Although that novel, too, is told in the first person, the invented voice lacks idiomatic presence and is in fact a disguised third person voice, a figure remembering a scene from his past. He is a detached observer, and the lack of authority and energy is evident when the passages are set beside one another: "I turned and ran back in the opposite direction. When I reached Sixth Avenue, he was about fifty feet behind me. I vaulted the subway turnstile and shoved the cigarette package into the space at the side of a gum machine. I ran down one level and got a train up to the Square." Later, Lee "could feel the Federals moving steadily closer" (54, 56). Here, Burroughs' account is little more than a list of successive actions, in which language is assumed to be a transparent medium for transmitting "facts." The words have little expressive relation to the fear which the speaker presumably feels, but in *Naked Lunch* the distance between voice/word and action/experience is severely reduced; Burroughs adopted the present tense ("could feel" became "can feel"), and the idiom and syntax of the passage cease to obey the almost compulsive adherence to the truth of external reality ("into the space at the side of a gum machine") that renders the earlier version so prosaic.

The authority of the postwar voices resides less in what they have to say than in the breezy candor and comical self-demolition of their point of view. These looser, meandering speakers enact a form which is inherently suspicious of form—of any projected meaning—at the same time that the subject of their ruminations is always the necessity of some such projection if one is to play a role in the world. In this, the fiction of Barth and Burroughs was characteristic of the postwar conflict in liberal discourse between a suspicion of ideology and a desire for action. Todd, Jacob, Holden, Invisible Man, even Bill Lee are characters who express something authentic, if only in the legitimacy of their turmoil, but who are presented at the same time as lacking an integration of idea with experience. None of them is happy without a "picture" of the world, yet each of them suspects that any such picture is always a "distortion."

The political meaning of "immediacy" as a trope and aspiration of postwar writers thus emerges out of the dialogue which structures so much liberal discourse in those years. The conventional oppositions between idea and experience, form and spontaneity, social conformity and private consciousness that recur throughout intellectual history are appropriated at this time within the assumptions of postwar liberalism and cold war dualism. This binarism quite naturally generates—as it did for Trilling—the idea of a consciousness that mediates the extremes of social and political life. Within social and political history so construed, the development of a first person voice, often emotionally disturbed or divided against itself, is always at some level an expression of the "liberal" self caught within the dialectic of that history.

Though the first person voice must be situated within a perception of social history structured by liberal discourse, this narrative vantage nevertheless seemed to offer the postwar writer a new subject at the same time that it emphasized the immediate relation of consciousness to world. This was especially true of those voices which contributed a new idiom to United States fiction. These new idioms were in varying degrees subversive, and in some instances purposely so. A central feature of Beat writing, for example, was the injection into American literature of a new vocabulary. In *Advertisements for Myself*, Mailer provided a diagram of this vocabulary, divided into "Hip" and "Square" (389), but his experience of the "hipster" was secondhand and failed to note the subversive character of "hip" language, as Burroughs had done in a note appended to the glossary of his first novel, *Junkie*:

It should be understood that the meanings of these words are subject to rapid changes, and that a word that has one hip meaning one year may have another the next. The hip sensibility mutates. For example, "Fey" means not only white, but fated or demonic. Not only do the words change meanings but meanings vary locally at the same time. A final glossary, therefore, cannot be made of words whose intentions are fugitive. (158)

Burroughs saw the possibilities of an "illegal" language which expressed the need for authenticity, privacy, and freedom. Language helped the "hipster" evade the sober efforts of the "square" to fix the truth of life in this or that word.

In a quite different but related context, Percy's novel *The Moviegoer* deploys a similar opposition between realistic language that assumes an objective, stable reality, and the ephemeral truth of "subjective inwardness": when his aunt sympathetically tries to explain her nephew's antisocial behavior as a "*Wanderjahr*," she subordinates the immediacy of his experience to an abstract category. Binx thinks, "We do not understand each other after all. If I thought I'd spent the last four years as a Wanderjahr, before 'settling down,' I'd shoot myself on the spot." By the end of the novel, Percy has made it ironically clear that Aunt Emily has been right about Binx, in an objective sort of way, but her words never stick to Binx. Language and experience remain separate, or words must wait on experience, when it comes to private states of being and the self's journey through the stages on life's way. The reality of being remains "fugitive" (49).

The unifying and liberating effects of language were intimately related to the writer's private experience of American culture and politics. Bellow's first novel, *Dangling Man* (1944), was written in the first person, built according to the prevailing standards of well-made, well-crafted fiction; but like Burroughs' *Junkie* it didn't exhibit the personal voice which Bellow later developed. His next novel, *The Victim* (1947), told in the third person, begins to explore the dark, irrational realities of a divided self. The novel begins with a description of the central character, Asa Leventhal, missing his elevated stop: "the black door of the ancient car was already sliding shut; he struggled with it, forcing it back with his shoulder, and squeezed through" (3). The reader can expect the novel to concern Leventhal's fight with himself (who appears as the book's doppelganger), something "ancient" and "barbaric," which he must exorcize.

Many reviewers considered *The Victim* to represent a marked development over Bellow's first novel, but in his third novel, *The Adventures of Augie March*, Bellow made use of his immigrant upbringing in creating the first person voice of Augie, thus closing the distance between himself and his fiction. *Augie March* finds its authority within the major character's personality, whose cocky American self-reliance seems to have burst through

Leventhal's Kafkan nightmare: "I am an American, Chicago-born—Chicago, that somber city—and go at things as I have taught myself, free-style, and will make the record my own way" (3).

This declaration of individual freedom, questioned by both Howe and Roth at the end of the decade, was to some degree an illusion, but it permitted Bellow to develop his voice and his vision of how one might relate to American society, at a time when both writing and social vision were severely cramped. Augie is self-taught, and emphasizes his powers of freedom and improvisation, and none of this was available to the writer unless he or she could extend social scrutiny within the authority of a perceiving self.

In one way or another, the new idioms in the work of Ellison, Bellow, and Burroughs were a means of attempting to heal the fissure between sign and self, language and experience, idea and action. If, as was true for Trilling, consciousness was the area in which their divorce became most plain, the representation of that consciousness was also a means of bringing them together within a single voice. Language and point of view, insofar as they issued from and represented the same territory, helped heal that divorce by reuniting the truth of private experience with public expression.

The widespread use of the first person voice is one result of that conviction, but the underlying assumption of this mechanical device was that the way one felt, the tempo and mood of one's consciousness could, in the midst of the "age of conformity," remain "real"—that one could step outside the public narcosis by stepping inside to the ongoing dialectic of consciousness. Though such a move might seem to condone a political passivity, the social construction of that consciousness, the way in which society was conceived—as an "organization," a "mass society," an "age of conformity"—made such a move both logical and pertinent, culturally if not politically subversive. Such a move was a way of identifying difference, of locating an inside otherness.

The idiomatic voice was thus part of a widespread sense that the social mind needed renewal. If the voice was the immediate meeting place of self and world, it was also a means of uniting a discouraging past with an uncertain future, sign with object, idea with action, in the authority of the present experience. The first person voice was not only an instrument for redefining the matrix of reality; it was also the result of a generation's need to find its own way, free-style.

Clearly this need was one of the explicit reasons for the postwar popularity of jazz as a model for prose writing, for the musical language of the jazz solo promised the freedom of improvisation at the same time that it embodied the serious search for an ephemeral rightness or truth, which once "found"—held in a series of notes, reached through a player's experimental excursion—would disappear. "There was no poetic," Charles Olson said of that time. "It was Charlie Parker" (cited in Paul 39). The idea of "jazz," like the idea of "immediacy," was part of the postwar cultural politics, having acquired a subversive meaning by its engagement with the discourse of bureaucracy, conformity, and totalitarianism.

Parker represented a new break with the jazz conventions that the "age of conformity" had learned to admire, so that here again we see the transient quality of authority. In an essay titled "Remembrances of Bop in New York, 1945–50," Gilbert Sorrentino recalls the time a friend called him in to hear a new record: "He put on this 78 Savoy, I think it was, and I sat there as if someone had hit me over the head: it was *Ko-Ko*, by Charles Parker and His Re-Bop Boys." Much of the authority which Parker had for Sorrentino came from his music's indifference to official culture: "Be-bop cut us off completely, to our immense satisfaction. It was even more vehemently decried as 'nigger music,' but even to the tone-deaf it was apparent that it (the music) didn't care what the hell was thought of it—jazz had broken itself free of the middle-class world's *social* conception of what it should be" (72, 73).

It is fairly easy to explain the charisma of jazz in the postwar as it functioned within the discourse of conformity and its Stalinist reverberations. "Jazz and the jazz life are, after all, semi-illegal," James Jones said. "It's a pretty amoral sort of life really, and is one way of escaping the increasingly encroaching controls of a bureaucratic government. Jazz and jazzmen live pretty much on the edge of the law—no matter how the propagandists of any country try to drag them by their hair into the national morality" (*Writers*, 3d ser., 235).

Their experience outside the pale of official culture gave jazzmen authority in the eyes of their followers. Ellison recalls that when he was a young boy "the jazzmen, some of whom we idolized, were in their own way better examples for youth to follow" because "despite the outlaw nature of their art, the jazzmen were less torn and damaged by the moral compromises and insincerities which have so sickened the life of our country." In "On Bird, Bird-Watching, and Jazz," Ellison points out the significance of Parker's influence:

Parker operated in the underworld of American culture, on that turbulent level where human instincts conflict with social institutions; where contemporary civilized values and hypocrisies are challenged by the Dionysian urges of a between-wars youth born to prosperity, conditioned by the threat of world destruction, and inspired—when not seeking total anarchy—by a need to bring social reality and our social pretensions into more meaningful balance. (*Shadow* 227–28)

Nor was this merely a matter of theme, of expressing in print thoughts and experiences which the official culture considered taboo. For several writers, jazz became a model of how the prose itself might move in a sentence, departing from straight syntax and taking on aural rhythms to express the imagination's improvisatory immediacy. The most notable effort to use jazz in writing narrative fiction was made by Jack Kerouac. The persistent model to which he appealed for explanation of his "spontaneous prose" was jazz improvisation: "yes, jazz and bop, in the sense of, say, a tenor man drawing a breath and blowing a phrase on his saxophone, til he runs out of breath . . . that's how I therefore separate my sentences, as breath separations of the mind." For Kerouac, as for Ellison, jazz carried connotations for culture as well as technique; the two were inseparable: "There's the raciness and freedom and humor of jazz instead of that dreary analysis" (*Jack* 555).

In some respects, Kerouac is the representative writer of the McCarthy era, for although none of his work appeared in print until the publication of *On the Road* in 1957, it was during the late forties and early fifties that he wrote most of it. In Kerouac may be seen the characteristic swing toward the authority of subjective experience, and the effort to break through what Mary McCarthy had called the "masquerade" of formalist "ventriloquism." In him we observe two impulses at work, in which autobiography—John Clellon Holmes called him "The Great Rememberer"—merges with an interest in the reality of fiction, in which the reality and authority of the self coincide with the reality of the words on the page.

Kerouac wrote his books in opposition to the discourse of "technique," but they express a deflection of political radicalism into personal "experience" that he shares with that discourse. This common move generates the dynamic of opposition through which many writers saw themselves operating. Kerouac is but one instance of a widely perceived need to renew literary form, to make it capable once more of conveying a sense of the real. Kerouac's effort to integrate autobiography with "spontaneous prose" was thus an effort to align fiction with fact along some other metaphor than "the mirror," and achieve an authentic expression. Like Holden Caulfield and Binx Bolling, Kerouac felt an overwhelming insincerity at the heart of American existence, and he was determined—as were other writers in their own ways—to find a literary form that would break through the separation of "orthodox" art from the immediacy of their lives. "That was Kerouac's great discovery in *On the Road*," Allen Ginsberg has said. "In conversations with people whom we knew well, whose souls I respected, that the things we were telling each other for real were totally different from what was already in literature. . . . The problem is to break down that distinction" (*Writers*, 3d ser., 288).

Kerouac thus shows how the experiences and values of his generation could be used to create art. Sorrentino was one of those to whom Kerouac's example gave a great assist: "Kerouac did what we all knew *had* to be done, which was to incorporate our own experience into what we liked to think of as being serious prose. . . . He said, I listen to Charlie Parker and it's valuable. I'll put that right into my story. I mean the *idea* of Charlie Parker. And we read this . . . it was a kind of burst of light, that we could do such a thing" (Alpert 18). These testimonials not only indicate Kerouac's influence; they provide confirmation of how strained and paralyzed the times must have felt, how unwelcome to the new crowd and mood of the young. Nothing else can explain the hyperbole that we hear in both Sorrentino ("that we could do such a thing") and Pynchon ("allowed to exist!")—especially when we recall that the work they are describing is *On the Road*, *Temple of Gold*, and *The Adventures of Augie March*.

Kerouac's experiments with the immediacy of "spontaneous prose" developed after he had written his first novel, *The Town and the City*, a conventional third person narrative in the mold of Thomas Wolfe's *Of Time and the River*. As in the early careers of McCarthy, Mailer, and Bellow, Kerouac's illustrates a shift in perspective from third person omniscience to first person expressiveness. Like *The Naked and the Dead*, Kerouac's first novel was an effort to provide the social stratification and generational scope of the "big social novel" he admired in Wolfe, Dos Passos, and Steinbeck. The first paragraph of the book announces Kerouac's intention to write something like Wolfe's *Of Time and the River*:

> The town is Galloway. The Merrimac River, broad and placid, flows down to it from the New Hampshire hills, broken at the falls to make frothy havoc on the rocks, foaming on over ancient stone towards a place where the river suddenly swings about in a wide and peaceful basin, moving on now around the flank of the town, on to places known as Lawrence and Haverhill, through a wooded valley, and on to the sea at Plum Island, where the river enters an infinity of waters and is gone. Somewhere far north of Galloway, in headwaters close to Canada, the river is continually fed and made to brim out of endless sources and unfathomable springs. (3)

The early Kerouac is clearly obeying what he took to be the rules of writing—relaxed a bit to accommodate his poetic imitation of Wolfe and his own sentimental associations with Lowell, Massachusetts.

Beginning the book in this way, Kerouac was paying his respects to Wolfe, trying to write with some degree of orthodoxy and seeking a niche in tradition. There is even evidence that he thought of his Merrimac as an echo of the River Liffy that runs through Phoenix Park, and that he hoped to give his novel something of the quality of *Finnegans Wake*. In a letter written to Charlie Sampas, in preparation for the publicity of his book, Kerouac said he had come full circle, bringing "us by a commodious vicus of recirculation past River Eve and Adam back to the nights when we'd all bump on the Square" (McNally 124).

The Town and the City received reviews that should have been encouraging to a young writer. Though reviewers complained that the "long-winded nonsense of its intellectuals is well-nigh unreadable" and found its attack on the city "exaggerated," they also said it was "almost a major work" and "a rough diamond." As Sorrentino wrote later, Kerouac "could have parlayed that reception, as many young writers do, into a second novel, just as dead, just as silly. Instead, he wrote *On the Road*, which took many years to be published" (Barone 238).

Even before publication, Kerouac hadn't been satisfied with his first novel. He told Holmes in 1948, "Well, I've decided I wrote it because I wanted fame and money and . . . love, not for any sterile artistries. I was just wooing the world with it, being coy" (McNally 110). Kerouac had already begun working on a book that started where the first one ended— Peter Martin hitchhiking—but this one would eliminate some of the gap between Kerouac's voice and the experiences recorded in the novel. In the new book's first sentences can be heard the characteristic chords of the first person melancholy so typical of the fifties voice: "I first met Dean not long after my wife and I split up. I had just gotten over a serious illness that I won't bother to talk about, except that it had something to do with the miserably weary split-up and my feeling that everything was dead" (5).

Typically, the importance of *On the Road* is attributed to Kerouac's experiments with spontaneous prose, but the significance of "spontaneity"— whatever one thinks of it as a strategy for writing—was generated by its dialogue with the language of conformity and the programmed consciousness the writer was determined to escape or replace with a true alertness. Kerouac was seeking a literary form that would provide a fresh sense of reality in the writing itself. In attempting this, Kerouac was not only advancing in the typical direction of the fifties toward a first person voice vaguely disguising the private life of the author; he was evolving a sense of style as primary reality, and of the novel as experience rather than reflection or picture. At its best, his "prose" was not a picture of an experience, but the experience itself, just as the jazz solo is not mimetic but creative: "you simply give the reader the actual workings of your mind during the writing itself" (*Jack* 541).

As published, *On the Road* is the least "spontaneous" of Kerouac's early writing. For more thorough experiments with "spontaneous prose," one must turn to *The Subterraneans* (1958), "The Railroad Earth," and *Visions of Cody* (1960). While Kerouac was working on *Cody*, he wrote to John Clellon Holmes, "What I'm beginning to discover now is something beyond the novel and beyond the arbitrary confines of the story . . . wild form, man, wild form" (McNally 145). Unlike Mary McCarthy, Kerouac was perfectly willing to jettison the novel as an outmoded form if "novel" meant a sterile set of conventions that excluded his consciousness of the world.

In the way he executed them, Kerouac's ideas about writing were almost designed to fail, for he cared less about a polished piece of work than about the authenticity of creation, and he knew that writing as "blowing" will have its moments, like a jazz musician reaching for "IT." One night in Chicago, Sal Paradise and Dean Moriarty wander into a club where several musicians begin to "start blowing." Sizing up the band, Dean tells Sal about one of the men, "You see, man, Prez has the technical anxieties of a money-making musician, he's the only one who's well dressed, see him grow worried when he blows a clinker, but the leader, that cool cat, tells him not to worry and just blow and blow—the mere sound and serious exuberance of the music is all *he* cares about. He's an artist" (*Road* 197).

Many writers of Kerouac's time had that same anxiety over technique. Kerouac was perhaps the most extreme in his move toward "wild form"; certainly for many readers, Kerouac's moments of successful blowing have seemed too few, but in his conviction that writing had to close the gap between experience and language, had to move within to the immediacy of mind and body, Kerouac was a man of the postwar years.

The sharp outlines of Kerouac's career help clarify some of the central problems and strategies of the writer after World War II. In his work may be seen the effort to thrust aside the "charade" of orthodox fiction and triumphant "technique" that had troubled McCarthy and Bellow. In turning to the first person of his second novel, Kerouac was typical of his time, even though other writers made this move with greater deliberation, retaining greater degrees of control and elements of indirection often characteristic of invented first person narrators. The pervasive use of the first person form—all along its spectrum of possibilities—was undeniably an appeal to the priority of consciousness and perceived experience as a source of fresh material for fiction, and a point of view from which the writer claimed some coherent authority. At the same time, this conscious dismissal of the immediate literary past, in which the third person ideological point of view had achieved preeminence in American letters, was one of the most explicit ways in which the suspicion of social realism and naturalist ideology, shared with New Critic and Old Left alike, was manifest in the new writing.

Although the specific relations sketched here between writer and critic and among the writers themselves by no means describe a unified movement, within them may be noted the essential terms of postwar discourse: the pervasive search for a new authority, the effort to evade a naive politics, and the renewed appeal to resources of the self—including the moral imagination—which came to dominate the narrative fiction of the fifties and sixties.

Part 2

5

From Ranter to Writer

Ellison's Invisible Man and the New Liberalism

The essence of the word is its ambivalence.

"Twentieth Century Fiction," 1946

There is an argument in progress between black men and white men as to the true nature of American reality.

"Harlem Is Nowhere"

I

Because Ralph Ellison began writing *Invisible Man* in the aftermath of African American disillusionment with the left, it should come as no surprise that his essays and fiction from this period share a great deal with the anti-Stalinist discourse of the new liberalism. In Ellison's writing of this time, as in literary culture generally, one notes the characteristic rejection of naturalism and social realism as adequate forms of representation, and a redefinition of personal identity and social history as tragic, complex, ambivalent, and ironic. Further, during this period Ellison gave increasing significance in his fiction and essays to psychological terms of social analysis, and gave these terms priority over economics and class consciousness as the dominant discourse of change.

Although at many points indistinguishable from the centrist discourse to which both New Critics and New York intellectuals contributed, Ellison's redefinition of social reality emerged from interests and experiences very different from those of southern Agrarians and disenchanted white liberals, a difference nowhere more evident than in the fact that when Ellison began to write, black Americans did not yet have "social equality" under the law. While "contradiction" and "irony" might be constitutive of human existence and history for Cleanth Brooks and Lionel Trilling, for black Americans these terms described their experience within a political system that promised freedom and equality for all but in practice failed to deliver those rights to a tenth of its citizens. In writing *Invisible Man*, Ellison made this long-standing hypocrisy a central theme of his novel, but his determination to make the experience of his central character resonate universally for all readers had the effect of mediating historical and political urgencies within the ahistoricism of mythic form and tragic vision so typical of postwar critical thought. Because *Invisible Man* is constituted by the dynamism of these incompatible discourses, the novel has generated a good deal of controversy for several generations of readers.

The close fit between Ellison's analysis of the black American situation and the analysis of human nature set forth in the conservative discourse of the dominant criticism was at once a major source of the novel's success and its infamy. Many of the competing discursive pressures from that time emerged into clarity and arrayed themselves in stark opposition in the first reviews *Invisible Man* received. The new conservatism of the literary liberal is immediately recognizable in many of these, for the novel's first admirers openly praised *Invisible Man* for going "beyond" social realism and the protest novel. R. W. B. Lewis, for example, noted with favor the novel's contentment with "its own being" and the absence of any impulse within it "to atone for some truculence in nature or to affect the course of tomorrow's politics" ("Eccentrics," 145). Postwar liberalism's contempt for the naive politics of the thirties also informs Richard Chase's approval of the novel's portrait of "mystery, suffering, transcendent reality, and the ultimate contradictions of life" ("A Novel," 678–84). In the *Listener*, Stephen Spender was more explicit: "His great achievement is that he is not content to be a 'social realist' learning the lesson of oppression and building up a solid case against social evil" (115). At the end of the fifties, Leslie Fiedler argued that *Invisible Man* was "superior to any of the passionate, incoherent books of Richard Wright" precisely because Ellison "bypassed all formulas of protest" (*Love* 493).

Predictably, the novel has been attacked by those on the left and those within the African American community for the very same reasons. Irving Howe's review in the *Nation* was full of praise, but he took issue with the hero's assertion of freedom: "Though the unqualified assertion of individuality is at the moment a favorite notion of literary people, it is also a vapid one" ("A Negro," 454). Abner Berry wrote in the *Daily Worker* that Ellison's book is "written in vein [*sic*] of middle class snobbishness—even contempt—towards the Negro people" and that it "manipulates his nameless hero for 439 pages through a maze of corruption, brutality, anticommunism slanders, sex perversion and the sundry inhumanities upon which a dying social system feeds." Writing for *Freedom*, John O. Killens called the book "a vicious distortion of Negro life" and attacked Ellison for appealing to the popular conservatism of the time: "mix a heavy portion of sex and a heavy portion of violence, a bit of sadism and a dose of redbaiting (Blame the Communists for everything bad) and you have the making of a bestseller today" (quoted in Neal 34–36).

This opposition was rekindled in the mid-sixties by the new orientation of Black Nationalism and the Black Aesthetic (see Cruse 505–12; Neal 31–37; and Baker, *Afro* 140–59). Among these more recent critics, Ernest Kaiser, whose essay provides a useful survey of social criticism of Ellison, argued that Ellison had abandoned the Marxist viewpoint when he fell "under the influence" of the New Criticism (56), and had taken as his models writers "who see nothing but eternal tragedy in the human condition which no revolution can change, and art and writing as man's only triumph over tragedy" (58). He described *Invisible Man* as a "contrived novel about phony innocence and against Communism and for the existential notion that each person must solve his own problems" (81–82).

Kaiser's picture of an abrupt shift is not, as Robert O'Meally has shown, a fair account of Ellison's development, for even the first review he wrote, "Creative and Cultural Lag," expresses critical values Ellison has continued to hold, such as his insistence that writers explore "the rich deep materials of the Negro" and differentiate the "psychology" of their characters (90–91). At the same time, this review "reflects so thoroughly the black leftist sensibilities of the times" (O'Meally, *Craft* 40ff.), for as Ellison himself noted thirty years later, he was writing "what might be called propaganda" (*Going* 294). In this review, for example, Ellison uses the Marxist discourse of totality to assert that the black writer must "utilize yet transcend his immediate environment and grasp the historic process as a whole" (91).

In book reviews for *New Masses* from 1939 to 1941, this Marxist perspective remains a central element. In "Ruling Class Southerner," for example, he faults the author for failing to make his central character "the personalization of the sociological facts" and argues that "no matter how powerful an individual may become, he is dependent upon others with similar interests; it is this group's consciousness of itself as a class . . . that is responsible" (27). In "Anti-War Novel" Ellison suggests that *Spring Offensive*, a novel by Herbert Lewis, is unlikely to receive attention from "the capitalist press," and admires the book for showing "a degree of class consciousness" and "nuances of American class struggle" (29–30). Similarly, Ellison praises Len Zinberg's novel *Walk Hard, Talk Loud* for showing a boy's coming to see his relation to a "diseased social order" and notes that the success of

Zinberg, a white writer, derives from his "Marxist understanding of the economic basis of Negro personality" ("Negro Prize Fighter," 27).

Looking back through these first essays, one notices not only that Ellison easily accommodated Marxist ideology with other themes that he has since retained, but also that within the context of that time, his determination to situate the black American within the terms of universality was far from reactionary. Ellison was preoccupied with the need to displace "stereotyped roles which ignore Negro problems and Negro reality" with roles and portraits that acknowledged a greater "range of emotion." "It was a long Broadway tradition," he notes in his review of Theodore Ward's *Big White Fog*, "that the Negro should never be shown as capable of the universal emotion of love" (22). In "Stormy Weather," his review of Langston Hughes's autobiography *The Big Sea*, Ellison faults the author for avoiding "analysis and comment . . . that unity which is formed by the mind's brooding over experience and transforming it into conscious thought." Had Hughes supplied such commentary, "we would be shown the processes by which a sensitive Negro attains a heightened consciousness of a world in which most of the odds are against his doing so" (20–21). In formulations such as this one, which seem to anticipate so explicitly the project of *Invisible Man*, the Marxist terminology of "historic process" gives way effortlessly to the growth of mind as the territory within which social change must occur. "It will be the spread of this consciousness," Ellison concluded, "added to the passion and sensitivity of the Negro people, that will help create a new way of life in the United States" (21).

In itself, this modernist move toward the interiority of psychological realism might have proven uncontroversial, but such readers as Kaiser, Addison Gayle, and Houston Baker, Jr., have seen in Ellison's version of the "heightened consciousness" a Eurocentric view of the artist which subordinates African American culture to "conscious" art and separates that art from politics (see Smith 25–26). In his essay "To Move without Moving: An Analysis of Creativity and Commerce in Ralph Ellison's Trueblood Episode," Houston Baker, Jr., attempts to recover *Invisible Man* from these charges by arguing that "the distinction between folklore and literary art evident in Ellison's critical practice collapses in his creative practice" (829).

Though Ellison has always maintained that art and politics are different realms, it is worth recalling that Ellison developed as a writer during a time when the separation of art and politics not only seemed possible, but, in view of recent events, necessary. There have been many accounts of the experience of black Americans with the Communist Party, but most of them agree on the essentials which Ellison summarized years later: "The Communists recognized no plurality of interests and were really responding to the necessities of Soviet foreign policy, and when the war came,

Negroes got caught and were made expedient in the shifting of policy" (*Going* 296; see Cruse). In this development, Ellison's experience was not unlike that of Rahv, Trilling, and Chase; like them he understood political literature to be a form of propaganda, while "art"—being faithful to the ironic complexities of experience—was inherently anti-ideological.

Today this position seems at once naive and reactionary, but once relocated within the discursive context from which it emerged, the separating of art and politics becomes a more complex event, and regains some of its original plausibility. More than that: within the African American community that distinction participates in a strategy of withdrawal from centers of power, both democratic and communist, that was provoked by a crisis in black American leadership during World War II. The story that Ellison has told on several occasions about the origin of *Invisible Man* always involves the failure of this leadership, so that students of the novel have long recognized that the book details the difficulties of a young black man who seeks to become a leader. But accounts such as those by M. K. Singleton and John S. Wright, as useful and eloquent as they are, pursue the mythic discourse of the novel and follow the lead given them by Ellison's references to Lord Raglan and Kenneth Burke. In doing so, they foreground the contemplative character of the novel and lose sight of the controversy over "Negro leadership" which supplies access to Ellison's contemporary history and to the more active and political dimension of the novel. Returning to this discourse helps us work against the novel's universalism and its explicit tendencies to veer toward caricature and allegory, away from contemporary reference.

After all, Ellison found Raglan's book relevant only because he had been thinking for years about leadership and the nature of the hero. He provides the most specific motive for that meditation in the essay "On Initiation Rites and Power":

> during the historical moment when I was working out the concept of *Invisible Man* my people were involved in a terrific quarrel with the federal government over our not being allowed to participate in the war as combat personnel in the armed forces on an equal basis, and because we were not even being allowed to work in the war industries on an equal basis with other Americans. This quarrel led to my concern with the nature of leadership, to the nature of Negro leadership, from a different and nonliterary direction. I was very much involved with the question of just why our Negro leadership was never able to enforce its will. (*Going* 44)

Ellison's concern was one of the dominant preoccupations in the African American community during the forties, because it was during this period that the stimulus of the war and its rhetoric of freedom and equality helped produce the sustained unrest and militancy that led to the civil rights successes of the fifties and sixties (see Dalfiume; Bernstein; Chafe 18). Walter White, executive secretary of the NAACP, noted that "World War II has immeasurably magnified the Negro's awareness of the disparity between the American profession and practice of democracy" (quoted in Chafe 29).

This "disparity" was the immediate political meaning of "contradiction" in the "Prologue" to *Invisible Man*, where the narrator asks how he can be "responsible" to a culture which denies him "social equality." This was a question, as Richard Dalfiume shows in "The 'Forgotten Years' of the Negro Revolution," being asked throughout the African American community. Dalfiume supplies a number of representative reactions to wartime rhetoric which appeared in the black press: an editorial in *Crisis* responded, "the hysterical cries of the preachers of democracy for Europe leave us cold. We want democracy in Alabama and Arkansas, in Mississippi and Michigan"; a columnist for the Pittsburgh *Courier* insisted that "our war is not against Hitler in Europe, but against the Hitlers in America" (Dalfiume 522). As O'Meally has noted, this comparison between the Nazis the United States was pledged to defeat and the "Hitlers at home" was an analogy that Ellison himself made (*Craft* 53), but this analogy enjoyed a wide currency (see Dalfiume 524).

These responses were part of a conscious strategy to exploit the occasion of the war: "What an opportunity the crisis has been," exclaimed the Pittsburgh *Courier*, "for one to persuade, embarrass, compel and shame our government and our nation . . . into a more enlightened attitude toward a tenth of its people!" (Dalfiume 525). As managing editor of the *Negro Quarterly*, from its second issue in 1942 to the end of its brief run in 1943, Ellison was directly involved in this controversy, because the relationship of "American Negroes . . . to the Four Freedoms" was the dominant subject of the editorials and essays in the quarterly's four numbers, and the theme throughout was that "Negro leaders, the government and labor, have thus far failed to understand the real mood of the Negro people" (ii).

In the editorial for the last issue, which clearly bears his stamp, Ellison suggested not only the form which leadership might take, but also the eventual conclusion of the novel he was yet to write. Ellison sided with those who rejected an unconditional support of the war effort as "a crime, not only against Negroes, but against all true anti-Fascists," and went on to approve of William Hastie's resignation from the War Department, which he described as a "tactic of withdrawal." Hastie's action had special meaning for Ellison because it was prompted by the effort to "palm off" an air school at Tuskegee "as the real thing" (*Negro Quarterly* 299). Founded by Booker T. Washington, Tuskegee was one of the major black American institutions, and so stood in Ellison's mind not only as his alma mater but also as the symbol of a leadership that had failed to "represent the Negro community" (*Shadow* 18). As Richard Dalfiume notes, the president of Tuskegee Institute in 1943, Frederick D. Patterson, had "made it clear in his newspaper column and in talks with administration officials that he believed in all-out support for the war effort by Negroes regardless of segregation and discrimination" (529, n. 55). In sharp contrast to the compromises of a "subsidized Negro leadership" (*Negro Quarterly* 301), Hastie's withdrawal "made his name meaningful among thousands of Negroes, bringing eligibility for that support which is the basis of true leadership" (*Negro Quarterly* 299).

The specific relevance of this event to the actions of Bledsoe, president of the college which expels Invisible Man, and of Norton, the northern white trustee who subsidizes the school, should be immediately apparent, but Ellison's thinking about the "tactic of withdrawal" as a form of leadership made necessary by the constraints of power within current institutions may well have suggested to him the overall form of the narrative as well: the successive disillusionment with institutional power that constitutes *Invisible Man*. Like the masses of black Americans at that time who took the "opportunity" of the war to "embarrass" the government, Invisible Man— speaking from the position of withdrawal—finds the terms of his critique within the charter of the United States, turning its rhetoric against itself, "compelling it," as Ellison wrote in the editorial for the *Negro Quarterly*, "untiringly toward true freedom" (*Negro Quarterly* 298).

Viewed from a position between Soviet-centered communist policy that abandoned the interests of black Americans, and fascism both at home and abroad, Ellison's strategy appears less accommodating than it might today. The striking fact, perhaps, is that although the device of withdrawal emerged from Ellison's thinking about a specific history of failed leadership and was stimulated by its contemporary ineffectuality, Ellison should have decided to remind readers of the nation's promise of equality within a modernist ideology of art which at all points threatens to lift the novel out of historical circumstance and subordinate its central figure to a frame that is more metaphysical than political.

After all, the novel's Prologue frames the story of its hero within the characteristic tropes of new liberal discourse: "the world moves," Invisible Man says, "by contradiction" (6), and those contradictions constitute his consciousness, because "incompatible notions" have reduced him to a state of paralyzed alertness. Invisible Man contains within himself, to recall Trilling, "the very essence of the culture," for he does not "submit to serve the ends of any one ideological group or tendency" (*Liberal* 9). Ellison's analysis of American culture in "Twentieth Century Fiction," an essay written in 1946, expresses a similar translation of Marxist terminology into psychological dialectic. "The struggle between Americans," he wrote, is part of a "democratic process" in which "conflict" is producing "a delicately poised unity of divergencies" (*Shadow* 26). Huck Finn is a figure of great humanity, he argues, because he "embodies the two major conflicting drives operating in nineteenth-century America" (33). This embodied conflict is what Trilling, in his essay on *Huckleberry Finn* two years later, called "the dialectic of Huck's great moral crisis" (*Liberal* 112).

It should be remembered that Ellison's overriding preoccupation, even in his reviews for *New Masses*, was with the adequate representation of the black American; from his point of view, the people of his community had rarely been "drawn as that sensitively focused process of opposites, of good and evil, of instinct and intellect . . . which great literary art has projected as the image of man" (*Shadow* 26). *Invisible Man* sought to redress this omission by offering an alternative that is not so much an image as a voice: an articulate consciousness, that from its opening self-assertion, "I am an invisible man," expresses Ellison's determination to "explore the full range of American Negro humanity and to affirm those qualities which are of value beyond any question of segregation, economics or previous condition of servitude" (*Shadow* 17)—which is to say, beyond those "deterministic" terms which white and black alike have used to interpret black culture and identity. Though this was a reordering of definitional priorities enjoying renewed currency within the Christian realism of Reinhold Neibuhr and the politics of George Kennan and Arthur Schlesinger, it was seen by them as a reminder of moral complexity that twentieth-century liberals—especially in the thirties—had forgotten. From Ellison's point of view, on the other hand, this had been a "complexity" denied to the black American, especially since Reconstruction. His use of the terminology we associate with the dominant critical discourse of that time was always mediated by his position as part of a community denied social equality; his "moral imagination" (*Shadow* 37) should be not collapsed with Trilling's, but engaged with it to release the political torque or difference alive within that common discourse.

Ellison thought that much modern writing failed to acknowledge the universal complexity shared by black Americans as well as white, but twentieth-century American fiction, in particular, was inadequate to the "diversity of American life" generally, and had shown itself especially inept (and irresponsible) in portraying the realities of black American life, which, Ellison argued, had been largely absent from American realist and naturalist fiction. "When the white American," Ellison wrote in 1946, "holding up most twentieth-century fiction, says, 'This is American reality,' the Negro tends to answer . . . 'Perhaps, but you've left out this, and this, and this. And most of all, what you'd have the world accept as *me* isn't even human" (*Shadow* 25).

Here as elsewhere Ellison's position exhibits a striking double-voiced parallelism with the established critics, for his view of twentieth-century writing harmonizes with similar assessments of this fiction by Schorer, Trilling, and Rahv. Though Ellison focused on the absence of "the full, complex ambiguity of the human" (*Shadow* 25) in portraits of black Americans, all of them thought that naturalist writing relied upon a naive objectivity and spoke a superficial monologue that made it the ally of ideology and propaganda. Unlike Trilling, however, Ellison was trying to wrest reality not only from the Stalinists (Krupnick 64), but from the misperceptions of all white Americans.

Ellison drew a connection between the Jim Crow legislation that followed upon Reconstruction and the virtual disappearance of the black American from the fiction produced by the dominant white writers in American culture. Before the time of Reconstruction, the use of the black American to symbolize Man, Ellison argued, is "organic to nineteenth-century literature," and "occurs not only in Twain, but in Emerson, Thoreau, Whitman and Melville" (*Shadow* 32). The "Negro" had begun to "exert an influence upon America's moral consciousness," and "during the nineteenth century it flared nakedly in the American consciousness, only to be repressed after the Reconstruction" (29). Instead, the "Negro" becomes in twentieth-century fiction "an image of the unorganized, irrational forces of American life" (41). By comparison with "this continuing debasement of our image," Ellison declares in another essay, "the indignities of slavery were benign" (*Shadow* 48).

This judgment, of course, also constitutes another instance of that skewed or uneasy parallel I have been trying to isolate, for Ellison's attention to the moral ambiguities of nineteenth-century literature is part and parcel of the literary community's shift from the dominant naturalistic prose of the twentieth century, and the scientific as well as Marxist assumptions they associated with it. Trilling, for example, in his influential definition of culture as a dialectic, noted of the nineteenth century that "an unusually large proportion of its notable writers . . . were such repositories of the dialectic of their times—they contained both the yes and the no of their culture, and by that token they were prophetic of the future" (*Liberal* 9).

Consciously or not, Ellison deployed this valuation in behalf of the culture and personality of the black American. While "our naturalistic prose," Ellison wrote in 1946, is "perhaps the brightest instrument for recording sociological fact, physical action, the nuance of speech," it becomes "dull when confronting the Negro" (*Shadow* 26). For Ellison, the rise of naturalism, with its emphasis upon the crushing influence of the environment, is a literary corollary of the growing influence of "contemporary science and industry" which has obscured the "full, complex ambiguity of the human" (25).

As a technique and system of assumptions, naturalism could narrow and dilute the power of a writer. In Ellison's thinking, Richard Wright's *Native Son* had reinforced the image of the black man as a victim, and, since it was written by a black American who characterized himself as a "scientist in a laboratory" (xxi), helped demonstrate the shortcomings of the naturalist method. Ellison had begun to write under Wright's prompting, but when he came to write his own fiction he felt that Wright's interpretation of the Negro experience had been too sociological, for his character Bigger Thomas possessed none of the consciousness or imagination which Wright had in large measure: "I felt that Wright was over committed to ideology—even though I, too, wanted many of the same things for our people. You might say that I was much less a social determinist" (*Shadow* 16).

Certainly Henry Louis Gates, Jr., is right to insist that in making the move from naturalism to modernism, Ellison doesn't reject Wright so much as "signify" upon him (245–46), but this keeps our sense of Ellison's novel within a tradition of "black narrative forms" (246), when in fact the targets of his signifying, as O'Meally has pointed out (*Craft* 78), are seemingly without limit, and occur within discursive systems that cannot be contained within "black narrative forms."

Ellison thought the limitations of Bigger Thomas were in part a consequence of the narrative form Wright elected to use, for the naturalist mode, like the wrong channel, simply bypassed other frequencies of being, which he wanted to air. Because Ellison associated "naturalistic prose" with exterior detail—"sociological fact, physical action, the nuance of speech"— he felt it was disposed to offer only "counterfeit" images of the black American's humanity, which was hidden by the black mask and its stereotypical associations in the "white folk mind." Because black humanity and its problems with white America are "psychological," an adequate image of the black man can emerge only from interior modes of expression (*Shadow* 26–27). Wright's image of Bigger Thomas only confirmed "what whites think of the Negro's reality," he wrote in "The World and the Jug" (1964). "Here environment is all—and interestingly enough, environment conceived solely in terms of the physical, the non-conscious" (*Shadow* 114).

Because Ellison felt that Wright's scientific attitude didn't allow for ways in which the individual might deviate from the generalizations and group comparisons of sociology and economic determinism, *Invisible Man* is full of parodies of scientific confidence. One example is the hospital scene in which Invisible Man undergoes shock treatment. Resting inside a glass box, wires attached to his head and navel in a mechanistic parody of fetal life, Invisible Man overhears the conversation of the doctors above him:

> "The machine will produce the results of a prefrontal lobotomy without the negative side effects of the knife," the voice said. . . .
> "But what of his psychology?"
> "Absolutely of no importance!" the voice said. "The patient will live as he has to live, and with absolute integrity. Who could ask for more? He'll experience no major conflict of motives, and what is even better, society will suffer no traumata on his account."

Reflecting upon this experience, Invisible Man recalls that "some of it sounded like a discussion of history" (231). This scene is meant to be a satire on communist pretensions, in Niebuhr's words, "to bring the vast forces of history under the control of any particular will" (*Irony* 79); but it serves at the same time to lay bare the system of cold war perception, in which science, medicine, and industry all figured as expressions of naive rationalism, unable to explain or contain the ineradicable conflicts within the self, society, and reality. In this way the scene also anticipates the next major section of the novel, where Ellison's hero is told by the Brotherhood, "We are all realists here, and materialists"; "We follow the laws of reality" (300, 491).

This dialogue also sets forth the novel's opposition between the confidence in description—the belief in an external reality that may be described with approximate objectivity—that the new liberal attributed to conventional realism, and the freedom of psychological reality to evade such description. Written in the late forties, this passage shows how realism, by becoming identified with a materialist view of human behavior, had lost its authority. Implicitly, Ellison's novel proposes a psychological narrative form—at places surreal and expressionistic—as being more "realistic" than the naturalism it supplants.

The uneasy dynamic between the political specificity of Ellison's conception and its expression within a discourse that obscures those politics characterizes the entire novel. Invisible Man ends his Prologue by telling his reader that what follows will be an explication of the blues he feels and his own responsibility for them: "But what did *I* do to be so blue?" Houston Baker has identified the blues as the cultural "matrix" specific to the African American community, but Ellison has defined the blues in terms drawn from Western culture, as "a near-tragic, near-comic lyricism" (*Shadow* 78). At the same time, Ellison has already provided a more political explication of the blues within the Prologue, dramatized in Invisible Man's descent into the music of Louis Armstrong.

This italicized passage from the Prologue is a kind of historical overture that sketches the background to the contemporary manifestation of the blues within the hero's brief lifetime and is enigmatic, to say the least, but it appears to dramatize, through an intertextual tour de force, a theory of personal and social identity produced through a history of conflict and contradiction. The blues dream identifies the origins of American cultural conflict in the scene of a slave auction, and in the contradictions of "blackness" within that culture. Later in the dream Invisible Man encounters a "singer of spirituals" who tells him that she loved her master because he gave her several sons: "I learned to love their father though I hated him too" (9–10). Whatever else remains murky here, fairly clearly Ellison means to figure the emergence of American culture—of self, society, and social history—as the ambivalent offspring of conflict between the races. Culture "is nothing if not a dialectic," Trilling insisted in "Reality in America," but Ellison's version of that dialectic, at least in this passage, was anchored in the specific historical circumstances which produced the conflict structuring the hero's psychology.

The problem for the novel was that this specificity jockeys with a collateral tendency to present such conflict, as it became entangled in the discourse of cold war dialogics, as a tragic and eternal fact of human existence. When Schlesinger admonished his reader, "You cannot expel conflict from society any more than you can from the human mind" (*Vital* 255), he was addressing Stalinism, perceived to be a system that promised its members a life free from anxiety. In the hospital scene cited above, Ellison was speaking within that same discourse by satirizing such attempts as a form of lobotomy, but in deploying this discourse the novel threatens to transform history into natural truth, as Invisible Man does in the Prologue: "that (by contradiction I mean) is how the world moves" (6). The self-contradiction that Ellison built into his character was for him, as for Trilling and other prominent critics in the postwar, the faithful representation of human circumstance, even though this inner division, for the African American community, had causes that were reinforced by federal and state law and thus existed well within range of human intervention.

These related but distinct discourses, woven into the fabric of the novel, are united by the mode of irony because the entire interior narrative is told by Invisible Man at the expense of his former self, who may be interpreted, within this discussion, as a palimpsest of radical malaise—mediated through the terminology of the blues, but significantly resonant with liberal disenchantment. For the better part of the novel, Invisible Man plays the role of naive liberal, as he struggles with the transition between two ideas of reality: one that portrays society as a solid world in which he wishes to play a part, and one that renders the depth of that social world mere surface, and in which no action short of charlatanism seems possible. In the first of these ideas, "reality" remains merely external, and it is this epistemological naiveté which Invisible Man must outgrow, just as Trilling in his attack on Vernon Parrington insisted the liberal must do.

For Ellison, the words "society" or "social reality" referred—as they did for Rahv, Trilling, Howe, and other contemporaries—not to an external world that the novel might "mirror," but to some collective "idea" or nightmare held in common by and helping to produce the social world. Ellison had long argued that no social change would be possible unless it evolved by recognizing the dream-life of the nation: not only the "emotion-charged myths, symbols and wartime folklore" of "the black masses" (*Negro Quarterly* 301–2), but also the fantasies and myths of the "white folk mind" (*Shadow* 48, 304).

Because of the cultural dominance of whites, black Americans, as Ellison wrote in his review of Gunnar Myrdal's *An American Dilemma*, have had to endure "the nightmarish fantasy of the white American mind" in which they exist as phantoms of everything the white man seeks to "repress" (*Shadow* 304, 48). This produces the condition Du Bois called "double consciousness," the initial and unproblematical expression of the psychological reality Ellison sought to represent: "you often doubt if you really exist. You wonder whether you aren't simply a phantom in other people's minds. . . . You ache with the need to convince yourself that you do exist in the real world" (*Invisible* 3–4). In "Harlem Is Nowhere" (1948), Ellison described the effort of a psychiatric clinic in Harlem to ameliorate the psychopathology of blacks who had "no stable, recognized place in society." Sometimes their feeling of being "nowhere" erupts in mass riots—Ellison cites the Harlem riots of 1935 and 1943—but this seething explosiveness has been ignored because "there is an argument in progress between black men and white men as to the true nature of American reality" (*Shadow* 300, 301). This was, he argued, a "psychological problem":

> For in our culture the problem of the irrational, that blind spot in our knowledge of society where Marx cries out for Freud and Freud for Marx . . . has taken the form of the Negro problem. (311)

Ellison's adoption of narrative modes that depart from the conventions of realism and manners thus has a political motive, though it is expressed in the characteristic accents of new liberal discourse: his use of interior, psychological forms is an effort to take part in the redefinition of reality by presenting the effective reality of the "sense of unreality that haunts Harlem" (302).

Invisible Man is a figure of that psychopathology; his written confession is a form of therapy which issues, finally, in the greater calm and readiness for action claimed in the novel's "Epilogue." His education is progressively radical, one which continues even as he tells his story, for though it begins as a naturalistic revelation of social manipulation, the novel evolves in the Rinehart chapter to a modernist suspicion of the contradictions underlying all identity: that identity is only a mask, that "truth [is] always a lie," and that all action may be "betrayal" (482, 487, 495).

At the same time, one of Ellison's challenges in writing his novel was not only to expose the apparent reality as a set of fictions sustaining a social order, but to do so without supplying in its place another fiction, equally monolithic. To achieve this, Ellison invented a narrative form that would emerge from within and confirm the insights of his major character. This is merely to state the obvious: having struck through the social mask and found a cosmic charade in process, Invisible Man loses even the illusion of his bodily substance and is left only with his invisible, psychological reality. From this vantage, *Invisible Man* tells its story from the inside out, so that "reality" is not merely "out there" to be found lurking among visible signs, but within the perception that constitutes—for each person—the relation of self and world. Here Invisible Man and *Invisible Man* coincide, as the book's words and its hero's "disembodied voice" stand as the only reality presented to the reader.

II

From this position of strategic retreat, Invisible Man tells his story as a form of leadership, a prolonged dramatic discourse upon the ambivalence of the word: its "potency to revive and make us free" as well as its "power to blind, imprison and destroy" (*Shadow* 24). This means that the literal world Invisible Man inhabits must be converted into symbol; that is, to put the case more radically, the social world and its institutions must be revealed as only symbols, the true "reality" of both concrete and custom— what gives these things the appearance of immutable givens—being their foundation in folk ideology. Invisible Man must discover that he walks not among skyscrapers but within a nightmarish wilderness of archetypal symbols that constitute a collective dream or linguistic structure, of which the social world he inhabits is merely the *expression*.

But Invisible Man comes to this realization—and makes use of it as a writer—only by first exhausting the options for leadership which he thought were available to him. The dismantling of his naive ambitions begins in the first chapter of the interior narrative with an oblique reference to Booker T. Washington's "Atlanta Compromise," Lincoln's Emancipation Proclamation, and to the wording of *Plessy v. Ferguson*, the Supreme Court decision which gave legal sanction to the proposition that black Americans could be separated from white, without narrowing or reducing the equality of their rights and opportunities.

When Ellison began to write *Invisible Man* in 1945, *Brown v. Board of Education* (1954) was still nine years in the future and the "separate but equal" doctrine of *Plessy v. Ferguson* (1896) still obtained. In the opening to chapter 1, when Invisible Man reflects upon the false promise of manumission, however, he alludes not only to that doctrine, but to the speech which provided the critical distinction that *Plessy* upheld, the "Atlanta Compromise" (1895): "About eighty-five years ago they were told that they were free, united with others of our country in everything pertaining to the common good, and, in everything social, separate like the fingers of the hand. And they believed it" (15; see Washington 156). The span of eighty-five years directs us back in time from 1947 to 1862 and to Lincoln's proclamation, but the words are Booker T. Washington's, and they prefigure Invisible Man's own willing complicity in what enslaves him. Ellison refers to both documents simultaneously to bracket the period of Reconstruction when the moral role blacks had occupied in American culture was "shut off and forgotten," not only because blacks were "shackled to almost everything [the white folk mind] would repress from conscience and consciousness" (*Shadow* 48), but because under Washington's leadership they acceded, in Du Bois' word, to such "submission" (see Du Bois 42–54).

This is the diachronic reference to a tradition of failed leadership, originating, as Du Bois argued, with the "ascendancy" of Washington (42ff.); and the persistent influence of Washington is the first target in the novel's critique of black leadership. After the bitter irony of the chapter's first paragraphs, the hero begins his story with the account of his humiliation in a social ritual that expresses in compact form the system of social relations in which all of the members of the society participate. This scene of "The Battle Royal" is much commented upon, especially for the moment after the young men have fought each other blindfolded, when Invisible Man at last gives his speech. This speech turns out to be a carefully memorized crib from Washington's "Atlanta Compromise" (see Singleton 13; Callahan 62–65; and John S. Wright 164–66). Invisible Man outrages his audience of town fathers when, flustered by their heckling, he yells the word "equality" instead of "responsibility."

But the language of "separate but equal" also operated within a contemporary system of reference to public and highly charged issues of Jim Crow in the national politics of World War II. These terms were central to what Ellison called "the terrific quarrel" taking place when Ellison composed the scene, for the compromise that Washington had negotiated was beginning to unravel under the intolerable hypocrisy of wartime rhetoric. Parts of Washington's speech that Ellison did not include in the novel acquired the ironic relevance of a bad joke in the context of continued Jim Crow policies in defense industries and the armed forces. Black Americans, Washington assured his white audience, were "ready to lay down our lives, if need be, in defence of yours" even though they were not granted social equality. "The wisest among my race," he continued, "understand that the agitation of questions of social equality is the extremest folly" (156, 157).

Du Bois notes in his chapter on Washington that "Negroes resented, at first bitterly, signs of compromise which surrendered their civil and political rights" (47), though this resentment was given little voice and Washington's leadership was accepted. By 1944, Richard Dalfiume reports, black Americans were far less willing to accept the terms of the compromise, and the language of "social equality" was uppermost in their minds. When a number of eminent black Americans from both the South and North were asked what they thought black Americans wanted they answered overwhelmingly, "full political equality, economic equality, equality of opportunity, and full social equality with the abolition of legal segregation" (Rayford W. Logan, ed., *What the Negro Wants*, quoted in Dalfiume 531).

Nevertheless, Washington's assurance remained the guiding assumption of many powerful white Americans well into the nineteen fifties. As Barton J. Bernstein has noted of President Truman's position on "social equality" for black Americans, many "decent men of his generation" thought that "equality before the law could be achieved within the framework of 'separate but equal' " (539). He cites Truman's statement to the Convention of the National Colored Democratic Association, in the summer of 1940: "I am not appealing for social equality of the Negro. . . . The Negro himself knows better than that. . . . Negroes want justice, not social relations" (539). In 1948, when northern liberals, led by Hubert Humphrey, forced the Democratic convention to endorse a civil rights plank that "called for federal laws guaranteeing political participation, equal opportunity in employment, security of person, and equal treatment in the services," the plank still "did not directly attack Jim Crow: it did not promise social equality" (555). Despite the pervasive agitation within their community to press for social equality, the black leaders supported Truman in 1948, thinking he was their best hope and fearing that if they didn't support him future presidents might be even more reluctant to advocate civil rights (Bernstein 555).

Ellison was impatient with such logic, but Invisible Man's position at the end of his confession presents a dubious alternative: unlike Hastie's, his retreat seems to represent less the principled stubbornness of a point of view than the paralyzed awareness of competing viewpoints—a position uncomfortably reminiscent of Trilling's reading of Hyacinth Robinson. In part, this echo of Trilling is produced by the logic of novel, in which Ellison represents all positive, energetically prosecuted viewpoints as so much charlatanism. Especially within the context of Invisible Man's development from a "rabble rouser" to a writer, the scene of his performance before the town fathers incorporates the critique of Washingtonian leadership into the novel's general rejection of imposed order and its specific critique of radical simplification and communist discipline. Through such implications, Invisible Man's mimicking of Washington also signifies within the liberal narrative as an image of the naive optimism that the "new" liberalism attributed to the prewar radicalism of the "old."

In this way, Invisible Man's blunder represents a Freudian slip that not only suggests the repressed humanity which Washington thought could be set aside, but also stands as another instance in which Freud's "tragic realism"—the phrase is Trilling's—was used as a reprimand to Marxian materialism. In his review of Myrdal's book on race relations, Ellison had written, "Marx cries out for Freud and Freud for Marx." Invisible Man's transition from the rote memorization of Washington to the complex writing of his confession may be read as a form of self-psychoanalysis which exemplifies the pervasive complication and displacement of Marx by Freud, especially in the discourse of the new liberalism. One has only to recall Trilling's essay on Freud to see how perfectly Ellison's conception coincides with that discourse: "When, for example, we think of the simple humanitarian optimism which, for two decades, has been so pervasive, we must see that not only has it been politically and philosophically inadequate, but also that it implies, by the smallness of its view of the varieties of human possibility, a kind of check on the creative faculties" (*Liberal* 56–7).

Invisible Man's disastrous performance also implies a critique of speech-making itself as a form of leadership in which the ambiguities of the word may be collapsed into the monologue of ideology. In this scene, for example, Invisible Man not only fails to reproduce Washington's talent for accommodation, he is reprimanded for evoking the complex relationship of "responsibility" and "equality" which Washington kept separate. Quite evidently in the chapel scene that follows upon Invisible Man's mishandling of Mr. Norton, the northern trustee, speech-making is shown to be a form of leadership especially suited to demagoguery. The students assemble for chapel, "uniforms pressed, shoes shined, minds laced up, eyes blind like those of robots" (36), and once inside they listen to Homer Barbee "renewing the dream" in their hearts (116). Through the amusing use of hand imagery, Ellison transforms Barbee into the ghost of Washington, for he makes a "cage" of his hands, as he begins to talk, later "spreading his fingers palm down before him" (118). Though his performance is one of the most eloquent and powerful in the novel, the function it serves is propaganda: Invisible Man feels his "emotions woven into his words as upon a loom" (118); when a member of the audience cries out "My God, yes!" her voice is added "to the structure of his vision" within the hero (120); by the time he finishes speaking, Barbee has made him "see the vision" (131). Describing himself walking away from the chapel, Invisible Man is figured in the objective correlative of the campus street lamps, "each light serene in its cage of shadows" (132).

In the course of his development, Invisible Man's own speech-making, as John S. Wright notes, gradually evolves from reproducing Washington's discourse to a greater self-assertion, whose accents are modeled on the figure of Frederick Douglass (166; see also Du Bois 47, and Stepto, "Literacy and Hibernation," 112–41). Under the emotional pressure elicited by the eviction of an old couple in Harlem, Invisible Man draws upon the power of collective memory, "not so much of my own memory as of remembered words, of linked verbal echoes, images" (266), and communicates that power, much to his surprise, to the listening crowd outside the tenement. He is "thrilled" by their response and continues to speak without "thinking about the nature of [his] action" (275). Similarly, in his first speech for the Brotherhood, he is so moved by the songs and chants which give the political rally the feeling of a "southern revival" that he "gave up trying to memorize phrases and simply allowed the excitement to carry [him] along" (332).

As Callahan and Wright have shown so compellingly, these and other speeches he gives constitute "frequencies of eloquence" (Callahan) in an evolving "calculus of leadership" (Wright). But my point has less to do with tracing that evolution than with situating it within the story postwar liberalism told about its own development from radicalism to tragic realism, from collective action to individual freedom—figured here in the plot of the novel as the move from the spoken word of the "rabble rouser" to the written word of modernist aesthetics. Writing in 1946, Ellison argued that the intrinsic "ambivalence" of the "word"—its ability to mean opposite things at the same time—made it the ideal medium for conveying "the full, complex ambiguity of the human." In this point of view we see how the aesthetics of postwar modernism were for Ellison perfectly compatible with the project to establish a more adequate image of the black American. Thus the story of Invisible Man's fruitless efforts to lead his people as an orator is framed by his recollection of that period captured in the written word. This is the visible proof of his growth and of his "transformation"—as Ellison wrote later of his character—"from ranter to writer" (*Shadow* 57).

Insofar as the novel's quite obvious social critique is mediated through the expression of ambivalence, as both a psychological state and an aesthetic structure, *Invisible Man* was essentially in step with the politics of literary culture at this time. The novel oscillates between two insistencies: on the one hand upon the invented character of identity and social institutions; on the other, upon the universal and eternal nature of chaos and conflict. This oscillation never stabilizes; in fact, the novel appears to confirm that instability as the aesthetic form of the insights it has to offer. As a result Invisible Man's analysis of the social contradictions he has experienced constitutes a form of raised consciousness that threatens to predicate a mythic vision instead of political action.

Much of the novel presents a succession of ambiguous signs that produce a corresponding ambivalence within Invisible Man, but that succession is also ordered as a series of mythic repetitions. He remembers standing before the Founder's statue at the College: "unable to decide whether the veil is really being lifted, or lowered more firmly in place" (36). Later in the novel, when he is beginning his work for the Brotherhood, this ambiguous veil reappears: "I had the sense of being present at the creation of important events, as though a curtain had been parted" (298). These veils, in turn, are part of a recurrent focus upon the symbolic implications of the white woman in black/white relations: mesmerized by the naked dancer hired by the town's leading citizens—an American flag tattooed on her belly—Invisible Man "wanted . . . to caress her and destroy her, to love her and murder her" (9); in a repetition of this early moment in the novel, when one of the Brotherhood's wives seduces him, her red robe parting "like a veil," Invisible Man "wanted both to smash her and stay with her" (405).[1]

1.   One of the persistent figures in Du Bois' *The Souls of Black Folk* is the "veil" that shuts out the "Negro" from the world: "the Negro is a sort of seventh son, born with a veil, and gifted with second-sight in the American world—a world which yields him no true self-consciousness, but only lets him see himself through the revelation of the other world" (16). An apter description of Invisible Man's condition is hard to imagine, and indeed, Du Bois' imprint is everywhere in Ellison's book. Consider the "Sorrow Songs" which head each of Du Bois' chapters, which are perhaps the origin of Ellison's "music of invisibility" and of his idea of the novel as a "blues" autobiography. Also Du Bois' emphasis upon "self-assertion"

Because the entire novel is built out of such repetitions (the "Battle Royal" in the first chapter, for example, is repeated in the riot that closes the interior narrative) the novel balances between a representation of mythic recurrence from which there is no escape, and the identification of the social contradictions (between the assertion of equality and its denial, for example) of which the mythic structures are structural effects. Certainly the mythic highlighting given to social ritual can be read backward as an exposé of social structure. Such is the case with the early scenes in which Bledsoe, Norton, and Trueblood are meant to explicate the structure of a system: to show the distribution of power, the effects of liberal subsidy and its misbegotten motivations—which include repressing the reality of the sharecroppers who live outside the campus. The "Battle Royal" may be the most successful instance of this anthropological politics in the novel. There Ellison reproduced as art an actual initiation ritual—a theatrical performance in its own right—which explicates the social system in which all the members of the rite, i.e., the young black men, the naked blonde with the American flag, the leading citizens of the town have their designated places, know the terms by which their coexistence is negotiated and the spoils (sex and money) distributed.

Ellison has said of this scene that he didn't have to "invent" it: "the patterns were already there in society, so that all I had to do was present them in a broader context of meaning" (*Shadow* 174); but this can become a circle in which social structure expresses timeless myth rather than the other way around. He himself has described the artist as one who recognizes "social forms" in order to "raise them to the level of art." It is just this tendency that has disturbed so many of Ellison's readers. On the one hand he sees the Battle Royal as "a ritual in preservation of class lines"; on the other, this specific social reading becomes more general and innocuous: "It is also the initiation ritual to which all green horns are subjected" (*Shadow* 174).

Because Invisible Man is the blind buffoon, a clownish ficelle who flushes these systems from their protective thickets, all the institutions of the novel—the College, the Paint Factory, the Hospital, the Brotherhood—are

(47)—which he sees originating in Frederick Douglass—and his belief that the future of the "darker races" rests "so largely upon this American experiment" are both fundamental ideas informing *Invisible Man*, as well as phrases and wording that Ellison repeatedly uses to discuss his fiction. Perhaps, finally, Ellison set himself the task of answering the white man's question, which Du Bois poses at the beginning of his essay: "To the real question, How does it feel to be a problem? I seldom answer a word" (15). Though little has been written on the relationship between Du Bois and Ellison, Stepto's *From Behind the Veil* offers an excellent discussion of Ellison's alteration of Du Bois' characteristic figures and strategies.

mediated through the ritual patterns of his mythic journey, patterns which also absorb the stark social critique of Jim Crow legislation on the one hand, and of black leadership on the other. Ellison circles furthest from the political and social motivations of his novel when Invisible Man is immersed in the confidence man mysteries of identity and absence that he learns from the mythic figure of Rinehart. At the same time, though circumscribed by this obligatory confrontation with Proteus, Invisible Man's experience helps advance the novel's meditation on leadership and racist order within the psychologized Marxism typical of new liberal discourse.

When Invisible Man is confused with Rinehart, he finally realizes the fluid reality of illusion and the illusion of objective reality: "If dark glasses and a white hat could blot out my identity so quickly, who actually was who?" (482). His discovery of the many masks of Rinehart leads him to the suspicion that Rinehart himself is only a mask, one of Proteus' many changes. "Could he himself be both rind and heart? What is real anyway?" he asks, and then concludes admiringly,

> His world was possibility and he knew it. He was years ahead of me and I was a fool. I must have been crazy and blind. The world in which we lived was without boundaries. A vast seething, hot world of fluidity, and Rine the rascal was at home. Perhaps *only* Rine the rascal was at home in it. It was unbelievable, but perhaps only the unbelievable could be believed. Perhaps the truth was always a lie. (487)

That is, order is always a fiction, but nonetheless real. Surface in this sense has depth—has the substantial power to ignite action and reaction, to produce lived history.

Following upon this realization, Invisible Man's outrage at the Brotherhood's claim to be following the "laws of reality" (496) reproduces Trilling's attack on Parrington and the "tendencies of liberalism to simplify, . . . to organize the elements of life in a rational way" (*Liberal* xiv). The figure of Invisible Man thus inscribes the characteristic circle of the "new liberalism": on the one hand, what he learns from Rinehart is in some sense a Marxian recognition that frees him from the bourgeois confusion of the current order with a timeless or natural state of affairs; on the other, that recognition is at once converted into a metaphysic of transcendence. Ellison seems to use the Rinehart episode to ground "social equality" not on the rights of man but within a metaphysics of illusion which applies to all institutional and personal identity, without regard to race, creed, or color.

The novel's critique of what we might call positive or unambiguous order culminates in the last confrontation between Invisible Man and Ras the Exhorter. Ras is a character whose degeneration over the course of the novel helps isolate for us the system within which order, speech, and ideology are shown to be related facets of totalitarian simplification. Ras has been a powerful voice in the novel, seemingly in possession of the blueprint to the maze in which Invisible Man wanders. In the middle of a fight among Ras, Clifton, and Invisible Man, Ras cries out: "Three black men fighting in the street because of the white enslaver? Is that sanity? Is that consciousness, scientific understanding? . . . Is it self-respect—black against black? What they give you to betray—their women? You fall for that?" (363). Ras here identifies the dynamics of the Battle Royal long before Invisible Man figures them out. In this early confrontation between them, Ras gets all the good lines: "Recognize you'self inside and you wan the kings among men" (364).

By the last time they meet, however, Ellison has stripped his character of that wisdom and made him a victim of the same Battle Royal structure that had fooled Invisible Man for so long. As if spoken eloquence carries within itself the entropic tendency toward fascist monologue, Ras is no longer merely an Exhorter but is now "the Destroyer" who rides a "great black horse" leading "a tight-knit order, carrying sticks and clubs, shotguns and rifles" (544). This language immediately situates Ras within the set of all those characters and scenes in the novel that embody order and repression: the college students that "drilled four-abreast" (35), the failure of "medical science" which drives Norton toward his "first-hand organizing of human life" (42), the crowd at the eviction scene asking to be organized (269), and the Brotherhood's formation "into columns of four" when they take the stage (330). The novel signals Invisible Man's lowest point when he "organize[s] a drill team of six-footers whose duty it was to march through the streets striking up sparks with their hob-nailed shoes" (370–71). Ras has been tucked within the discourse of totalitarianism, which, in the writings of such thinkers as Schlesinger and Hannah Arendt, conflated the left and right as opposites so extreme that both occupied the same territory.

One might argue that Ras is converted into a blind villain precisely because he is organized, because he believes—and acts upon what he believes. Without hesitancy or ambivalence to redeem his leadership, Ras's eloquence collapses into the literalism of propaganda, and is subordinated to the novel's representation of speech-making as the scene of manipulation, in which the hypnotic, imprisoning power of the spoken voice lures both the masses and the naive liberal. This particular scene frames Ras's organization as an illusion manipulated by the Brotherhood, which is itself an organization similarly unaware of social history's uncontrollable complexity: "they want the streets to flow with blood; . . . so that they can turn your death and sorrow and defeat into propaganda" (545). As always in postwar discourse, "propaganda" is the absent word and explicit background, both historical and contemporary, toward which all those other fifties words—ambiguity, irony, paradox—point.

The power of the spoken word to rouse and organize the masses—the power he himself has claimed throughout the novel—is violently rejected by Invisible Man when he thrusts Ras's own spear through his cheeks, locking his jaws. From the beginning, the two men have been doubles of each other; in silencing Ras, Invisible Man says good-bye forever to his own dreams of leading through oration. Recounting that moment in the more supple medium of the written word, he is able to capture the mythic paradox of Christian realism: "it was as though for a moment I had surrendered my life and begun to live again" (547).

In this late and crucial pivot from speaking to writing we must see the effects not only of modernist aesthetics, but also of those constraints upon positive action operating at the time that Ellison's novel was germinating and taking shape. Because Ellison wrote at a moment of great disillusionment within the African American community with those institutions within which leadership might occur, he chose to frame his portrait of the leader as a young man in negative terms. Throughout the novel Invisible Man has wanted to be a leader, but he is increasingly paralyzed by his paradoxical inability to lead without by that very act compromising his mission. All his efforts have brought him into contact with the major institutions of society and acquainted him with their corrupt and naive leaders: school (Norton, Bledsoe), industrial capitalism (Emerson), political parties (Brother Jack), and race organizing (Ras the Exhorter). Thus Invisible Man is able to lead only when he conceives of his project negatively, as a form of withdrawal. Facing Ras the Exhorter and his men, Invisible Man "recognized them at last as those whom I had failed and of whom I was now, just now, a leader, though leading them, running ahead of them, only in the stripping away of my illusionment" (546).

Bringing his hero through this series of unmaskings, Ellison's narrative voices the new liberal version of demystification, for Invisible Man has "*become acquainted with ambivalence,*" as he says in the Prologue (10). He has developed a new tolerance for contradiction and ambiguity, and thus for a complicated idea of freedom and action, without which human action— "liberal" as well as fascist or communist—remains a kind of sleepwalking, "making a mess of the world" (558).

This is the logic upon which the book bases its critique of all formal structures except those of modernist aesthetics, as they were defined in postwar critical discourse. Invisible Man's story is the story of empowerment, but it is an empowerment figured as a loss that fills itself only in the "full, complex ambiguity" of the written word. Within the discourse of new liberalism, such ambiguity is really the power of awareness itself, but a power that can be exercised only in the realm of art. When Invisible Man falls into the "dimensionless room" at the end of his interior narrative, he lies in a "state neither of dreaming nor of waking, but somewhere in between, in which [he is] caught like Trueblood's jaybird that yellow jackets had paralyzed in every part but his eyes" (556).

Ellison's effort to situate the grounds of responsible political action within the space between extremes provides the literary instance of similar exhortations in the writings of Schlesinger and Trilling, for Invisible Man transforms his paralysis into a "vital center" through the power of art. Purposely or not, Ellison presents his character—and himself, it seems impossible to deny—as one of those artists Trilling praised for containing "the yes and the no of their culture" (*Liberal* 9). In the Epilogue to his story, Invisible Man notes that the act of writing has "confused" him and "negated some of the anger" he has felt, so now "I condemn and affirm, say no and say yes, say yes and say no . . . I approach it"—life, action, the national culture and politics—"through division" (566–67). This is nothing if not the "moral imagination" of which Trilling in 1947 said the novel of the last two hundred years has been the most "effective agent" (*Liberal* 222).

Though many admirers of *Invisible Man* have argued in support of Ellison's own position that high art in general and his own novel in particular are "acts" of protest (see for example, essays by Callahan, Wright, and Schaub), they can be construed as such only by accepting the appropriation of "protest" by postwar discourse as a reaction against extremist subversion, and as a support of what was soon recognized as a liberal consensus. Arthur Schlesinger may have thought that "the spirit of the new radicalism is the spirit of the center" (*Vital* 256), but one could say so only by redefining what was meant by "radicalism." Though Invisible Man says that "the old fascination with playing a role" has returned (566), Ellison seems to have cut the political ground from beneath his character, for the social reality upon which the novel is so evidently predicated has had its apparent depth gutted by the hero's penetrating insight, and the hero—having accepted his invisibility—seems to hanker for activity on a stage of social theatrics in which he no longer believes.

Insofar as the narrative provides any synthesis to these dialectic oscillations, it lies within the complex weave of discourses orchestrated in its closing paragraphs. Within them, the attempt to supply a new face—a new "image"—for the black American through the agency of art has produced a disembodied voice poised on the edge of reincarnation in the body politic of social history. In the rap talk rhyming of his "buggy jiving," Ellison and his character improvise upon the ambiguities of "playing" as both social role and private performance. In the idiom of the black "DJ," they invite the reader to tune in to a lower frequency on a neglected part of the band, to find there in the very midst of what Trilling called the "culture's hum and buzz of implication" (*Liberal* 206) a public station broadcasting a message relevant to all.

These "lower frequencies" provide a last opportunity to note the transformation of radicalism within liberal discourse, for the provisional benediction with which Invisible Man brings his story to an end also invokes a social vision that should remind us of Richard Wright's belief in "solidarity among men." Though only thirteen years separate the collective "we" that Steinbeck's Okies learn on their trip to California from the plural "you" that is the last word of *Invisible Man*, in the discourse of the new liberalism that circulates through Ellison's novel solidarity has become universality, and class conflict an expression of moral contradiction shared equally by all.

6

Christian Realism and O'Connor's
A Good Man Is Hard to Find

> Whenever the public is heard from, it is heard demanding a literature
> which is balanced and which will somehow heal the ravages of our times.
> In the name of social order, liberal thought, and sometimes even Chris-
> tianity, the novelist is asked to be the handmaid of his age.
>
> Flannery O'Connor, "The Grotesque in Southern Fiction"

> America has a history. It is only that the tragic aspects and the ironic
> implications of that history have been obscured by the national legend of
> success and victory and by the perpetuation of infant illusions of inno-
> cence and virtue.
>
> C. Vann Woodward, "The Irony of Southern History"

No one would accuse Flannery O'Connor of being a liberal, yet we cannot
fully understand her fiction unless we read it as a response to liberalism.
Though her religious skepticism toward the claims of humanist rationality
would seem to be essentially ahistoricist, maintaining a religious point of
view is not something one does outside a culture, but is a historical act
participating in the dialogue of its time. Because O'Connor's contempt
for liberalism was shared by many liberals during the post–World War II
period, who were attempting to revise what was meant by "liberalism," her
conservative fiction is useful here precisely because it provides a counter-
example of how relevant the discourse of liberalism was to the work of a
writer who had no interest in being radical. Her fiction—noted by the *Time*
reviewer for its "sardonic brutality"—often proved congenial exactly because it reinforced the "new realism" which liberalism was in the process
of claiming as its own.

O'Connor's understanding of "liberalism" hardly attends to the varieties of social thought the term evokes, and certainly doesn't reflect the
postwar scramble among liberalisms that historians have documented. For

O'Connor, "liberalism" was barely distinguishable from "the modern idea" itself, formed primarily by Enlightenment thought and the material advancements of modern science. At any rate, this is the definition she provides Cecil Dawkins, in November of 1958:

> The notion of the perfectibility of man came about at the time of the Enlightenment in the 18th century. This is what the South has always opposed. "How far we have fallen" means the fall of Adam, the fall from innocence, from sanctifying grace. The South in other words still believes that man has fallen and that he is only perfectible by God's grace, not by his own unaided efforts. The Liberal approach is that man has never fallen, never incurred guilt, and is ultimately perfectible by his own efforts. Therefore, evil in this light is a problem of better housing, sanitation, health, etc. and all mysteries will eventually be cleared up. . . . Of course there are degrees of adherence to this, all sorts of mixtures, but it is the direction the modern heads toward. (*Habit* 202–3)

O'Connor saw herself as a heretic in a culture increasingly standardized by "the Liberal approach" and thus increasingly immune to her vision. "The novelist with Christian concerns," O'Connor wrote in 1957, "will find in modern life distortions which are repugnant to him, and his problem will be to make these appear as distortions to an audience which is used to seeing them as natural" (*Mystery* 33). Throughout the few years of her life as a successful writer asked to give talks and readings, O'Connor repeated this view of herself as a Catholic writing "for a hostile audience."

O'Connor's reaction to liberalism often took comic form, expressing a consistent skepticism toward the role of ideas and experiment in altering human manners. To Betty Boyd Love, a close college friend, she wrote, "My advice to all parents is beat your children moderately and moderately often; and anything that Wm. Heard Kilpatrick & Jhn. Dewey say do, don't do." When John Dewey died, she said to Russell Kirk, author of *The Conservative Mind* which O'Connor admired, "I hope there're children crawling all over him" (*Habit* 29, 112). O'Connor saw herself writing as a shouter, a cartoonist, a gothic crank whose freakishness would be "not merely an eccentricity" but a "reproach" (*Mystery* 44).

Informally, she described herself as a practical joker, setting ambushes for the liberal reader. "You can't clobber any reader while he is looking," she advises one correspondent. "You divert his attention, then you clobber him, and he never knows what hit him." To another aspiring writer she offers similar advice: "The thing for you to do is write something with a delayed reaction like those capsules that take an hour to melt in your stomach. In this way, it could be performed on Monday and not make them vomit until Wednesday, by which time they would not be sure who was to blame.

This is the principle I operate under and I find it works very well" (*Habit* 202, 349).

This "delayed reaction" metaphor appears in more serious contexts also. Speaking of her story "A Good Man Is Hard to Find," O'Connor imagines that the Grandmother's gesture of kinship "will grow to be a great crow-filled tree in the Misfit's heart, and will be enough of a pain to him there to turn him into the prophet he was meant to become" (*Mystery* 113). And when Lucynell's mother, in the story "The Life You Save May Be Your Own," tells Shiftlet the truth ("there ain't any place in the world for a poor disabled friendless drifting man"), the "ugly words settled in Mr. Shiftlet's head like a group of buzzards in the top of a tree" (*Good* 62). Her fictions were designed to be such "ugly words"—not a bad definition of the "grotesque"—the sort that would live in the minds of her "hostile audience."

Unlike such contemporaries as Norman Mailer and Ralph Ellison, O'Connor wasn't responding directly to the specific naiveté of liberalism in the thirties, which—from her perspective—was only a variant on a general failure of vision inherent in the "Liberal approach." Nor was she alienated by the difficulties of being radical in conservative times, for she counted herself among those southern writers who still had the advantages of a regional community: "They are not alienated, they are not lonely, suffering artists gasping for purer air. The Southern writer apparently feels the need of expatriation less than other writers in this country" (*Mystery* 53).

Furthermore, O'Connor appears to admire the fiction of manners and dramatic form against which so many of her contemporaries were in open revolt. Like Trilling, O'Connor emphasized the importance of manners for the novel: "Manners are of such great consequence to the novelist that any kind will do. Bad manners are better than no manners at all" (*Mystery* 29). She often told her audiences that fiction depends for its reality upon the internal, dramatic interplay of manners: "fiction has to be largely presented rather than reported. Another way to say it is that though fiction is a narrative art, it relies heavily on the element of drama" (73–74). She repeatedly echoed James's injunction to "dramatize"; her belief in "selection" as the means by which an author "makes his statements" is the customary advice of Conrad and Ford.

In sharp contrast to the stated attitudes of such writers as McCarthy and Kerouac, the work of Henry James was one of O'Connor's principal models, as it was for the critical community in the postwar. Modern literary history, in her view, originated with James: "along about the time of Henry James, the author began to tell his story in a different way. He began to let it come through the minds and eyes of the characters themselves, and he sat behind the scenes, apparently disinterested" (*Mystery* 74). In 1955 she wrote to Ben Griffith that *Understanding Fiction*, by Cleanth Brooks and R. P. Warren, had been of "invaluable help" to her, and to another correspondent recommended Percy Lubbock's *The Craft of Fiction* as "a very profound study of point of view" (*Habit* 83, 192).

Because O'Connor thought the writing of fiction was always to some degree mysterious, she was skeptical of merely technical approaches to writing. "When [most people] realize that they aren't writing stories," she said in one of her talks, "they decide the remedy for this is to learn something that they refer to as the 'technique of the short story' or 'the technique of the novel' " (*Mystery* 66–67). Still, her ideas about fiction writing were largely in agreement with those of the dominant critics in the postwar, and like them she saw the major challenge to her work coming from the popular culture. If her Christian belief exempted her from the characteristic political ennui of the postwar years, it did not remove the problem of the writer's authority in relation to society, but intensified it instead:

> Today many readers and critics have set up for the novel a kind of orthodoxy. They demand a realism of fact which may, in the end, limit rather than broaden the novel's scope. They associate the only legitimate material for long fiction with the movement of social forces, with the typical, with fidelity to the way things look and happen in normal life.

Because O'Connor was explicitly opposed to the spirit of scientific materialism, she rejected its expression in "naturalism" and the "realism of fact" that made "the deeper kinds of realism . . . less and less understandable" to "the public mind" (*Mystery* 38–39).

Her strategies for taking on liberal culture were wonderfully attuned to the tastes of New Critic and new liberal alike. In 1958, when William Van O'Connor discussed her work in the course of an article titled "The Grotesque in Modern American Fiction," he defined the "grotesque" as a response to modernity comparable to the central terms of postwar criticism: "It is not fortuitous that the terms *irony, paradox, ambiguity, synthesis, tension,* and so many others are the staple terms of modern criticism" (346). In her own essay on the grotesque, "The Grotesque in Southern Fiction," O'Connor saw the "romance-novel" as the central tradition in American writing, and she valued such writers as Hawthorne for the same reasons that Trilling, Chase, and Schlesinger did: "When Hawthorne said that he wrote romances, he was attempting, in effect, to keep for fiction some of its freedom from social determinisms, and to steer it in the direction of poetry" (*Mystery* 45–46). Such was the political content of terms like "grotesque" and "romance" during this period, and they functioned the same way for O'Connor as they did for the new liberal.

Because O'Connor was addressing a national audience with whom she did not share a set of manners and beliefs, she found it necessary to break with those conventions of fiction so long associated with a liberal humanist confidence, in order to create forms that would have the abrupt impact of reality upon her readers. The "realism of fact" encouraged its audience to confuse the material world with "the deeper kinds of realism," so O'Connor determined to violate the conventions of mimetic realism: "a literature which mirrors society would be no fit guide for it" (46). Her favorite tactic for exposing that confusion was to show that material reality in its distorted aspect: "You have to make your vision apparent by shock," she insists. "To the hard of hearing you shout, and for the almost-blind you draw large and startling figures" (*Mystery* 34). In college, O'Connor drew cartoons for the magazine she edited, and as a senior submitted a sheaf of them to the *New Yorker*.

Though the caricatural aspect of O'Connor's work is familiar to readers, she went through an apprentice period during which her work more nearly imitated the technical accomplishments of the greatest modern writers. Her eventual departure from many of those techniques was inseparable from her rejection of liberal humanism. In one of the stories she wrote while enrolled in the Iowa Writer's Workshop, and published as "The Train" in *Sewanee Review* (1949), O'Connor demonstrates how well she learned the lessons of the masters. As Frederick Asals has noted, the story owes a considerable debt to Faulkner. In particular, the rhythms, names, and syntax of Faulkner have yet to be expunged from her prose, as is evident in the following passage:

> For a minute he couldn't move off the porter for thinking it was Cash and he breathed, 'Cash,' and the porter pushed him off and got up and went down the aisle quick and Haze scrambled off the floor and went after him saying he wanted to get in the berth and thinking, this is Cash's kin, and then suddenly, like something thrown at him when he wasn't looking: this is Cash's son run away; and then: he knows about Eastrod and doesn't want it, he doesn't want to talk about it, he doesn't want to talk about Cash. (*Complete* 60)

Though this passage is especially reminiscent of both *As I Lay Dying* and *Absalom, Absalom!*, the narrator's position is indebted more generally to what James called the "central intelligence" or, in Mary McCarthy's terms, "*style indirect libre*." The language in this passage exists in that curious border area, where the third person voice of the narrator is sustained, but limited in large measure to the intonations, knowledge, and idiom of the "central intelligence"—described by Bakhtin as "inner speech" (319).

By 1948, when O'Connor was enrolled at Iowa, this narrative device was already part of the "craft of fiction," and she had learned the trick of this ventriloquism, used so successfully to realistic effect four decades earlier by Joyce, and before Joyce, by James and Turgenev. When Joyce writes of Stephen Dedalus, for example, the third person narrative voice absorbs the idiom of the young boy: "He was alone. He was happy and free; but he would not be anyway proud with Father Dolan." In using this device, Joyce was advancing or developing psychological realism by inventing language that seemed to issue from the thoughts and emotions of the depicted character. O'Connor introduced the major character of "The Train"—Hazel Wickers—with just such a fusion of outside frame and inside perspective: "The man in the station had said he could give him a lower and Haze had asked didn't he have no upper ones." With this device the author maintains her control and omniscience over the story, but acquires the heightened "realism" of proximity with and sympathetic access to the character's thoughts: "He remembered when he was a little boy, him and his mother and the other children would go into Chattanooga on the Tennessee Railroad. His mother had always started up a conversation with the other people on the train. . . . My mother was a Jackson, Haze said to himself" (*Complete* 54–55).

By the time O'Connor revised this story for *Wise Blood*, where it appears as the first chapter, all the echoes of Faulkner were removed, and the sympathetic insight of the narrator point of view was entirely obstructed: "Hazel Motes sat at a forward angle on the green plush train seat looking one minute at the window as if he might want to jump out of it, and the next down the aisle at the other end of the car." No longer privy to Haze's consciousness, we are forced to view him as a strange object, so that we share the impatient inquisitiveness of the passenger seated opposite to him: "She wanted to get close enough to see what the suit had cost him but she found herself squinting instead at his eyes, trying almost to look into them. They were the color of pecan shells and set in deep sockets. The outline of a skull under his skin was plain and insistent" (*Three* 9).

These passages show the results of O'Connor's decision to turn her original conception into something less understandable and far more grotesque —what Asals has described as the evolution of her style from "psychological realism and mild satiric comedy to the nonmimetic mode of the grotesque" (11). In moving away from the troubled consciousness of her character, O'Connor withdrew from using the humanist, liberal explanations of behavior in a deliberate effort to evoke "mystery." As a result, many readers share the confusion felt by Haze's landlady at the end of the novel: "She felt as if she were blocked at the entrance of something. She sat staring with her eyes shut, into his eyes, and felt as if she had finally got to the beginning of something she couldn't begin, and she saw him moving farther and farther away, farther and farther into the darkness until he was the pin point of light" (*Three* 126). For the writer who "believes that our life is and will remain essentially mysterious," O'Connor once said, "the meaning of a story does not begin except at a depth where adequate motivation and adequate psychology and the various determinations have been exhausted" (*Mystery* 41–42).

Though O'Connor associated "the Liberal approach" generally with these "various determinations," she viewed her own work within the specific context of recent literary history, and rejected the determinist assumptions governing much of the fiction written before World War II at the same time that northern liberals were also rejecting them, or diluting their force. "In the thirties we passed through a period in American letters when social criticism and social realism were considered by many to be the most important aspects of fiction. We still suffer with a hangover from that period." Again, like many of the postwar liberals she rejected the explanatory power of purely economic, psychological, and naturalistic models: "the social sciences have cast a dreary blight on the public approach to fiction," she declared in another lecture (*Mystery* 164, 38).

Understood in this context, many of her characters may be interpreted as caricatures of the "Liberal approach." Her story "Good Country People," for example, satirizes abstract ideas and the inadequacy of philosophy and science to account for the evil in human nature. Joy-Hulga—the primary figure in this story—is a young woman with a wooden leg and a Ph.D. in philosophy but living at her home in the South because of a weak heart. Hulga "made it plain that if it had not been for this condition, she would be far from these red hills and good country people. She would be in a university lecturing to people who knew what she was talking about" (*Good* 175). The reader is given to understand that Joy-Hulga is something of a logical positivist. When Hulga's mother opens one of Joy's books, she comes upon this passage: "Science, on the other hand, has to assert its soberness and seriousness afresh and declare that it is concerned solely with what-is. Nothing—how can that be for science anything but a horror and a phantasm? If science is right, then one thing stands firm: science wishes to know nothing of nothing. Such is after all the strictly scientific approach to Nothing. We know it by wishing to know nothing of Nothing." When Hulga steps out with the Bible salesman, Manley Pointer, intending to seduce him, she tells him, "I don't have illusions. I'm one of those people who see *through* to nothing" (176, 191).

Manley Pointer, as his name suggests, is a kind of evil hunting dog, able to sniff out innocence and penetrate the facile liberalism of Hulga's existential positivism, confronting her with the actual experience of nothingness and the complexity of those good country people Joy had thought so simple: "And I'll tell you another thing," Manley tells her as he makes off with her wooden leg, "you ain't so smart. I been believing in nothing ever since I was born!" (195). Hulga is left without a leg to stand on.

This ironic reversal, the characteristic movement in O'Connor's stories, is another quality congenial to the revisionist liberal spirit, which interpreted recent history as an ironic reproach to the naive radicalism of the thirties. These visitations of evil reality are almost always associated with masculine force, as here with Manley Pointer (a name meant to echo the original hunting accident in which her father's gun blew away his little girl's leg). The same is true of the farcical story "A Stroke of Good Fortune," in which the cynical young woman refuses to admit that she has become pregnant. Indeed, *A Good Man Is Hard to Find and Other Stories* is, as a collection, extraordinarily gender-marked.

People have typically read the title—*A Good Man Is Hard To Find*— as a reference to Christ as the "good man" so hard to find in the midst of contemporary degeneracy, and no doubt this was one of O'Connor's intentions. But the recurrent sexual motifs of this collection—the pistols, wooden legs, pointers, and automobiles—lead us to recall that the title is taken from a song by Eddie Green, made popular in 1927 by Bessie Smith, explicitly about the sexual potency of the male. The song is a version of the exhortation to count one's blessings, for in it the woman with a good man is told to "hug him in the morning, kiss him at night, give him all your loving, treat him right"—because "a good man is hard to find." The women of *A Good Man Is Hard to Find* are shot to death, abandoned at a roadside stand, impregnated, embarrassed, burned out, and finally completely undermined (in "The Displaced Person"). Only at the hands of such rough, masculine treatment do these characters become "good women."

Throughout her fiction, it isn't too hard to see that for the most part these violent conversions are meant to operate as much against the liberal reader as against the central character. O'Connor almost always makes the figure of naiveté the most appealing character in the story, appealing because most reasonable, most cynical, often the most witty, most "normal" to a liberal, secular sensibility. Though Joy-Hulga is decidedly freakish, she is far more sympathetic than either her mother, Mrs. Hopewell, or the tenant farmer's wife, Mrs. Freeman. Clearly, O'Connor had her liberal audience in mind when she constructed such social scenarios—traps, as it were— egging the reader on, encouraging readers to share in the fun of Joy-Hulga's barbs at "good country people," only to pull the rug from under her character and readers. At the end of the story, Mrs. Hopewell, whose social acuity and attention to the mystery of manners and what they reveal are as weak as her daughter's, muses upon the figure of Manley Pointer as he disappears into the distance (with her daughter's wooden leg), "I guess the world would be better off if we were all that simple." But Mrs. Freeman's gaze—as penetrating and masculine as Manley Pointer's—*"drove forward* and just touched him before he disappeared under the hill" (italics mine). "Some can't be that simple," she says to Mrs. Hopewell. "I know I never could." Here the "good country people" of the South turn out to have a sharper understanding of human behavior than the university-trained Joy-Hulga, whose views it turns out are merely *ideas* (and whose behavior is governed by her cultural past). The story, then, is in part a working out of the superiority of history, culture, and experience over ideas, which are shown to be simple, reductive, producing more illusion than reality. Significantly, Mrs. Freeman (free-man: insight always associated with the male, as is violence and reality itself) is pulling an "evil-smelling onion shoot . . . from the ground" (196).

In part because of her stated intentions and orientation toward the national culture, these typical devices, assumptions, and themes of O'Connor's *A Good Man Is Hard To Find* bear a remarkable resemblance to the discourse of revisionist liberalism. The imputation to culture and history of a complex ambiguity beyond the reach of reason and ideas, the assumption of human imperfection and the ineradicability of evil, the necessity to recognize the limitations of human control and aspiration, her repeated representation of brutal reality in masculine figures—all these elements are commonplaces in the discourses of cold war liberalism. Though she viewed her fiction as a dramatic reprimand to liberal assumptions, the revisionist liberalism of the postwar era was in many respects speaking her language. This dialogic irony not only helps underline the "Christian realism" which informs much of the politics, foreign policy, and historiography of the period, but also suggests the historical character of belief—that it must find expression in terms, figures, themes inextricably produced by, and engaged with, the dialogue of its time.

The historical conditions or provocation of this unintentional echo are commonly described as the crisis of liberalism after World War II. Those somewhat familiar with the discourse of the postwar years will note that O'Connor's view of her fiction employs many of the assumptions underlying a wide variety of postwar texts, from Niebuhr's theology to Kennan's foreign policy. The repeated reversals of O'Connor's fiction thus have a familiar feel to them, for they serve as allegories of the liberal confronted with the evil and violence that liberalism hadn't been prepared to acknowledge. Arthur Schlesinger, Jr., for example, had asked, "why was progressivism not prepared for Hitler?" and was explicitly willing to entertain theological explanations of human nature as premises for its new political "realism" (*Vital* 39).

Christian realism and political "realism" were never far apart in the years following World War II, discourses that often reinforced one another in the writings of such men as Schlesinger and Niebuhr. Ironically, then, the premises of O'Connor's work were remarkably consistent with those of the very audience she imagined withering under her attack. "The corruptions of power," Schlesinger wrote, "the desire to exercise it, the desire to increase it, the desire for prostration before it—had no place in progressive calculations." The "tragic movements of history in the twentieth century" had amounted—in a telling metaphor—to a "historical re-education" of liberalism (*Vital* 40, ix).

The typical refrains of revisionist liberalism may be found in *The Vital Center*, but here, too, is the machismo of the liberal anticommunist, dividing men into the "weak" and the strong. Democratic freedom, precisely because it allows each individual to make his or her choice, requires strength, or what Paul Tillich described in 1952 to his audience at Yale as the "courage to be." In her book *The Hearts of Men*, Barbara Ehrenreich points out that "communism kept masculine toughness in style long after it became obsolete in the corporate world and the consumer marketplace" (103). We see this machismo attitude working through Schlesinger's prose style when he describes the failure of the right. "The result," he says, "was to emasculate the political energies of the ruling class" (*Vital* 14). And the idea of a militant liberalism is explicit throughout, especially in the last chapter, titled "Freedom: A Fighting Faith." In yet another version of the attack on liberalism's past naiveté, Schlesinger tells the reader that "today democracy is paying the price for its systematic cultivation of the peaceful and rational virtues" (245). When *The Vital Center* was advertised in the *New York Times Book Review*, the display pictured a clenched fist raised between the left and the right.

The idea of "the South" and of "southern writing" also helps to situate O'Connor's collection of stories, for during the fifties specific political and cultural meanings were attributed to the southern experience. When Walker Percy won the National Book Award in 1961 for *The Moviegoer*, he was asked why the South was contributing so many fine writers. He answered, "Because we lost the War." O'Connor gave her interpretation of Percy's meaning in an essay she contributed to *Esprit*: "He didn't mean by that simply that a lost war makes good subject matter," O'Connor wrote. "We have gone into the modern world with an inburnt knowledge of human limitations and with a sense of mystery which could not have developed in our first state of innocence—as it has not sufficiently developed in the rest of our country" (*Mystery* 58–59). This is a summary identical to those we can find in the writing of Hartz, Niebuhr, and Vann Woodward—all of whom used the experience of the South as a source of directives for United States foreign policy.

There is some evidence that O'Connor's interpretation of Percy's comment paraphrased C. Vann Woodward's thesis in "The Irony of Southern History." O'Connor wrote to "A" on May 25, 1963, "I have taken up with reading C. Vann Woodward. Have you ever read this gentleman—*The Burden of Southern History* is what I have but I intend to order off after more. Southern history usually gives me a pain, but this man knows how to write English" (*Habit* 522). Though O'Connor apparently did not read Vann Woodward's essay until 1963, he delivered the lecture in 1953 as an elaboration of Reinhold Niebuhr's thesis in *The Irony of American History*, published the year before.

One of the architects of postwar foreign policy, George Kennan, had defined this irony in terms similar to Niebuhr's. In the forward to *American Diplomacy*, Kennan described the ironic aura of the Allied victory: "one had the inescapable fact that our security, or what we took to be our security, had suffered a tremendous decline over the course of the half-century. A country which in 1900 had no thought that its prosperity and way of life could be in any way threatened by the outside world had arrived by 1950 at a point where it seemed to be able to think of little else but this danger" (vii).

The thesis of Vann Woodward's lecture, given in 1953, was part of a widespread conviction in the intellectual community that American foreign policy must recognize its limitations. One reads this in Schlesinger's *The Vital Center*, and in Louis Hartz's *The Liberal Tradition in America* (1955), which asserts the "innocence" (and unconsciousness) of American liberalism, and argues that cold war conflicts may force Americans to understand "liberalism" as but one ideology among others: "which is to say that America must look to its contact with other nations to provide that spark of philosophy, that grain of relative insight that its own history has denied it" (7, 287).

Vann Woodward's essay first restated "the ironic incongruities of our position" and then explored this irony in light of southern history. In Vann Woodward's opinion, the southern historian can bring a special point of view and experience to these national ironies, and therefore is capable of making "a special contribution to the understanding of the irony of American history." For "the historian of the South can hardly escape the feeling that all this has happened before." The point of vantage for the southern historian, of course, is established by the South's having lost the Civil War, an experience setting it apart from the national experience: never having "known what it means to be confronted by complete frustration" has led to ideas of American invincibility and a vague belief that "history is something unpleasant that happens to other people" (168, 169). In sharp contrast, the South has something in common with Europe that the rest of the country does not. Hartz drew a similar lesson from southern history, though he focused upon the failure of the North to learn anything from the "Reactionary Enlightenment" (145–77). Vann Woodward makes explicit the regional assumptions informing O'Connor's fiction, assumptions which she herself later articulated in terms evolved from cold war discourse.

Vann Woodward's essay helps historicize or situate a pervasive southern conviction within a specific postwar context. The irony of O'Connor's antiliberalism is the success of her vision, its marvellous coincidence with dominant discourses of cold war liberalism. One may be perfectly willing to grant the ahistorical legitimacy of O'Connor's religious objections to the modern temper—without, in doing so, ignoring the historical discourses which O'Connor's language intersects and reinforces. O'Connor's good fortune, it may be said, was to be working at a time when her own objections to liberal thought were widely shared by the liberal audience that would have to make up her readership, if she was to have one at all. She and they shared for a time the emphasis upon "realism," innocence, evil, ambiguity, limitation, tragedy, and so forth. I think it fair to say that once we array this discourse beside O'Connor's work of the early fifties, there are many places at which the liberal self-critique and O'Connor's critique of liberalism overlap. This historicizing allows us to read aspects of her work with an enlarged sense of their cultural dialogue.

Revisionist liberalism is not so explicitly inscribed within the title story of *A Good Man Is Hard to Find* as in O'Connor's satire of Joy-Hulga in "Good Country People." The qualities that make this story so identifiable with the postwar era are more complex, powerfully embedded in ironic reversals and the themes they accentuate. This is especially clear if we read the fiction through its allusions to Margaret Mitchell's *Gone with the Wind*, which bring the irony of southern history to bear upon the Grandmother and her son's family.

In the story "A Good Man Is Hard to Find," the Grandmother's desire differs from her son's: instead of vacationing in Florida, she wants to visit her "connections" in east Tennessee. Her son and his family seem to be interested only in comics, in the "funny papers" and the sports page; they have no eye for beauty in the landscape, no respect for family relations. As in so many of O'Connor's stories, the character who is going to take the hardest fall—here the Grandmother—is made to look good by contrast with her son and his family. Bailey is a bald, taciturn father, wearing a Hawaiian shirt with parrots on it. The mother, who is virtually mute, has a face "as broad and innocent as a cabbage" and a kerchief on her head with "two points on the top like rabbit's ears" (9). The children are disobedient brats who speak in screams and shrieks. In this context, the Grandmother's vitality, her interest in things, however shallow, is refreshing. If we smile at her, we also feel the family line has degenerated a bit. She is stuck with a pretty slow crew. Their lives are a vacuity, they are always on "vacation," and they are headed for Florida, then beginning to incarnate the emptiness and deregionalization of American culture.

The Grandmother is so taken up with her desire to visit her relations that during the ride she begins to associate the scenery they are passing through with her girlhood landscapes, and this association is a recollection at once of her past and of the Old South before the Civil War. When they pass a cotton field with an "island" of graves in the center she says, "that was the old family burying ground. That belonged to the plantation." Her son's boy, John Wesley, asks where the plantation is and the grandmother makes a joke: "Gone With the Wind," she laughs. O'Connor left the words capitalized in order to emphasize their reference to Mitchell's novel and the film adaptation that won an Academy Award for best picture in 1939.

Like the fact that she has named her cat "Pitty Sing" after a character in Gilbert and Sullivan's *The Mikado*, the grandmother's reference to *Gone with the Wind* further identifies her as a character whose consciousness is in some degree manipulated by the kitsch of democratic-liberal culture. Though the Grandmother elaborates her harmless allusion no further, her joke participates in a complex system which O'Connor extends throughout the rest of the story and which dramatizes the serious consequences of mass cultural representation. The allusion at once tells a truth and refers to the transformation of southern history into representation, into writing and film—sign of that history's having lost its substantial meaning, of its conversion now to a diluted, glorified sentimentality. O'Connor herself had little interest in or patience with the South's antebellum nostalgia or with the war itself. She asks one of her correspondents, "What you want to read *A Stillness at Appomattox* for? Buy it for me but don't send it to me. I never was one to go over the Civil War in a big way . . ." (*Habit* 309). The literal representation of history was of less interest to O'Connor than the ahistorical and spiritual truths which the Grandmother's nostalgia overlooks.

For John Wesley to ask "where's the plantation?" is to ask where is the South? Where is its wealth and pastoral, Edenic promise? The past as a time when men were gentlemen and children respected their elders is a constant theme of the old woman. To quiet the children, the Grandmother tells them a story of her youth "when she was a maiden lady . . . courted by a Mr. Edgar Atkins Teagarden." Clearly, O'Connor wants us to understand the old lady's revery as a dream of lost paradise: her gentleman caller is named for the very "garden" that has been lost, and his initials—E.A.T.— are clearly meant to remind us of the story of the Fall. Mr. Teagarden was in the habit of leaving the Grandmother a watermelon with his initials carved on it. The old lady doesn't read the spiritual fact within the accidental name, and identifies her loss with the money Teagarden made from his Coca-Cola stock.

In many ways, "A Good Man" is a story about eating, about appetites and the Garden of Eden, and about nature's appetite, which swallows rich and poor alike. In fact, the children have just finished the lunch the grandmother has made for them when the family stops for barbecued sandwiches at Red Sammy's. While Sammy and the Grandmother discuss "better times" and complain about the Marshall Plan ("the way Europe acted you would think we were made of money," she tells Red Sammy), the children watch a monkey in the chinaberry tree outside, who is "busy catching fleas on himself and biting each one carefully between his teeth as if it were a delicacy" (16).

O'Connor further elaborates the Civil War allusion in the scene which follows, describing the soporific car ride after lunch and the confused recollection the Grandmother has of "an old plantation that she had visited in this neighborhood once when she was a young lady. She said the house had six white columns across the front and that there was an avenue of oaks leading up to it and two little wooden trellis arbors on either side in front where you sat down with your suitor after a stroll in the garden" (16). To induce her son to look for this old house she invents a lie that elaborates and projects her antebellum nostalgia: " 'There was a secret panel in this house," she said craftily, not telling the truth but wishing that she were, "and the story went that all the family silver was hidden in it when Sherman came through but it was never found' " (16–17). The "secret panel" idea is a hit with the kids and Bailey is forced to capitulate.

The "secret panel," like the memory generally, is a facile representation of an undefiled South, a secret access to a recoverable past. But as with the explicit reference to *Gone with the Wind*, O'Connor turns the Grandmother's nostalgic allusions against her. For the woods, beside which their overturned car finally comes to rest, are (from Frost) "tall and dark and deep" (20), and once the Misfit and his gang appear—outside "Toombsboro" in a "big black battered hearse-like automobile"—the woods become even more threatening: "behind them the line of woods gaped like a dark open mouth" (21). The family's mindless, animal appetites here re-emerge as instances of nature's appetite, red in tooth and claw, ready to consume. The ironic allusions to Mitchell's novel find their fulfillment in the pistol shots announcing the death of her son Bailey and the boy John Wesley, for the Grandmother "could hear the wind move through the tree tops like a long satisfied insuck of breath" (25). Bailey and his son are gone with the wind, and this is no joke, but the irony of southern history.

The language of this scene implies not only a malign and unforgiving nature, but also the spiritual inadequacy of the "Liberal approach" based upon naturalist beliefs, such as that articulated by John Dewey and Sidney Hook in their "Failure of Nerve" essays: that the world of natural human history and society is a sufficient amphitheater for human aspiration, reason, and perfection. The two major players in the final scene of the story—its last third—are the Grandmother and the Misfit, both of whom are struggling within and coming to recognize the limitations of this "modern idea." Certainly the Misfit is more aware of this than is the Grandmother, whose "liberalism"—if we may ascribe such to her—is a watered-down set of mass cultural "banalities" (*Habit* 389). She keeps a record of their mileage, encourages an aesthetic appreciation of the countryside, prattles on about education and the need to be "broad," and imagines a time when there used to be "good men." The lack of good men follows from a decline in culture or politics ("Europe was entirely to blame for the way things were now," she tells Red Sammy), instead of following from the idea—as O'Connor expressed it to Cecil Dawkins—that "man has fallen and that he is only perfectible by God's grace."

The Misfit, too, bears traces of "the Liberal approach." His "silver-rimmed spectacles" give him a "scholarly look," and he turns out to be a precise, literal man, outraged by the incommensurability of his crimes and punishments. He, too, is a record keeper, ready to acknowledge the claims made upon him by "papers" and accounts. "That's why I sign myself now," he tells the Grandmother. "I said long ago, you get you a signature and sign everything you do and keep a copy of it. Then you'll know what you done and you can hold up the crime to the punishment and see do they match and in the end you'll have something to prove you ain't been treated right" (27–28). This language is as close as O'Connor comes to acknowledging the song which gave her story its title. The Misfit is a man who hasn't been "treated right." The love he lacks, one supposes, is God's love, which his rigid rationalism prevents him from receiving. The Misfit's accounting house tropes may remind us of liberalism's origins in the rise of the middle class, as well as of the Grandmother's regret that she failed to marry into Teagarden's Coca-Cola wealth.

But cold war discourse denied that the bookkeeping of capitalism, its ideas of fairness and contracts, had any basis in the truth of human nature or social and political history. In his lecture "Diplomacy in the Modern World," Kennan argued the deficiencies of the "legalistic approach"—expecting the world's nations to subscribe to a common law and judicial process—especially because of "the inevitable association of legalistic ideas with moralistic ones" and the military indignation that follows from a conviction of moral superiority. "It is a curious thing," he wrote, echoing Lionel Trilling's conclusion to "Manners, Morals, and the Novel," his Kenyon talk on the novel, "that the legalistic approach to world affairs, rooted as it unquestionably is in a desire to do away with war and violence, makes violence more enduring, more terrible, and more destructive to political stability than did the older motives of national interest." On this subject there was a marvellous consistency to the discourse of the liberal center. Niebuhr's language echoes Trilling's even more perfectly: "Our moral perils are not those of conscious malice or the explicit lust for power. They are the perils which can be understood only if we realize the ironic tendency of virtues to turn into vices when too complacently relied upon. The ironic elements in American history can be overcome, in short, only if American idealism comes to terms with the limits of all human striving, the fragmentariness of all human wisdom, the precariousness of all historic configurations of power, and the mixture of good and evil in all human virtue." Niebuhr goes on to cite Kennan's book, which appeared the year before Niebuhr's, drawing a moral-religious lesson from history rather than stopping short with one of "national self-interest" (*American* 100–101; *Irony* 133, 148).

The Misfit's violence, of course, is a form of moral indignation that his experience and his morality do not "match," and his inability to remember his first crime suggests that the Misfit is human rationality itself, unable to comprehend the affront of mortality as a punishment for man's original "fall." "I done something wrong and got sent to the penitentiary. I was buried alive," he tells the Grandmother. In the "Liberal approach" there is no escape hatch from this mortality, and our natural environment becomes a prison house. " 'Turn to the right, it was a wall,' The Misfit said, looking up again at the cloudless sky. 'Turn to the left, it was a wall. Look up it was a ceiling, look down it was a floor. I forget what I done, lady' " (25–26).

The Misfit's symbolic penitentiary reveals how thoroughly O'Connor has invested her story with images of enclosure: the "black valise" imprisoning the Grandmother's cat, Pitty Sing; the gravestones the family sees at the beginning of their trip; the name Toombsboro; the "black, battered, hearse-like automobile"; the prison walls which enrage the Misfit; the dark open mouth of the woods. Even the name of the Grandmother's son, "Bailey," means the outer wall of a castle or the court enclosed by it. These are all images of enclosure producing the violence of history: as when Pitty Sing "rose with a snarl" from the valise and "sprang onto Bailey's shoulder"—causing the accident and the family's extinction. This movement is repeated later when the Misfit asks his sidekick for Bailey's Hawaiian shirt: "the shirt came flying at him and landed on his shoulder" (26). Clothing himself in "Bailey"—as it were—the Misfit imprisons himself in the false paradise of the natural world. For him there is "no pleasure but meanness," and "his voice had become almost a snarl" (28). The fiction itself operates as a place of punishment and retribution, imprisoning its characters in the straitjacket of moral reality.

At the same time, to see them as images only of enclosure is to misread the natural text—as the Grandmother misreads the initials carved on Tea-garden's watermelon—for these images participate in a vast ironic reorganization of meaning, accessible to us through another image of enclosure, the Grandmother's fictive "secret panel." She imagined that inside this nonexistent panel they would find the "family silver," and family silver is exactly what she does find. The Misfit's hair is "silver-gray," he is wearing "silver-rimmed glasses," and one of his accomplices has a "silver stallion" embossed on his sweatshirt. (Now and then O'Connor ended her letters with the closing, "hi yo silver.") Readers may recall that the "trees" earlier in the story "were full of silver-white sunlight and the meanest of them sparkled" (11). This is also "family" silver because when the imminence of death "cleared her head for an instant" she recognizes the Misfit as "one of my own children!" (29)—though not one of the "connections" (9) she wanted to make in east Tennessee. When she touches "him on the shoulder"—in the second repetition of the cat's escape from prison—the Misfit recoils and shoots her three times in the chest. The Misfit here is a kind of black Lone Ranger, a mixture of good and evil, whose (phallocentric) "meanness" saves the Grandmother's life by killing her: "She would of been a good woman," he tells Bobby Lee, "if it had been somebody there to shoot her every minute of her life" (29). In the religious register of the story, the secret panel has become a doorway to the kingdom of heaven.

The stress this ending places upon the family is the culmination of the story's thorough reorganization of natural accident into the design of a spiritual parable. O'Connor repeatedly insists upon the family's belief in the power of accident: the Grandmother has taken the cat along because she is afraid he will "accidentally asphyxiate himself" (10); she dresses formally for the trip so that "in case of an accident, anyone seeing her dead on the highway would know at once that she was a lady" (11); when the car overturns, the children scream "We've had an ACCIDENT!" in a "frenzy of delight" (19, 21). They shout this three times, perhaps as a sign of the spiritual denial their lives represent. Just as their vacation is revealed to be an antipilgrimage, and the digressive sidetrip down the dirt road becomes a spiritual journey taking them into the same woods in which Dante lost his way, so here the Grandmother's sense of familial connection is entirely and radically altered under the pressure of the Misfit's presence. One system is displaced and reorganized into another as O'Connor's irony converts a world of reason without ground to an irrational world grounded in Christ.

The Grandmother's recognition of the Misfit as one of her own children, uniting the world's people beyond the bonds of blood and locality, signifies two central assumptions of revisionist liberalism—human depravity and the universality of human circumstance. In his essay on *The Family of Man* photographic exhibit at the Museum of Modern Art in the 1950s, Eric J. Sandeen described the collected images as an "elaborately conceived argument for the validity of the photograph as a persuasive document, as well as for the liberal sentiment that 'mankind is one' " (369). When Steichen invited photographers to submit their work, he told them, "It is essential to keep in mind the universal elements and aspects of human relations and the experiences common to all mankind rather than situations that represented conditions exclusively related or peculiar to a race, an event, a time or place" (Sandeen 373). Sandeen offers this contextualization of those directives: "Like the liberal historians of the '50s, [Steichen and Miller] assumed that culture worked to bring humans together rather than to differentiate them. . . . Steichen believed in the psychic unity of mankind and used qualities of life, accessible to a mass audience, to get at this deeper level of confluence" (376).

Such displacement of racial and class differences by a universalizing perspective was one of the more conservative implications of the new liberalism. Of course for O'Connor this subordination of race and class to the family of man was consistent with her religious focus and her Agrarian belief in the organic development of culture. "The South has to evolve a way of life in which the two races can live together with mutual forbearance," she told an interviewer in 1963. "You don't form a committee to do this or pass a resolution: both races have to work it out the hard way" (*Mystery* 234). O'Connor's fiction represents the relations of race and class in the South, but always as a means of demonstrating the universalism of the human condition. Several of the stories in the *Good Man* collection end with this reminder of universality: Mr. Head and his grandson "could both feel [the artificial Negro] dissolving their differences" (128); Mrs. Cope's face, at the end of "A Circle in the Fire," "looked as if it might have belonged to anybody, a Negro or a European or to Powell himself" (154); and the old black man in "The Displaced Person" tells Mrs. McIntyre, "Black and white . . . is the same" (224).

Reviews of *A Good Man Is Hard to Find* often praised O'Connor's characters as "part of the human tragi-comedy" (*Booklist* 248). The *New York Herald Tribune* reviewed the book on page 1 of its book review section and praised O'Connor for her "use of the regional to communicate the universal" ("Flannery O'Connor: A New Shining Talent"). The *Commonweal* reviewer noted that "here, in rural miniature, are the primary intuitions of man" (Greene 404). Certainly O'Connor herself thought in just these terms. She wrote Ben Griffith about her story "The Artificial Nigger" that she meant "to suggest with the artificial nigger . . . the redemptive quality of the Negro's suffering for us all" (*Habit* 78); nine months later, when she recalled the story's origin, O'Connor gave the statue a more specific cultural and historical significance: "It's not only a wonderful phrase but it's a terrible symbol of what the South has done to itself" (*Habit* 140).

We needn't forget that O'Connor's demonstration of universality was rooted in Christian mystery, but this point of view not only had some currency within the postwar liberal community but also supplied a foundation for the social responsibility indigenous to "liberal sentiments" (Trilling, *Liberal* xi). O'Connor's explanation of what happens at the end of "A Good Man" suggests how her story might easily be read within the terms of the liberal narrative: "Her head clears for an instant and she realizes, even in her limited way, that she is responsible for the man before her and joined to him by ties of kinship which have their roots deep in the mystery she has been merely prattling about so far" (*Mystery* 111–12).

Within the postwar context the Misfit is really a double figure: on the one hand he is a defenseless liberal intellectual, guilty of what Trilling said was liberalism's tendency "to organize the elements of life in a rational way" (*Liberal* xiv); on the other he is the reality of violence and evil for which the liberal is unprepared. He is the reality of "history" itself—Stalin, Hitler, European evil showing up on the red dirt back road of the Georgia countryside—indeed, he is the greater evil that results from the astonished innocence of liberalism. His is the violence of a simplifying reason imposing its punitive logic upon the recalcitrant complexities of human nature and history.

Before encountering the Grandmother, the Misfit had developed a logic by which he could live, but it was a logic that required disbelief: if Jesus didn't raise the dead, he explains to her, "then it's nothing for you to do but enjoy the few minutes you got left the best way you can—by killing somebody or burning down his house or doing some other meanness to him" (28). The possibility that Jesus might have raised the dead throws "everything off balance" (27) and destroys the logic of his behavior. The Grandmother's gesture testifies to her belief, and it is for this reason that the Misfit is described springing back "as if a snake had bitten him." The Grandmother's gesture violates the consistency of the Misfit's protective logic and removes his last line of defense against the mystery of existence: "The Misfit's eyes were red-rimmed and pale and defenseless-looking" (29).

Understood in this way, "A Good Man Is Hard to Find" turns out to enact one of the central parables of cold war thinking and the "end of ideology"— that the naive rationality of liberal idealism produces a greater violence than a belief which recognizes the reality of evil in human behavior. Introducing this story to her audience at Hollins College in Virginia (1962), O'Connor told them, "I have found that violence is strangely capable of returning my characters to reality and preparing them to accept their moment of grace" (*Mystery* 112). This is Christian realism with a vengeance.

The true authority of this story resides within the narrative action itself, which brings its characters and readers to a perception of human mortality and depravity—that is, to a perception of the silent authority of reality, presented here in the relentlessness of the criminal, and engineered throughout by O'Connor. Indeed, all the stories in *A Good Man Is Hard to Find* may be read as depictions of the "family of man" in need of its "father." The collection's title reminds us that there are almost no fathers in any of the stories, and none who exert authority. In "A Good Man," the Misfit is a man who has lost his father, Bailey is an ineffectual father, and we hear nothing at all of the Grandmother's husband, alive or dead.

The need for authority is one she herself felt. "If you live today you breathe in nihilism," she told one correspondent. "If I hadn't had the Church to fight it with or tell me the necessity of fighting it, I would be the stinkingest logical positivist you ever saw right now." Similarly, to another she wrote, "I know that [baptism] had to be given me before the age of reason, or I wouldn't have used any reason to find it" (*Mystery* 112; *Habit* 97, 131). The Misfit appears to be her imagination of how mean she could be without the faith. At the same time her faith seems to permit her the violence she wreaks upon her characters.

Inscribed within that violence was one of the repeated admonitions of revisionist liberalism—that we must return to "reality"—just as it was part of the liberal narrative (the story told by many liberals) that history ("all the lessons of modern history," Schlesinger wrote) had violently alerted them to the simplifications of liberal ideology. Despite O'Connor's expressed alienation from liberal culture, the "ugly words" of her fiction reproduce in another register the recurring injunctions of cold war discourse. All seemed to agree: it's time to establish a new realism, a less idealistic approach to domestic culture and foreign affairs, because a good man is hard to find.

7

Rebel without a Cause

Mailer's White Negro and Consensus Liberalism

> Fantasy may serve a curious purpose for the American political mind, for it may well be the only technique whereby it can seize any kind of perspective other than the liberal perspective which has governed it throughout its history.
>
> Louis Hartz, *The Liberal Tradition in America*, 1955

> Our motto must therefore be: Reform of consciousness not through dogmas, but through analyzing the mystical consciousness, the consciousness which is unclear to itself, whether it appears in religious or political form. . . . So, we can express the trend of our journal in one word: the work of our time to clarify to itself (critical philosophy) the meaning of its own struggle and its own desires. . . . It is a matter of *confession*, no more.
>
> Karl Marx to Arnold Ruge, 1844

When analysts of the cold war period in the United States write of a "consensus" culture, they mean that a collaboration of business, government, and labor established a dominant center which either saw no need for extreme and divisive positions or actively worked to suppress them. In the view of one writer, "the shared agreement between corporate liberals and conservatives (however reluctant) on fundamental premises of pluralism, was—outside, perhaps, of the H-Bomb—the fifties' most important product" (Biskind 20). This "vital center," in Arthur Schlesinger, Jr.'s, phrase, represented itself as beyond ideology—a kind of neutral, natural being, in harmony with the complex realities of the postwar world. Something of the ideological blindness of this center is conveyed by David Riesman's 1961 introduction to *The Lonely Crowd*, already quoted, which serves as a retrospect to the period his study helped introduce: "*The Lonely Crowd* was one of a number of books which in recent years have eschewed dogmatism and fanaticism and preferred openness, pluralism, and empiricism" (xxxiii).

Cold war studies usually concede that consensus had its discontents, often shown to flower and become dominant, in turn, during the subsequent decade. Mailer's essay "The White Negro," published in 1957, as an example of such discontent, is commonly read as one of the most radical expressions of disagreement with the prevailing "conformity" of its era and as a prophetic description of the disruptive and liberating cultural events during the sixties. Such readings perceive Mailer and his context through a pattern of opposition essentially in league with his attempt to project an image of beleaguered, autonomous subcultures at war with their society. In such an approach, our understanding of both dissent and conformity is distorted.

A more adequate understanding of this period emerges if we investigate this celebrated text of discontent, not merely to elucidate Mailer's intended point of view, but to show that view entangled with the culture it criticizes—to check the boundaries dividing Mailer and his culture for signs of osmosis and erosion. Within his essay, for example, one can trace a complex of influences that Mailer uses to breathe life into "the white Negro" and to establish the social importance this figure may soon have for our culture. At the same time, these influences are a set of exposed discourses from the forties and fifties, which we may read as evidence of culture speaking through Mailer, just as a geologist may read the sedimentary striations of canyon walls to learn the earth's history, the canyon being merely a convenient point of access. To do this is to see "The White Negro" transformed into an expression of culture inhabiting Mailer, who has, in varying degrees, thus lost the reins to his own thought—so that one's consciousness understood as private property ("own thought") becomes less and less adequate a characterization of the essay's origin. To say this is not to jettison altogether the idea of an author acting in time with ideas and arguments, but to suggest the difficulty one has in thinking beyond the assumptions of one's time. As we shall see, "The White Negro" is not only an expression of discontent with consensus liberalism, but a record of the ways in which Mailer's radical intentions were subverted by the prevailing discourses of the liberal culture he wished to repudiate. "The White Negro" is a hodge-podge, a confused piece of writing, but for that very reason a useful cross-section of cold war discourses and a record of the radical imagination's difficulty in reinventing the possibility of significant social change.

This confusion begins with the title of the piece, for "The White Negro" promises to be an essay about desegregation—arguably the most prominent cultural issue of the fifties. Though Chief Justice Warren had declared in 1954 that "the doctrine of 'separate but equal' has no place" in public education and had ordered (the following year) that desegration take place with "all deliberate speed," school integration was deliberately resisted throughout the South (not to mention the de facto segregation in northern urban areas). In one account, southern resistance "was reflected in massive efforts of legislative bodies to evade implementation—or at least to delay it as long as possible. In the decade following *Brown*, the Southern Education Reporting Service found that the seventeen southern and border states enacted 475 acts and resolutions relating to the segregation or desegregation of public schools" (Barker and Barker 185–86).

In such a context, the title "The White Negro" appears as a metaphor of radical integration, though a deeply ambivalent one since it summons not only the fully mixed figure of a society racially at rest, but also the figure of the black man "passing" as white. But the ostensible subject of his essay, though relevant to integration is not exactly "integration." When Mailer republished "The White Negro" in *Advertisements for Myself* (1959), he affixed a preface explaining, among other things, that the idea for the essay originated in a bet with Lyle Stuart, owner of the monthly newspaper the *Independent*, that he could write something about "integration" that "no large newspaper would ever [print]" (307). Mailer chose to write about the volatile subject of integration, that is, because of an argument "about how much freedom there was in the mass-media" (307). To be able to write something unacceptable to what C. Wright Mills called "the cultural apparatus" would prove that such an "apparatus" existed as a repressive, conformist manipulator of culture. At the same time, by thinking outside the assumptions of that culture, Mailer would demonstrate his ability to "imagine non-conformity" (in Lionel Trilling's phrase), to assert his own freedom, difference, and rebellion.

Civil rights and nonconformity would seem to have much in common, especially if we think of conformity as contributing to the perpetuation of racial stereotypes and oppositions. In Mailer's first draft of the essay— three paragraphs he wrote before going to bed the night of the bet—he tried to state baldly the root of southern resistance to integration: "the comedy is that the white loathes the idea of the Negro attaining equality in the classroom because the white feels that the Negro already enjoys sensual superiority. So the white unconsciously feels that the balance has been kept, that the old arrangement was fair. The Negro had his sexual supremacy and the white had his white supremacy" (307). While the issue of "conformity" is barely present in this statement—existing perhaps as the deluded consciousness of white men, unaware of what they are "unconsciously" feeling—the essay which later evolved gave priority to the subject of conformity: "our collective condition is to live with instant death by atomic war, relatively quick death by the State as *l'univers concentrationnaire*, or with a slow death by conformity with every creative and rebellious instinct stifled" (312).

The "white Negro" is the nonconforming "hipster" who may show the way out of repressive social consensus. The hipster is an amalgam of sociological categories: "the bohemian and the juvenile delinquent came face-to-face with the Negro, and the hipster was a fact in American life" (314). The hipster is a figure of the urban "wilderness" who lives in "the enormous present" (314). He is awash in the "intensity of his private vision . . . that no rational argument . . . can explain away" (316); he tries to "create a new nervous system for himself" (316); he fights for the "sweet" of "energy" and "orgasm" (322); and because he divorces himself from "the Super-Ego of society"—"to do what one feels whenever and wherever it is possible"—he widens the "arena of the possible" not only for himself but "reciprocally for others as well" (327).

Mailer's invention of the "white Negro," then, is a romantic strategy of converting a struggle between racial colors into an opposition between self and society, imagination and ego repression. Mailer's affirmation of "infantile desire" is a postwar Freudian version (through Reich) of Wordsworth's return to the unsocialized self of childhood as a source of renewal. For this being to emerge, all social restraint must be removed: "the divorce of man from his values, the liberation of the self from the Super-ego of society" (327). The hipster is Mailer's poet, who finds in the lingo of the urban rustics—the black, the psychopath, and the juvenile delinquent—a language more pure for its foundation in the permanent forms of being. Mailer's savage may not be as good as Rousseau's, but the idea is the same: the ineradicable mixture of good and evil that recent history has revealed within us all is far more benign than the collective violence of the state. Mailer attempts to give these romantic qualities a contemporary and radical point by associating them with marginal groups and converting their marginality into the matrix of a future society.

The final essay was titled "The White Negro," but, as the above summary suggests, the metaphor had less to do with the integration of classes than with the latent origins of a revolutionary nonconformity. In itself this would be insignificant, were it not for what this transformation reveals about the problematic character of Mailer's radical nonconformity. The conscious source of this transformation in Mailer's focus may have been the bet with Lyle Stuart, but a more important and thorough cause was that Mailer began to think about "conformity" and a way out of its subtle restraints in pretty much the same way the liberal-conservative consensus had been thinking about them for over fifteen years.

The reasons for this may be traced to a widespread conviction of the thirties and forties, already in decline when Mailer wrote "The White Negro," that the world was witness to a new political phenomenon known as "totalitarianism." For example, Mailer's avowed contempt for rational argument—and the hipster's embrace of visionary mysticism—shared with consensus culture the essentially conservative and conservative-making obsession with totalitarianism, widely theorized as rationalism gone awry. Mailer may have thought his rejection of "good liberal reason" distinguished him from such cold war liberals as Sidney Hook, but consensus liberalism wasn't all that homogenous. Arguably, it was far more common for liberals to confess the naiveté of their former belief in reason. The accumulated horrors and hypocrisies of the Spanish Civil War, Stalin's purge trials and nonaggression pact with Hitler, the revelations of the Holocaust, and the dropping of the atomic bomb on Japan all signified to many liberals that their belief in "good liberal reason" (330) and the possibilities for social control and planning that might derive from rational beings was naive and misplaced. Their new view of human nature as "fallen," or inherently "limited" and "tragic," as composed of an inseparable and paradoxical "good-and-evil," is what made them conservative liberals and part of what defined them as belonging to the "vital center." This reconstruction of liberalism, as I have written earlier, was part of the rhetoric of "new realism" one finds in all the discourses of the forties and early fifties, from Reinhold Niebuhr's theology to George Kennan's foreign policy.

Nor was Mailer's emphasis on the totalitarian character of United States culture especially unconventional. For many it might have been an example of hyperbole, but sober (as well as shrill) analysts of American culture had been warning of the threat from within as early as the late 1930s. In all these admonitions, conformity is taken to signify an advanced stage of totalitarian infiltration. "The serious threat to our democracy is not the existence of foreign totalitarian states," John Dewey wrote in 1939. "It is the existence within our own personal attitudes and within our own institutions of conditions similar to those which have given a victory to external authority, discipline, uniformity and dependence upon The Leader in foreign countries" (*Freedom* 49). Introducing *Escape from Freedom* (1941), Erich Fromm announced his intention to focus upon those "factors in the character structure of modern man, which made him want to give up freedom in Fascist countries and which so widely prevail in millions of our own people" (6). The psychiatrist Robert Lindner (whose importance to "The White Negro" essay will be discussed later) was less restrained: "In our own United States, especially, we are confronted with a demand for conformity that not a single agency or institution opposes. . . . the making of Mass Man is in process" (*Prescription* 193). "Conformity is growing,"

Paul Tillich warned his Yale audience in 1952, but then reassured them, "it has not yet become collectivism" (*Courage* 104).

Thus when Mailer declared, "one is a rebel or one conforms, one is a frontiersman in the Wild West of American night life, or else a Square cell, trapped in the totalitarian tissues of American society, doomed willy-nilly to conform if one is to succeed" ("The White Negro," *Advertisements* 313), he was merely indulging a commonplace of the cold war consensus, familiar to mass, mid, and high culture alike. Everyone feared the insidious effects of conformity. Everyone lionized the "individual." The problem, as Lionel Trilling noted in *Freud and the Crisis of Our Culture* (1955), was that when everyone proclaimed himself a nonconformist, how did one "imagine non-conformity" (51–52)?

Though antitotalitarianism made conservatives of nearly everyone, Mailer tried to remain radical by proposing the existence of a growing hipster subculture at war with America's square conformity. The term "hipster" was not new, since the type had already been described in Nelson Algren's novels (*Walk on the Wild Side*, *The Man with the Golden Arm*), Kerouac's *On the Road*, and John Clellon Holmes's *Go*, and the word itself appeared in blurbs advertising Chandler Brossard's *Who Walk in Darkness*. The figure reached a wider popular audience in films like *The Wild Ones* (starring Marlon Brando) and *Rebel without a Cause* (starring James Dean and Natalie Wood). The catlike nimbleness and finger-snapping "cool" of *West Side Story*'s teens have a pedigree similar to that of Mailer's hipster. Hipsters and beatniks were subjects of essays in *Life* and *Harper's Bazaar*.

For our understanding of "The White Negro," the most influential portrait of the hipster came from Robert Lindner's study of psychopathology, *Rebel without a Cause* (1944), since many of the characteristics, much of the makeup, and not a little of the phraseology of Mailer's piece come from Lindner's introductory essay to his study. Throughout the forties and fifties, Lindner made a career out of explaining psychopathology and juvenile delinquency and relating these phenomena to America's worst fears: the rise of Mass Man and totalitarianism within its own borders. Of course, for Lindner the psychopath was neither a hero nor an exception. Instead, he described the psychopath as a prototype of "mass man" in the making. He then hybridized the psychopath with the juvenile delinquent and theorized that the "mass man" of communism and fascism has his breeding ground in the "mutiny" of youth. The psychopath is a "frontiersman" repressed by society, "encysted" within the urban environment now that the frontier is settled. As I will point out later, Lindner was typical of his time in attacking society for repressing its members, and attacking as deviants those who rebelled against society.

Lindner's juvenile psychopath is the predecessor of Mailer's "frontiersman in the Wild West of American night life," but Mailer chooses to treat Lindner's composite as Natty Bumppo, moving silently through the mean streets of an urban wilderness. Mailer's strategy appears to have been to radicalize the "hipster," not only by reinventing him as a mixture of the most marginal and threatening images to white American culture—the black man, the juvenile delinquent, the bohemian, and the psychopath—but by projecting "himself into essential sympathy" with them as well (318), that is, by seeing in these popular figures of magazine articles and films the smoldering embers of an individualism ready to burst into nihilistic, apocalyptic conflagration.

This radical brew was not only romantic but meant to stand in for the absence of a revolutionary class. In the year after "The White Negro" was published, Alfred Kazin remarked that Mailer's essay was the "adaptation to the hipster of the myth of the proletariat. Mailer's essay is a completely Marxist-revolutionary essay" ("Psychoanalysis," 4–5).

Kazin made the connection as a way of vitiating the essay's substance, and he listed Mailer with a group of writers he thought were looking for something to be angry about. The terms and conditions of Marx's thought no longer apply, Kazin asserted: "there *was* a proletariat once, and a bourgeoisie," but now "there is no authoritative moral tradition that [the rebel] can honestly feel limits and hinders his humanity" (5, 13). Kazin's assumptions about American culture, while far from cheerful, participated in the consensus view which included *Life* magazine's boast that the United States had "gone further than any other society in the history of man toward creating a truly classless society" (Sept. 12, 1955), and Pauline Kael's grumpy admission, "The United States has now achieved what critics of socialism have always posited as the end result of a socialist state: a prosperous, empty, uninspiring uniformity" (45). For a more cheerful expression of these assumptions, one could listen to Norman Podhoretz, who was convinced that young people were discovering "that 'conformity' did not necessarily mean dullness and unthinking conventionality, that, indeed, there was great beauty, profound significance in a man's struggle to achieve freedom *through* submission to conditions" (see Wechsler 21–22).

Such self-congratulation was but one of many legitimate targets of Mailer's criticism. Among them one must list such structural realities of American society as an economy dependent upon the manufacture and sale of arms, a tolerated level of unemployment, the denial of civil liberties to minorities, the McCarran Internal Security Act (which made provision for detention camps to hold subversives), and the only recently quieted witch hunts of HUAC. When Mailer wrote in the first section of "The

White Negro" that "these have been years of conformity and depression" in which a "stench of fear has come out of every pore of American life," he was hardly overstating the case, nor was he inventing something to be angry about.[1]

But the primary target of his essay was the lethargic, grudging rapprochement with the American status quo on the part of former radical liberals and fellow intellectuals. Even so, Mailer shared with them the dilemma of a socialist vision with no revolutionary class to ˙xecute it. "The monotony and bleakness of the future have become so engrained in the radical temper," Mailer wrote midway in the essay, "that the radical is in danger of abdicating from all imagination" (330, 331). What Mailer meant by this ("bleakness of the future") partially accords with Kazin's view that Marx's "proletariat"—which was to be the agency of social revolution—no longer existed. In part, this was because collective solutions were inherently suspect: after Hitler and Stalin, no one wanted to see masses of people united on behalf of anything, especially revolution. Less abstractly, American hopes for socialist advances, which had relied upon the growth in numbers and militancy of the labor union movement, were effectively dismantled by 1948, the year in which the Truman victory signified the willingness of labor to work within the compromises offered them by government and business. In an article published the following year, "American Socialists: What Now?" Daniel Bell concluded that "whereas the fundamental outlook of nineteenth century utopian unionism . . . was to change capitalist society, the fundamental drive of twentieth century unionism is to assure a place and some weight in that social order" (*Modern Review* 351–52; cited in Brick 187). Addressing a British audience in 1961, C. Wright Mills summarized the problem:

> For socialists of almost all varieties, the historic agency [of change] has been the working class—and later the peasantry; also parties and unions variously composed of members of the working class.
>
> I cannot avoid the view that in both cases, the historic agency (in the most advanced capitalist countries) has collapsed or become most ambiguous: so

---

1. The evidence here is overwhelming, but perhaps unknown to many readers. See David Caute, *The Great Fear*; Miller and Nowak, *The Fifties: The Way We Really Were*. For the similarity of terms he uses, it is worth citing Louis Hartz, *The Liberal Tradition in America*, on the anticommunism of the postwar era: "there can be no doubt that it represents the most frightening closing down of 'Americanism' at home that we have yet experienced. It is keener than the Palmer drive precisely in proportion as the Communist threat which elicits it is keener. It is wider than the Dies hysteria just as the element of reality it involves is wider. It has charged the atmosphere of national life with a fear that has become familiar" (306).

far as structural change is concerned, *these* don't seem to be at once available and effective as *our* agency any more. (254–55)

In effect, aspiring radicals like Mailer were confronted with the need to discover or invent a new revolutionary class. At the same time, Mailer was not inclined to think in terms of class or collective action, since, like everyone else, he associated such action with the failures of Russian communism and the Old Left in America. Because "the attempt failed in its frontal revolutionary attack," he wrote in the published debates provoked by "The White Negro," it is necessary to go "backward toward being and the secrets of human energy, not forward to *the collectivity which was totalitarian in the proof*" (emphasis mine, *Advertisements* 335–36).

Here, as throughout the essay, Mailer's thinking is infiltrated by the same totalitarian discourse that was helping to shape so many aspects of the consensus culture he sought to set himself apart from. This is especially visible in his shift of focus from the integration of blacks and whites to the social implications of a mythical figure—the hipster. One might have expected Mailer to seize upon black discontent as a potential agency of social change (which, in fact, it was), but instead his interest in their discontent was channeled by the assumption that collective action was futile, and that rational planning itself ("the Faustian urge to dominate nature") had contributed to the imminence of nuclear death and conformist restraints which, he declared, define our "collective condition" (312).

The result was that Mailer looked to psychological types, states, and qualities, rather than to socio-economic groups, for the germinating bed of a new revolutionary time. As we shall see, this too was a characteristic response of liberals to totalitarianism, and one at many points perfectly in keeping with consensus culture. The problems black people were having getting places at the front of the bus or at desks beside white children were secondary to the ways Mailer's psychological stereotypes about African Americans could help him go "backward toward being." Blacks in this essay aren't representative figures so much as a "source of Hip" (313), because their conditioning as marginal figures in American society, ever alert to the presence of violence and death, has developed psychological skills that are now of use to us all in the atomic age, having to live "with instant death" (312). Accordingly, the black man's psychology was more in tune with "being": having retained the "art of the primitive" and living in "the enormous present," having relinquished "the pleasures of the mind for the more obligatory pleasures of the body" the black man had developed the "existentialist synapses" appropriate for our time.

At this point in the essay Mailer's interest in the "Negro" virtually ceases until the last pages, and he now pivots to the hipster, the white man who appropriates the psychic skills of the black: "so there was a new breed of adventurers, urban adventurers who drifted out at night looking for action with a black man's code to fit their facts. The hipster had absorbed the existentialist synapses of the Negro, and for practical purposes could be considered a white Negro" (315). Mailer should have titled his essay "The Negro White," since what he describes is the white man "passing" for (his version of the) black. In a "Footnote to 'The White Negro,'" Mailer is even more explicit, if less prudent: "the psychic style" of the hipster "derives from the best Negroes to come up from the bottom" (*Advertisements* 346).

Mailer's use of the black man is influenced by a psychological orientation he shared with the consensus culture he hoped to unnerve by brandishing the image of the "white Negro." Thus when he thinks about the black man he thinks not of a class of people but of a reservoir of psychological and instinctual capacities. This orientation is established in the opening declaration of his first paragraph: "Probably, we will never be able to determine the psychic havoc of the concentration camps and the atom bomb upon the unconscious mind of almost everyone alive in these years" (311). Throughout his analysis, his explanatory model has little to do with socio-economic status and everything to do with the damage and effects of repression—in the form of the suppression of knowledge of such facts as A-bombs and concentration camps, and in the form of the sexual inhibitions upon which civilization depends—from which the black man, "following the need of his body," is free (314). "Every creative and rebellious instinct," he says, is "stifled" (312), and the result is "anxiety," "boredom," and "therefore sickness" (313). Moreover, man experiences this repression in the service of intolerable "contradictions": primarily those between private values ("stable middle-class values") (319) and the collective violence of the state, and those of popular culture "where sex is sin and yet sex is paradise" (317).

These inescapable contradictions are creating the psychopath, "an embodiment of the extreme contradictions of the society which formed his character" (321). The psychopath, like the black man, is an image for Mailer of a man who does what he wants, who encourages the psychopath in himself (313), a man who tries "to remake a bit of his nervous system" (320) by living the "infantile fantasy" (319). The implicit confidence, in this strategy against the totalitarianism of culture, is that the violence of unrepressed individuals will be less harmful than the collective violence of nations whose citizens are repressed (328, 336, in his reply to Malaquais). Mailer concludes his essay by speculating upon the great advantage it would be to our next revolutionary period if "the crises of capitalism in the twentieth century [were] understood as the unconscious adaptations of a society to solve its economic imbalance at the expense of a new mass psychological imbalance." What we need is "a calculus capable of translating the economic relations of man into his psychological relations and then back again" (331).

Mailer puts all of this forward as a radical hypothesis which he expects to shock the complacent liberal and stir the dormant socialist. People like Irving Howe—editor of *Dissent*—and Norman Podhoretz were impressed with the piece, but Podhoretz' memory of its impact suggests something of the latent conservatism in Mailer's ideas: "with Marxism and all its variants closed off as an alternative, I saw in Mailer the possibility of a new kind of radicalism—a radicalism that did not depend on Marx and that had no illusions about the Soviet Union" (47). I have already pointed out that Mailer's antitotalitarianism was a conventional theme of the cold war consensus, including that antitotalitarianism directed against elements of conformity in the United States. But the effort to understand and predict political behavior through psychological analysis of individuals and groups, which Mailer attempted in "The White Negro," was also one of the fundamental strategies of liberal retrenchment in the face of Hitler and Stalin in the thirties.

For the Marxist radical, the appearance of these totalitarian states raised the technical question, why hadn't capitalism evolved into socialism? For the liberal, this new political phenomenon raised questions about how absolute was the love of freedom, how far could planning and central government overcome the complexities and capricious morals of individuals, and everywhere one looks the answers to these questions were framed in psychological terms. It is not too strong to refer to this as the psychologization of cultural analysis (or perception). In 1933 Wilhelm Reich published *The Mass Psychology of Fascism*, his analysis of why fascism, instead of socialism, had evolved from Germany's capitalist economic structure. Economic conditions had seemed ripe for a socialist revolution. His answer was that Marxist analysts had failed to take into account the "character structure of the masses": "Owing to its lack of knowledge of mass psychology, Marxist sociology set 'bourgeois' against 'proletariat.' This is incorrect from a psychological viewpoint. The character structure is not restricted to the capitalists; it is prevalent among the working men of all occupations. There are liberal capitalists and reactionary workers. *There are no 'class distinctions' when it comes to character*" (5, xxiv).

Across a wide spectrum of thinkers and over the next several decades, this shift in analytical models—from studies of the role which modes of production played in class conflict to studies of human character—was repeated so often that psychological explanations of social history quickly gained hegemony. "Any attempt to understand the attraction which Fascism exercises upon great nations," Erich Fromm wrote in 1941, "compels us to recognize the role of psychological factors" (7). The authors of *The Lonely Crowd* thought that "the older social sciences—history, political science, economics—gave far too little weight to the understanding of social change that might be gleaned from a better grasp of psychoanalytical psychology" (Riesman, xxii). The same kind of puzzlement and desire to explain the apparently irrational human behavior of recent history persists in William Barrett's comparison of Marxist and existential philosophies: "Marxism has no philosophical categories for the unique facts of human personality, and in the natural course of things manages to collectivize this human personality out of existence. . . . Existential philosophy, as a revolt against such over-simplification, attempts to grasp the image of the whole man, even where this involves bringing to consciousness all that is dark and questionable in his existence" (22).

At the same time that analysts of developments in Italy, Germany, and Russia wanted to explain the rise of totalitarianism, they also wished to prevent its spread, and this complementary reflex naturally led to a renewal of essentially romantic values and assumptions about the autonomy of individuals and the virtues of "spontaneity," and to conventional oppositions between self and society, nature and civilization, rebellion and conformity. One of the most influential and persistent theories to emerge from this period was Wilhelm Reich's idea that the totalitarian masses had succumbed to a "fear of freedom," inculcated in the individual by the family. *"Man's authoritarian structure . . . is basically produced by the embedding of sexual inhibitions and fear in the living substance of sexual impulses."* The result, he wrote, "is conservatism, fear of freedom, in a word, reactionary thinking" (30–31).

The most influential version of this theory was provided by Fromm's *Escape from Freedom*, a book one finds cited later in works by Reinhold Niebuhr, Arthur Schlesinger, Jr., Paul Tillich, and Robert Lindner. When Fromm describes the threatening qualities of freedom he begins to sound like a New Critic discussing metaphysical poetry: freedom is "ambiguous"; freedom forces men to live with "contradiction" and "anxiety"; freedom forces men to make choices; freedom leaves men independent, but isolated. In the handbook of the new liberalism, *The Vital Center*, Schlesinger bought Fromm's theory whole: "The eternal awareness of choice can drive the weak to the point where the simplest decision becomes a nightmare. Most men prefer to flee choice, to flee anxiety, to flee freedom" (52). Democracies require of their citizens, Tillich concurred, "the courage to be." Fromm's thesis appeared even in theories of modern art: "It is this terror of the new freedom," René d'Harnoncourt wrote in *Art News* in 1949, "which removed the familiar signposts from the roads that makes many of us wish to turn the clock back and recover the security of yesterday's dogma." Here, as in so many other commentaries, how one responds to this fear separates the men from the boys, the freedom-loving democrat from the totalitarian: "The totalitarian state established in the image of the dogmatic orders of the past is one reflection of this terror of the new freedom" (252).

It isn't too difficult to see the patterns of thought which structure this rhetoric: totalitarianism breeds weakness and passivity; democracy relies upon the strength and courage of its citizens. The free enterprise system may induce anxiety by requiring decisions and eschewing the security of a planned economy, but without the strength to endure the anxieties of choice and insecure income man loses his freedom. Here the rhetoric of romantic individualism always veers upon covert support of democratic capitalism. The whole scenario is staged in terms of a metaphysical drama of man in uncertainties—Keats's famous quotation about Coleridge's "negative capability" gained a widespread currency in such diverse thinkers as Charles Olson and Lionel Trilling—but this new rhetoric of being wasn't really an effort to start from scratch, from the natural sources of "being," so much as it was a defensive maneuver of a world that saw itself as under attack.

Since the economic system of capitalism was no longer thought to be impenetrable, or self-sustaining, and since freedom itself had been shown to take second place to other human desires—Dewey wrote in *Freedom and Culture* (1939), "the view that love of freedom is so inherent in man that, if it only has a chance given it by abolition of oppressions exercized by church and state, it will produce and maintain free institutions is no longer adequate" (7)—the new emphasis was upon the psychological dynamics of character in strong individuals, willing to grasp their freedom. Mailer's rebellious hipster is but one variant of the aggressively masculine individual to emerge from this defensive rhetoric. Arthur Schlesinger's radical "liberal," for example, is pointedly capable not only of staunch but of violent action. One is reminded of the admonition that the Christian can be a "fighter" too.

Seen in this briefly sketched context, "The White Negro" loses a considerable degree of its force as a radical critique of the consensus culture. Mailer ended his reply to Jean Malaquais with the conviction that "until the radical bridge from Marx to Freud is built, and our view of man embraces more facts, contradictions, and illuminations than any conservative view, and stares into such terrifying alternatives as totalitarianism or barbarism, we are doing no more than scolding ourselves" (338). But this bridge from Marx to Freud was the centerpiece of the liberal architecture Mailer wished to dynamite, and seemed inherently designed to deradicalize, to provide an escape or retreat from the political action of groups.

It was in making this trip that so many thinkers replaced metaphors of class with those of "mind" or "consciousness" or "imagination" (one thinks of *The Liberal Imagination*, for example), and the "masses"—once the hope of revolutionary change—became transformed into the disappointing and potentially threatening "mass society." "Alienation," once defined as the separation of the worker from the fruits of his labor, now became a badge of radicalism and autonomy—a sign that one was not a member of "mass society." Erich Fromm suggested that the "well adapted" person might be "less healthy than the neurotic in terms of human values" (139). Peter Viereck wrote a book in praise of "the unadjusted man" (1956). "Alienation," Daniel Bell argued in *The End of Ideology*, "is not nihilism but a positive role, a detachment, which guards one against being submerged in any cause" (16–17).

This redefinition of "alienation" was part of the transformation in Mailer's thinking which had begun after the publication of *The Naked and the Dead*. For young writers brought up on the social fiction of Steinbeck, Dos Passos, Roth, and Farrell, the evaporation of the naturalist and class-conscious assumptions on which that fiction was based presented as severe a problem as did the compromise of labor with business for socialists like Daniel Bell. "I was a socialist after all," Mailer said in the 1963 interview already quoted. "I believed in large literary works which were filled with characters, . . . and were developed, let's say, like the Tolstoyan novel." But by the time Mailer began writing *Barbary Shore* (1951), his imagination was already influenced by the discourse of totalitarianism, which included the apparent failure of Marxism and the radical isolation of the individual. Deprived of his ideology, the narrator of this novel—it is told in the first person—cannot imagine any other literary project except one in which an individual finds himself struggling with "an immense institution never defined" (42).

Like many writers of this period, Mailer tried to turn his own frustrations and paralysis into subject matter by writing about writers having difficulty writing. Seven years after his second book, Mailer remained at the same impasse: the apparent absence of political alternatives leaves him stalled within the minds of his characters. In the story "The Man Who Studied Yoga" (1959), the central figure, Sam Slovoda, is also a writer, but here Mailer explicitly makes the connection between the decline of socialist possibilities and the difficulties Slovoda experiences. "Sam is thinking of other things. Since he has quit the Party he has studied a great deal. . . . He is straddled between the loss of a country he has never seen and his repudiation of the country in which he lives" (*Advertisements* 167). This somewhat histrionic description of the alienation endured by the radical in the fifties is presented as the reason Slovoda can't write. Without the Marxist explanation of social history, of how society works, the "realistic" form Slovoda knows how to use is no longer suitable, because "reality is no longer realistic." " 'It's all schizoid,' Sam said. 'Modern life is schizoid' " (167).

Mailer's move from third person to first, from a transcendent analysis of the relations of classes—which he had presented in *The Naked and the Dead*—to a representation of a consciousness mired in its own divisions, is one of the clearest results of consensus liberalism. Just as Marxist analysis had provided the basis of the socialist's confidence in the evolution of History, so had class analysis been the basis of novelistic structure in Mailer's first book. Once the coherence and adequacy of Marxist analysis were thrown into question, Mailer found it impossible to assume the confident voice of the naturalistic narrator. Reflecting upon those years following publication of *The Naked and the Dead*, Mailer tied narrative point of view directly to an author's ability to comprehend contemporary history: "I must have felt at that time as if I would never be able to write in the third person until I developed a coherent view of life. I don't know that I've been able to altogether" (*Writers*, 3d ser., 265).

While writing *Barbary Shore*, Mailer oscillated between the impulse to write social history on the one hand, and the desire to dramatize a reality defined in psychological terms on the other. As a result the book literally teeters between chapters full of sexual innuendo and chapters of tedious political theorizing. "My conscious intelligence," Mailer recalls, ". . . . became obsessed by the Russian Revolution. But my unconscious was much more interested in other matters: murder, suicide, orgy, psychosis, all the themes I discuss in *Advertisements*" (*Writers*, 3d ser., 263).

It must have been at this time that Mailer read Trotsky's *History of the Russian Revolution*, because a scene from that vibrant history reappears in the reflections of Lovett, the novel's speaker:

> I had come this far, remembered this much, and felt again a faint glow of the ardor with which I had waited for the inevitable contradictions to burn the fuse. The proletariat which crawled to glory beneath the belly of a Cossack's horse, the summer flies of Vyborg, I could see it all again, and know with the despair which follows fervor that nothing had changed, and social relations, economic relations, were still independent of man's will. (117)

Readers familiar with the literature of the Russian Revolution will recognize this passage as an echo of Trotsky's famous description of the "Five Days" in February 1917, when some twenty-five hundred workers at one of the principal mills of the Vyborg district—with Trotsky as one of their leaders—successfully demonstrated despite the presence of the Cossacks, aligned against them. For Trotsky, the scene was an image of newly found fraternity between the peasants and the Cossacks—"solid property owners"—who refused to fire upon them. He describes the relations of the two classes as a kind of mating ritual, the two sides at once suspicious, fearful, and coquettish: "Behind [the officers], filling the whole width of the Prospect, galloped the Cossacks. Decisive moment! But the horsemen, cautiously, in a long ribbon, rode through the corridor just made by the officers. 'Some of them smiled,' Kayurov recalls, 'and one of them gave the workers a good wink.' This wink was not without meaning. The workers were emboldened with a friendly, not hostile, kind of assurance, and slightly infected the Cossacks with it. The one who winked found imitators. In spite of renewed efforts from the officers, the Cossacks, without openly breaking discipline, failed to force the crowd to disperse, but flowed through it in streams. This was repeated three or four times and brought the two sides even closer together." As a last resort the officers aligned the Cossacks to block the demonstrators from getting to the center of the square. "But even this did not help: standing stock-still in perfect discipline, the Cossacks did not hinder the workers from 'diving' under their horses. The revolution does not choose its paths; it made its first steps toward victory under the belly of a Cossack's horse" (104–5).

Trotsky's description is worth citing at such length because it is a tableau of class relations that remained in Mailer's imagination, where it was psychologized and redeployed as the relations of schizoid divisions. The possibilities for fraternity are converted into hopes for overcoming schizophrenia, for achieving "the whole man" and a unified society, also conceived as a mental structure. Mailer preserves the socialist hope within another set of terms, in which the "proletariat" is transformed into the "unconscious" which must crawl to freedom beneath the jealous eye of the "Super-Ego." Trotsky's image, and Mailer's psychologization of it, are still present in Mailer's thinking when he describes his role in the march on the Pentagon in 1967 (published the next year as *Armies of the Night*). The entire account is presented within the psychoanalytical model of a nation and its individual citizens suffering from schizophrenia. Along the rope barricade separating the demonstrators from the National Guard the social divisions searing the country are described by Mailer in terms of the psychological stress the combatants experience, and the possibilities for wholeness provided by the confrontation. "If the troops were relieved that a pullulating unwashed orgiastic Communist-inspired wave of flesh did not roll right over them, . . . the demonstrators in their turn were relieved in profounder fashion that their rank of eyes had met the soldiers, and it was the soldiers who had looked away" (286–87). Most of the demonstrators

"were on the mouth of their first cannon, yet for each minute they survived, sixty seconds of existential gold was theirs" (288). When each draft
card burner gives his card to the fire, "his schizophrenia is burning and the
security of the future with it" (300).

This moral, psychological emphasis differs greatly from that of the Trotskyite scenario on which it is based, for no ultimate revolutionary victory
is contemplated, and the rewards are personal and moral. Mailer himself
crossed the line and engaged one of the guardsmen, who raised his club but
could not strike:

> Some unfamiliar current, now gyroscopic, now a sluggish whirlpool, was
> evolving from that quiver of the club, and the MP seemed to turn slowly away
> from his position confronting the rope, and the novelist [Mailer] turned with
> him, each still facing the other until the axis of their shoulders was now per-
> pendicular to the rope, and still they kept turning in this psychic field, not
> touching, the club quivering, and then Mailer was behind the MP. . . . (150)

For this brief heroism on behalf of a moral principle, Mailer earns a "clean
sense of himself"—a momentary healing of the divisions of hypocrisy and
guilt within: "what [Christians] must signify when they spoke of Christ
within them" he reflects (238). History, in this account, becomes a "moral
ladder" or ritual in which sin is atoned, or temporarily ameliorated by the
actions of its saints. Who is to say, he asks rhetorically, that "the sins of
America were not by their witness a tithe remitted?" (319).

The point here isn't simply that Trotsky's tableau persisted in Mailer's
mind but that Mailer transformed it into a psychological model, in which
the sources of revolutionary "agency" are now such elements as the "unconscious" and "instinct." In the schizophrenic persona that Mailer invents
for himself, this "unconscious" or "instinct" is the unpredictable "Beast"
that arrives unannounced and whose actions, though they may embarrass,
are finally what save him from the timid rationalizations of his more repressed self. This persona or character emerged from Mailer's frustrations
and experiments in the fifties and may be glimpsed in varying degrees in
the characters of Marion Faye in *The Deer Park* and Stephen Rojack in *An
American Dream*, as well as in such personae as the "Mailer" of *Armies
of the Night*, and New Journalist protagonists like Gary Gilmore in *Executioner's Song*. But Mailer's most explicit enunciation of his development
from Marx to Freud, and the way out of the stalemate of his own career as
a novelist, was in "The White Negro," where he first formulated for himself how the antisocial hipster might work as the revolutionary unconscious
of American culture (as well as a fictional character more interesting than
dead-end writers like Lovett and Slovoda).

I have been arguing that the radicalism of these efforts was blunted by the romantic conservatism they shared with the consensus discourses, and this aspect of "The White Negro"—already present in its obsession with totalitarianism and its focus upon psychological types rather than socio-economic groups—becomes undeniably explicit once we turn our attention to the essay's insistence upon sexual liberation. Here the hipster's affinities with classical economic liberalism make him something of a philosophe as gangster, physiocrat as urban entrepreneur. In the sexual role Mailer assigns the black man, we see most powerfully how the conservative undertow, which pervaded the new liberalism's self-scrutiny, reproduces stereotypes of the status quo instead of revolution.

The insistence upon sexual liberation was another theme in the radical-liberal critique of totalitarianism at home and abroad. One of the crimes for which Big Brother holds Winston and Julia guilty is the crime of sexual passion, with all the intimacy, privacy, and freedom this passion entails. When Irving Howe wrote about *1984* in *Politics and the Novel* (1957), he asserted, "that Orwell has here come upon an important tendency in modern life, that the totalitarian state is inherently an enemy of erotic freedom, seems to me indisputable" (246). Wilhelm Reich had argued in *The Mass Psychology of Fascism* that the sexual inhibitions first embedded in the family were the basis of the authoritarian character structure, and both Herbert Marcuse and N. O. Brown (in *Eros and Civilization* and *Life against Death*) argued, similarly, that social oppression has its roots in sexual repression.

Perhaps inevitably, the discourses of strong, democratic individualism and sexual freedom that were essentially gender-neutral often produced a male-dominated rhetoric, in which society (totalitarianism, conformity) was associated with an emasculating femininity, and the rebel was always a man. Sexual potency and nonconformity were never far apart in this rhetoric. In prescribing a cure for the swelling tide of Mass Man, Lindner assured his readers, "where the right of protest is recognized, however, and no imperative to adjust is permitted to emasculate the culture, [the phenomenon of Mass Man] will not appear" (*Prescription* 291). Spillane's figure Mike Hammer was perhaps at one extreme in the spectrum of the male-dominated rhetoric of the cold warrior. His *One Lonely Night* begins with Hammer's boast that he has killed thirteen communists, turned them into soft putty, sharply contrasting the passivity of the pinko and the aggressive individualism of the free man.

Mailer's hipster figure weighs in on the heavy end of this spectrum. The central characteristic of the various groups which comprise the hipster figure is sexual wilfulness. As we shall see, the importance of sexuality had roots in Mailer's private insecurities, but sexuality had a more general political resonance on which Mailer was drawing. Here, too, the distance between Mailer's radicalism and the conservative liberal is difficult to maintain, because liberalism had been trying to shed its soft, feminine, naive, fellow-traveling image for over fifteen years and this effort at redefinition easily fell into the gender biases latent in the sexual connotations of popular language. As Lasch pointed out in *The Agony of the American Left*, the liberal everywhere tried to toughen up his image, and this invariably involved appropriating to himself the cold war virtues of action, toughness, aggression, qualities associated in the culture with the male sex. The complement to this is the attack on "momism" that one finds in Philip Wylie's *Generation of Vipers*, in far more measured tones in Erikson's *Childhood and Society*, and throughout the popular culture of films and magazines (as Michael Rogin has shown in "Kiss Me Deadly").

What Mailer likes about the psychological types making up his hipster is their virility, for the hipster is a kind of white man who regains his potency by marrying into the erotic "wealth" of the black. This is a "wedding of the white and the black" in which it is the black who brings the "cultural dowry." Femininity is a floating term, attached wherever the sexual opposition requiring it is called into play. The white, who benefits from this dowry, is therefore the male figure in this wedding. Even though the black man is the source of unrepressed sexuality and logically the male figure, Mailer is always intent upon aggrandizing the male territory for the white man. Superficially, none of these connotations has any sustained consistency, but what lies beneath them is a more systematic and conventional relation of white and black, in which the hipster turns out to be a white man in the Congo, expropriating its raw materials, so that he may develop the "sophistication of the wise primitive in a giant jungle" (317).

Mailer asserts that the hipster's "psychic style" derives from the "best Negroes," but in the course of his analysis the black man is largely drawn upon for his sensual expertise ("the art of the primitive," "the more obligatory pleasures of the body," as one who follows "the need of his body"), and is displaced by the "psychopath" who is the willful, mental, component of the hipster's character. Blacks return to Mailer's attention only as the source of a "sexual impetus" and are briefly mentioned but once in the interior of the essay in relation to "white girls" (324, 330). The implication that the black has only body to offer and no mind confirms rather than subverts the psychology of segregation that Mailer argued in his essay's first draft: "The comedy is that the white loathes the idea of the Negro attaining equality in the classroom because the white feels that the Negro already enjoys sensual superiority" (307). The real radicalism of the civil rights movement for blacks, as Ellison foresaw, lay in declaring their complex humanity, separate from the simplifications and stereotypes of the white man's folk symbolism; but Mailer continued to use the black man as a metaphor of the white man's unconscious and as an image of his unrepressed sexuality.

Mailer's personal motives for this appropriation, this symbolic segregation, aren't difficult to locate. At the time he sat down to write "The White Negro," he was the author of a best-selling first novel and of two subsequent novels—*Barbary Shore* (1951) and *The Deer Park* (1955)—which satisfied no one, least of all himself, that he was the great writer which *The Naked and the Dead* had promised he was. By the spring of 1957, Mailer began to wonder if he had irrevocably squandered his talent: "I thought I might be paying for the years I had twisted my nerves with benzedrine and seconal. At times it would come over me that I could not keep away from writing much longer, and I began to live with the conviction that I had burned out my talent" (*Advertisements* 307). Mailer could not have been encouraged by the assertion of Caroline Bird a few months earlier, in her article "The Unlost Generation," that Mailer and Capote and Styron, while they have "numerous admirers," have not had an "impact on young intellectuals . . . remotely comparable to that made on a previous generation by Fitzgerald" (174).

We know Mailer read Bird's piece because he begins "The White Negro" with an edited version of the article's subsection "The Hipster," which follows immediately upon the passage I have quoted above. Mailer uses Bird's unsympathetic description of the hipster as a model of conventional contempt, which his own more experienced and thoughtful analysis will show to be superficial, but at the same time Mailer appears to have taken his cue from the concluding paragraph of Bird's piece (which he does not cite): "There is a chance that while the young seem tame, uncommitted, they may be invisibly moving in a direction so radical that we cannot as yet conceive it" (175). Mailer's "white Negro" was an effort to attribute a radical direction to the "young" and, at the same time, to prove to himself and his audience that he was still a talented writer. At least this is the implication of the "Sixth Advertisement for Myself," which serves as a preface to "The White Negro."

Mailer felt he had lost the ability to get anyone's attention, and he sought to regain center stage through a kind of writing-as-rape, which in its method would exhibit the same unrepressed journey (his essay, he tells us, was a "trip into the psychic wild of 'the White Negro' ") which the essay encourages—to "remake a bit of his nervous system" (310, 320). This was a nervous system not only "wired" by the Super-Ego of Society, but considerably damaged, he suspected, by his own experimentation with drugs.

(This is a story he tells again in the opening pages of *Armies of the Night*).
That the writing of the essay is also a sexual act consummated upon the
reader is implicit throughout in Mailer's use of the black man as a model of
rebellion, hipness, and sexual prowess, but in his preface Mailer makes this
explicit by leading us to believe that the greatness of insight he achieved was
made possible only by a descent into erotic experience ("I will not try to
give even a hint of that time," he teases), not merely in Mexico during the
weeks prior to the writing of "The White Negro," but in the entire period
to which *Advertisements* is meant as a translucent confession ("startling in
its candor").

The implicit strategy of Mailer's life during this period, like his portrait of
the hipster, is essentially romantic. Sexual excess (his biographers disagree
about this), drug use (confirmed by Mills and Manso), and impulsive behavior are all a kind of religious retreat for Mailer, his Walden and Windemere,
through which he hoped to escape the restrictions of society embedded in
his consciousness, and by which he could rejuvenate his imagination—not
to mention the lapsed imagination of the radical left wing. Throughout the
"Sixth Advertisement" Mailer draws the conventional connection between
the inability to write and sexual impotence, and this fear of impotence
supplied a strong motive in the attraction which the black, the juvenile
delinquent, and the psychopath exercised upon him. In one of the curious pockets of this advertisement Mailer recounts Faulkner's contempt for
the brief explanation of southern resistance that was his first draft of "The
White Negro." "Like a latent image in the mirror of my ego was the other
character Faulkner must have seen: a noisy pushy middling ape who had
been tolerated too long by his literary betters" (310). Mailer clearly sees
himself as the "white Negro," a white man who looks in the mirror and
sees a "noisy pushy middling ape" and decides not to repress the "ape" but
to give him increased stature: "I had at last no choice but to begin the trip
into the psychic wild of 'The White Negro' " (310). The "middling ape"
becomes in this Jekyll/Hyde scenario the American black man, a potential
King Kong preparing to storm the citadels of white repression.

The point of this brief digression into the personal agenda informing
Mailer's essay is to indicate how perfectly matched Mailer's own feelings of
impotence were with the prevailing liberal-radical effort to regain from the
right wing the high ground of toughness. The essay's strategies, foci, and
preoccupations are thus at once private inventions and public expressions
of discourse that speak through Mailer, since his essay is an artifact whose
"meaning" relies upon (or can be found only within) other discourses of its
time. Less abstractly, we may say that "The White Negro" should be read
as issuing from the same cultural discourse that produced Nicholas Ray's

film *Rebel without a Cause*, Sondheim and Bernstein's *West Side Story*, and Robert Lindner's *Must You Conform?* as well as Paul Goodman's *Growing Up Absurd* and Lionel Trilling's *Freud and the Crisis of Our Culture*—to mention but a few examples.

In varying degrees and with varying volume all these writers felt threatened by the emasculating controls of adjustment and conformity exacted of its members by society. In the film *Rebel without a Cause*, James Dean and another boy race their cars toward the edge of a cliff that rises from the Pacific Ocean, each testing the other in a "chickie run" to see who will be the first to jump from the driver's seat of his speeding car. The audience knows that Dean has agreed to participate because he is trying to "be a man" and that his need to prove himself is the result of his father's flaccid masculinity—that his father has not told him or shown him how to be a man. This question—How to be a man?—is one that reaches deep into cold war culture, underlying the popularity and prevalence of adolescent heroes in fiction and film: the political anxieties of the "adult" were played out upon the lives of the young.

The suicidal race of the teenagers in Ray's film is a test intimately bound up with gender, since cowardice—being "chicken"—is also feminine (girl as "chick" or "chickie"). Within the context of this gender-tagged discourse, Mailer speaks with the voice of his culture: "if you lapse back into being a frightened stupid child, or if you flip, if you lose your control, reveal the buried weaker more feminine part of your nature, then it is more difficult to swing next time" ("The White Negro," 324). Mailer's effort to define the "hipster" is related to James Dean's effort to "be a man," and both are expressions of the liberal-conservative scramble to demonstrate a new toughness. One of the prevailing opinions of postwar culture was that it was the softness of the New Dealers—not to mention the communist fellow travelers—that had gotten us into our "chickie run" with the Soviet Union. The weak parents of James Dean and Natalie Wood are in part portraits of soft liberals whose passivity helped steer their children into that race toward death to which the superpowers seemed to have committed their societies.

Nowhere in Mailer's portrait of the hipster is there any room for the feminine. (See Joyce Johnson's *Minor Characters*, about the women who were part of the beat scene, but who are left out of or demeaned in accounts of that scene by its male figures.) To "swing" is to be a man, to find and keep energy ("how to find his energy and how not to lose it," or, later, "one has amassed enough energy to meet an exciting opportunity with all one's present talents for the flip" [322, 323]). This point is always to be on the way "toward making it" (324). This is the language of capital acquisition rather than socialist redistribution and equality, and the sexual connotations fall neatly into place. The "feminine part" within is a threat to the masculinity of the hipster, but the feminine without is the most valuable territory of all because, as the object of acquisition, women certify the manhood of the hipster.

Mailer's determination to define the hipster's search for love as "the search for an orgasm more apocalyptic than the one which preceded it" (321)—a search thus stripped of bourgeois associations with marriage or conventional mating—takes him further right than consensus liberalism itself, to an expression of bourgeois economic liberalism of the nineteenth century. For love as orgasm is love as property, a thoroughly material conception in which the male is an adventurer always "on the make." Thus "making it" in Mailer's vocabulary is an activity exerted upon another, as in having "made" a woman. At the same time, this idiom of economic liberalism or laissez-faire capitalism also includes the discourse of creativity, since "making it" implies not only acquisition but actual creation. One wants to feel, in the rags to riches psychology, that one has "earned money the old-fashioned way." One doesn't merely come into it, or qualify for it: one "makes" it. So there is a simultaneous discovery and bestowal, nowhere more pointed than in a man's "making" a woman by possessing her; similarly, a woman "has" or "keeps" a man if her money has "made" him. There is hardly anything radical in the idea that one liberates the self by enslaving another. Mailer's radical hipster seems to require the repression of the "feminine part" in order to achieve the liberated psychology of the white Negro.

Thus all too clearly are the value-laden terms "nature," "wilderness," "creativity," and "liberation" brought into the service of man as frontier capitalist. It is a curious fact of this time that the effort to "imagine non-conformity"—to establish a truly critical point of view—so often was eroded by or unintentionally transformed into conservative, even reactionary viewpoints. Lionel Trilling was at least aware of the tightrope he was walking:

> Now Freud may be right or he may be wrong in the place he gives to biology in human fate, but I think we must stop to consider whether this emphasis upon biology, whether correct or incorrect, is not so far from being a reactionary idea that it is actually a liberating idea. It proposes to us that culture is not all-powerful. It suggests that there is a residue of human quality beyond the reach of cultural control, and that this residue of human quality, elemental as it may be, serves to bring culture itself under criticism and keeps it from being absolute. (*Freud* 48)

Mailer and other writers were less sensitive to the ways in which they might be speaking the unspoken assumptions on which consensus rested. Robert Lindner, for example, puts Trilling's point without any of its evasions: "Man is a rebel. He is committed by his biology *not* to conform, and herein lies the paramount reason for the awful tension he experiences today in relation to Society" (*Must You Conform?* 176). The response to conformity, in other words, tended all too often merely to underline the rhetoric of Wild West individualism that coincided nicely with American exploitation of the globe's resources, and touted a new masculinity that confirmed the prevalent repression of the feminine, which in political terms meant the weak: minorities, women, and young people.

Nothing is more indicative of how consensus psychology operated than the way these proponents of alienation, nonconformity, freedom, and rebellion consistently pulled back from the radical implications of their exhortations. After hundreds of pages in which he argues that totalitarianism will surely follow from the repression of the individual, the best that Fromm can propound as a cure is "positive freedom" and state planning. Robert Lindner is the classic consensus voice in this regard. He made a career out of attacking conformity and adjustment, but his description of the nonconformist was certainly reassuring to his middle-class audience: "The productive way toward non-conformity is the way of positive rebellion, of protest that at once affirms the rebellious nature of man *and* the fundamental human values. These values reside in the common treasury of humanity. They form the basic aspirations of all humans everywhere and are expressed most clearly in the great documents and contracts—such as our Bill of Rights—which men see fit to declare from time to time." Lindner concludes, "*Rebellion and protest in their name, and conducted in a fashion which does not in any way violate their spirit, is positive rebellion, authentic rebellion*" (177–78). Employing metaphors of economic liberalism ("the productive way," "the common treasury," "contracts"), Lindner appeared to have supplied the question "must you conform?" with a positive answer. Perhaps Arthur Schlesinger, Jr.'s, *Vital Center* is the *reductio* of this centrist double-talk: "The spirit of the new radicalism is the spirit of the center—the spirit of human decency, opposing the extremes of tyranny. Yet, in a more fundamental sense, does not the center itself represent one extreme?" (256).

In the course of Mailer's meditation upon "the white Negro," the figure of the hipster undergoes a similar transformation from one who might legitimately represent a threat to society to one whose antisocial behavior has liberal, socially responsible effects surprisingly in harmony with the assumptions and biases of consensus discourse. Despite every effort to the contrary, Mailer's concept of the hipster is finally a method through which full humanity may be achieved in a rational society. For example, though he identified the hipster as a mystic, loyal to the "very intensity of his private vision," he very quickly converted that loyalty to the "enormous present" into prudence and delayed gratification: "having converted his unconscious experience into much conscious knowledge, the hipster has shifted the focus of his desire from immediate gratification toward that wider passion for future power which is the mark of civilized man" (316, 317). The hipster is interested only in opening "the limits of the possible, for oneself, for oneself alone"—one can almost feel Mailer's radical delight in harping on the selfishness of the hipster—yet, "in widening the arena of the possible, one widens it reciprocally for others as well" (327). This is the radical turned liberal, the man whose search for method joins the romantic with the laissez-faire economist; for method is the point at which the imperatives of the self, in its intercourse with Nature, become relevant to and prescriptive for the body politic. Mailer's emphasis upon "reciprocity" is the liberal extension of that sublimation: "the hipster may come to see that his condition is no more than an exaggeration of the human condition, and if he would be free, then everyone must be free" (329). This is the familiar pattern of the liberal reconstruction during the postwar era: from spontaneity to social responsibility, from private desire to "human co-operation" (*Advertisements* 328).

Mailer's hipster, following the reasoning of imperialist liberal economics, is an entrepreneur of emotions in an economy of scarcity: "unstated but obvious is the social sense that there is not nearly enough sweet for everyone," and therefore "life is a contest between people in which the victor generally recuperates quickly and the loser takes long to mend, a perpetual competition of colliding explorers" (323). In C. Wright Mills's essay "The Competitive Personality," he notes how central the idea of competition is to liberal politics: "For liberals, competition has never been merely an impersonal mechanism regulating the economy of capitalism. It has been a guarantee of political freedom, a system for producing free individuals, and a testing field for heroes. These have been the alibis of the liberals for the hurt that competition has caused people ground between the big sharp edges of its workings" (*People* 263).

There is some contradiction in Mailer's apparent accession to, if not glory in, the idea of life as a "contest," since he is speaking here of "sweet" as sexual pleasure, presumably in short supply only because of the repressive society which the hipster may help overthrow. Mailer seems to have forgotten that his contemporary "affluent society"—in the assumptions of his argument—is the cause of a sexuality of scarcity, and the reason seems to be that Mailer is quite comfortable with the consensus answer to scarcity:

one fights for the sweet. The hipster is a capitalist, a frontiersman who thinks he can win a sufficient number of battles, a man who would not be a man or know what being a man meant unless life were a contest for limited sexual pleasures.

"The White Negro" ends in a vision of revolutionary apocalypse: "with this possible emergence of the Negro, Hip may erupt as a psychically armed rebellion whose sexual impetus may rebound against the antisexual foundation of every organized power in America." This rebellion will force the naive liberal to admit that "the amount of collective violence buried in the people is perhaps incapable of being contained, and therefore if one wants a better world one does well to hold one's breath, for a worse world is bound to come first" (329, 330). Of course this is not a rebellion of an underprivileged or alienated class, but a rebellion of alienated instincts and creative impulses, so that the scenario Mailer paints is one in which Freud's great allegory of Instinct locked in battle with Civilization is given a political reading, and one in which we would be better off to let instinct have its way against the reality principle. Here man's natural being, though far from inherently good, is liberated against the naive controls of "good liberal reason" (330).

In some respects the rise of the "New Left" in the late fifties and early sixties seemed to bear out Mailer's rejection of classes in favor of instincts and impulses that, as Reich had argued twenty-five years earlier, cut across class distinctions. The New Left, it might be argued, did achieve some unity around issues such as civil rights, capital punishment, free speech, and the Vietnam War which were often conceived in ways that appealed to diverse groups across the entire spectrum of American society. At the same time Mailer's thinking was unable to separate itself from the characteristic reflexes and assumptions of consensus liberalism in the cold war era, of which the conversion of class struggle into mental anxiety, of segregation into schizophrenia and romantic oppositions of black and white, unconscious and consciousness were central features. Especially in the way Mailer's promising metaphor of the "white Negro"—of a "wedding of white and black"—comes to represent not the integration of actual people in actual neighborhoods and classrooms but the psychological wholeness and bellicose virtues of the hipster do we see the latent dangers of his approach. Not very far beneath the surface of the essay's radical exhortations and predictions are the reactionary aspects of consensus thought.

8

Ahab at the Pepsi Stand

Existentialism and Mass Culture in Barth's
The End of the Road

> Thus I am brought to that paradox which is the perilous reef of all liberal
> politics and which Rousseau has defined in a single word: I must "force"
> the Other to be free.
>
> Jean-Paul Sartre, Being and Nothingness, 1943

> There is no reasonable doubt that existentialism will soon become the
> predominant philosophical current among bourgeois intellectuals.
>
> Georg Lukács, "Existentialism," 1947

In much fiction published during the mid-fifties, the dynamics of liberalism and its characteristic discourses became less urgent or prominent, as
political frameworks dissolved in the cultural categories of "mass society," "conformity," and the "existential" self alienated within that society.
Although the thematic attention to political ideas and activity that can be
found in Trilling's *In the Middle of the Journey*, Ellison's *Invisible Man*,
or Mailer's *Barbary Shore* was less and less common, the relationship between art and politics was translated into subjects, characters, and plots
which lack their full cultural resonance unless they are relocated within the
aesthetic politics generated in the postwar period.

John Barth's first two novels, *The Floating Opera* (1956) and *The End
of the Road* (1958), are good examples of the need for this translation,
not only because in them the political is entirely obscured by philosophical
discourse, but also because they were transitional works for Barth, written
when he was still unsure what direction his writing would take. In the foreward to a recent combined edition, *The Floating Opera and The End of the
Road*, Barth remembers trying to discover his "essential subject matter":
"Is your muse the lady with the grin or the one with the grimace? Are you

a realist or a fantast? Ought you to make art for its own sake or engage it in the service of some lofty cause? Are you more interested in the thing said than in its saying (the Windex approach to language) or vice-versa (the stained-glass approach)?" (v).

This very way of framing his options in pairs of mutually exclusive terms was a typical structure of literary thought in the postwar period, but those terms weren't entirely unmixed in Barth's early work, which may be read as a record of his struggle to sort them. By the mid-sixties, having published *The Sot-Weed Factor* and in the midst of writing *Giles Goat-Boy*, Barth had clearly opted for the "stained-glass approach" to fiction. "I didn't think after *The End of the Road*," he told John Enck, "that I was interested in writing any more realistic fiction—the fiction that deals with Characters From Our Time, who speak real dialogue" (11). In fact, since the publication of the experimental stories in *Lost in the Funhouse* (1968) and *Chimera* (1972), critics have tended to read Barth's first novels entirely outside of or disentangled from their social and historical moment, and find in them the origins of his later "metafiction" and postmodern experimentation. Such origins may be found there, but they are, I think, of a different character than is commonly argued.

An entirely different sense emerges if we read *The End of the Road* not as the beginning of a writer's career, but as a dramatic expression of an evolving literary discourse, in which the logic underlying the divorce of art and politics is tested, as it were, within the allegorical relations of three "Characters from Our Time." Though he told Enck that he wasn't "very responsible in the Social Problems way" (13), Barth's second novel suggests either that he hadn't been so sure or that the irrelevance of social problems to art was a proposition he had to prove for himself.

The End of the Road is the story—an autobiographical confession—Jacob Horner tells of his psychophysical paralysis, the efforts of an uncertified black doctor to cure him, his ménage à trois with Rennie and Joe Morgan, and the death of Rennie Morgan during an attempted abortion by Horner's doctor. Much of the dialogue in the book sets forth Joe Morgan's "non-mystical value-thinking"—his belief that one may be committed to particular values even though they have no absolute or transcendent origin, so long as one holds to them rationally, consistently, and seriously. Joe's wife, Rennie, has tried to adopt her husband's views and habits of rational thought and to participate with him in creating a utopian marriage, but Jake Horner, as his name suggests, plays devil's advocate and succeeds in exposing the weaknesses of her husband's convictions. Hence the adultery, the uncertain paternity, and the botched abortion which follow.

A number of steering mechanisms encourage readers to interpret this plot within the philosophical terms provided by the dialogue between Horner and Morgan, as though it were primarily a narrative about the inherent shortcomings of representation. Perhaps the most powerful of these is the novel's first-person narration: the ahistorical emphasis of the narrative is largely a rhetorical effect of the narrator's self-defense and an evasion of responsibility for his unethical behavior (having sex with Rennie). Throughout the novel, Horner argues for a "special kind of integrity"—a kind of loyalty to his "plurality of selves" (136)—and his "inability to play the same role long enough" to accept responsibility for the actions any one of them might commit (176). Not only does the novel's autobiographical confessor deflect the reader's inquiry in self-serving ways, Barth himself has consistently described the novel ahistorically, as the second half of a philosophical farce which carries "all non-mystical value-thinking to the end of the road" (Bluestone 586). Barth thinks his own interests to be primarily metaphysical rather than historical: "My argument is with the facts of life, not the conditions of it" (Enck 13). David Morrell, author of the single critical biography on Barth, calls *The End of the Road* Barth's only "novel of ideas" (16).

David Kerner, one of the first to review *The End of the Road*, was a bit closer to the mark when he described the book as a "novel of ideology," for this designation implies the historicity of its contents—that its trio of characters is a framing of "ideas" peculiar to the postwar period, and not a parable for all time. "The area Barth is working in," Kerner wrote, "was described by Lionel Trilling ten years ago" (59–60). In the essay "Art and Fortune" that Kerner cites, Trilling wrote:

> Nowadays everyone is involved in ideas—or, to be more accurate, in ideology. . . . Social class and the conflicts it produces may not be any longer a compelling subject to the novelist, but the organization of society into ideological groups presents a subject scarcely less absorbing. Ideological society has, it seems to me, nearly as full a range of passion and nearly as complex a system of manners as a society based on social class. Its promise of comedy and tragedy is enormous. (*Liberal* 274–75)

Though the rest of his review focuses upon the ideas in the novel, Kerner's use of Trilling's essay to describe the kind of book Barth wrote does begin to identify the literary discourse from which it emerged.

For the most part, subsequent criticism ignored that discursive context and has followed the leads suggested by Barth and his narrator, Jake Horner. As a result, most commentary on the novel has focused upon those passages in which Horner reflects upon the inherent—inevitable—violence that language (and its users) must inflict upon the world in order to live within it. Perhaps the most commonly cited of them is this representative rumination: "To turn experience into speech—that is, to classify, to categorize, to conceptualize, to grammarize, to syntactify it—is always a betrayal of experience, a falsification of it; but only so betrayed can it be dealt with at all" (112).

Certainly these ruminations within the novel have a pointed relevance to its author, but that potential allegory remains out of focus; instead, the book seems caught in a troubling oscillation between a dramatic critique of Horner and an admission that what he says is inescapably true. Thus many readers have felt an uneasiness not only with Horner but also with the novel's conceptual integrity. On the one hand Jake Horner is clearly designed to be the agent of Joe Morgan's destruction, and his nihilism is supposed to show the inadequacy of Joe's rationalism—his "non-mystical value-thinking." On the other, Horner is also a Little Jack Horner, who, finding himself in a corner, concocts an intricate philosophical defense of his behavior, so that the entire novel, or narrative confession, is nothing more than an extended rationalization: what a good boy am I (see Enck, "John Barth," 12).

Both Campbell Tatham and Tony Tanner, for example, not only reject the ethical consequences of Horner's conclusions, but also question Barth's attitude toward them. As Tanner notes, "it is of some importance whether we take that mind to be only Horner's—or Barth's as well. Not because one is interested in knowing whether there is anything autobiographical in the book, but because it influences our assessment of Barth's own attitude to that ambiguous license enjoyed by a mind for which words are no longer answerable to things" (Tanner 240; see Harris 44–49). In part, the conclusion to the novel seems to urge this ethical reaction, because the graphic description of Rennie's death stays with the reader as a dramatic rebuke to the inhuman theorizing of the two men who compel her divided loyalty. But this rebuke predicates the existence within the novel of something with constant value—animal life, vitality—and reinstates the necessity for conventions of social behavior to protect that value.

The narrative ends up implying the need for active intervention, for material changes in human law: for the right of black people to practice medicine or a woman's right to an abortion, either of which would have saved Rennie's life. Though written in the fall of 1955 (and not published until 1958), the novel is set in the three years prior to the court ruling against segregation in the schools, and of course well before dramatic advances in contraception technology, the legalization of abortion and widespread public acceptance of it. This is to say that the legal foundations upon which the plot depends might be read as insisting that the values inscribed within social conventions are not mystical; indeed, for a book whose subject is the arbitrariness of convention—underlying all social formations, including personal identity, language, and communicability—the inescapably social nature of the sign is curiously frustrated. The novel refuses the option of either Jake's nihilism or Joe's ideology: even though Rennie's death could have been averted by a reform of law and social convention about abortion, the impulse to make these changes is undermined by the Joe Morgan figure—who shows the violent consequences of applying ideas to behavior and that reason is a poor tool to use in tinkering with it—while contentment with the status quo is made impossible by Horner's pointed reminders that conventions are arbitrary. He weakens their claims by exposing them as conventions.

We may further isolate the self-contradiction of this book by noting that *The End of the Road* seems unable to extricate itself from Horner's point of view. Despite the fact that Horner is entirely discredited, his theorizing remains the aesthetic foundation of Barth's novel, and in fact many of Horner's assertions about language and reality, that must be read dramatically, appear in Barth's interviews as straight assessments of the artist's problems and compromises. Thus, for example, Horner's assertion that turning experience into speech is "always a betrayal" is often repeated by Barth, though stripped of the social significance it carries in his early novel. In 1968 Barth said that one way to come to terms with the difference between art and life "is to define fiction as a kind of true representation of the distortion we all make of life . . . a representation of a representation" (Prince 54); though Barth is here attempting to establish the autonomy of the artistic realm, his aesthetic doesn't successfully distinguish art from life, but instead finds its permission or license within an analogy to social relations that his artistic practice cannot escape.

By the mid to late sixties when he gave this and other interviews, Barth seemed more at ease with his finesse of social reality by art, but it was a stratagem that originated in *The End of the Road*, where the distinction between art and life is impossible to draw. His cheerful remarks to Alan Prince repeat almost word for word the pragmatic advice given by the black doctor in the novel written thirteen years earlier: "in this sense" he says, explaining the practice of "Mythotherapy" to Horner, "fiction isn't a lie at all, but a true representation of the distortion that everyone makes of life" (83). Once we accept this fact, Barth said in 1964, we can enjoy the tricks of art as "good clean fun" (Enck 6). *The End of the Road*, however, runs this reasoning in the other direction, through the glib remarks of Horner and their disastrous results: "Assigning names to things is like assigning roles to people: it is necessarily a distortion, but it is a necessary distortion if one would get on with the plot, and to the connoisseur it's good clean fun" (135).

This line of argument, which establishes representation as the transcendent cause of the social conflicts in the novel, not only reinforces the narrator's rationalizations for his part in a grisly death, but also conforms to the conservative modernism of literary culture in the fifties. The novel's concerns with representation and convention are variants on the pervasive hostility to ideology and to ideas of order generally, expressed earlier, for example, in the admonition with which Invisible Man ends his own narrative confession. In Barth's novel, however, the authority for ambiguity and irony is attributed to Sartrean thought—to the language of existential identity and "ultimacy"—rather than to the experience of political duplicity or Christian realism. Even so, the estimation of human nature held in common by both perspectives becomes a given within Barth's nihilistic farces, and his interest in satirizing "non-mystical value-thinking" is a transformation of postwar liberal discourses which opposed high art and sensibility to mass culture, and modernism to totalitarianism, whether Stalinist or domestic. These political and social discourses of the novel emerge quite strikingly from the "claptrap"—as Marx characterized bourgeois thought—of representation once we recognize "Joe Morgan" as a stock figure in postwar liberalism's morality play: the Naive Radical, the Old Liberal or Well-Intentioned Ideologue.

The chronological starting point, however, of the novel's plot is a scene which directs our attention to the "facts of life, not the conditions of it." As a result, the novel requires the reader to develop the social discourse of the narrative as the negative image with which it is in covert dialogue. Jake Horner suffers from something he calls "cosmopsis"—"the cosmic view." With his eyes "gazing on eternity, fixed on ultimacy," he is unable to carry on the day-to-day activities of social life. During attacks of cosmopsis Horner is paralyzed by the absence of any reason to act. Describing the onset of the disease, Horner tells his reader: "I simply ran out of motives, as a car runs out of gas." During these periods of immobility, Horner experiences a near-empty consciousness, filled only "by that test pattern of my consciousness, *Pepsi-Cola hits the spot*, intoned with silent oracularity" (69).

This mental event is described four times in the novel, the first occurring after Jake has accepted a dinner invitation from Rennie and Joe Morgan:

> I went back to my rocker and rocked for another forty-five minutes. From time to time I smiled inscrutably, but I cannot say that this honestly reflected

any sincere feeling on my part. It was just a thing I found myself doing, as frequently when walking alone I would find myself repeating over and over in a judicious, unmetrical voice, *Pepsi-Cola hits the spot; twelve full ounces: that's a lot*—accompanying the movement of my lips with a wrinkled brow, distracted twitches of the corner of my mouth, and an occasional quick gesture of my right hand. Passersby often took me for a man lost in serious problems, and sometimes when I looked behind me after passing one I'd see him, too, make a furtive movement with his right hand, trying it out. (36)

Almost any reader with a smattering of literary-intellectual history will spot a multitude of textual voices in this passage, from advertising, popular idiom, philosophy, and literature; but the kind of conclusions we may draw from them depends upon whether we read them as allusions that reinforce the steering mechanisms of authorial intention or as voices whose very presence signifies the historical specificity of the passage.

Asked to scrutinize the above lines in this way, Americanist readers might well observe in the words "inscrutably" and "wrinkled brow" a mediated reference to *Moby-Dick*, for these terms figure prominently and conjointly in Melville's novel, repeatedly attached not only to Ahab and Moby-Dick, but to the world and its representation as well.[1] There is some warrant for imagining that Barth wove this echo into his text with some intention, because he remembers wondering if he would "sing white whales or scarlet letters" (v); but to do so confines the reader within the ahistorical inertia of the narrative voice, because the Melvillean resonance easily coincides with the novel's existential discourse—just as it does in the above passage.

The centrality of existentialist discourse may be observed in the passage quoted above, especially in the sentence "I cannot say that this honestly reflected any sincere feeling on my part." [2] Though composed from everyday idiom, this sentence will be suspected by many readers as a formulation

1. In "The Chart," for example, we read, "While thus employed, the heavy pewter lamp suspended in chains over his head, continually rocked with the motion of the ship, and for ever threw gleams and shadows of lines upon his wrinkled brow, till it almost seemed that while he himself was marking out lines and courses on the wrinkled charts, some invisible pencil was also tracing lines and courses upon the deeply marked chart of his forehead." Moby-Dick, too, is "distinguished" by a "peculiar snow-white wrinkled forehead" in which Ahab sees an "inscrutable malice." It is that "inscrutable thing" Ahab hates, but he himself is branded "that inscrutable Ahab," and the rocking motion imparted to the lamp above his head is "borrowed from the sea; by the sea, from the inscrutable tides of God."

For the significance of Melville during the cold war, see Geraldine Murphy, "The Politics of Reading *Billy Budd*," and Donald E. Pease, "*Moby Dick* and the Cold War."

2. The only essay I know of which explores the philosophical positions of the novel with any adequacy is Jacquelyn Kegley's "*The End of the Road*: The Death of Individualism."

generated by Sartre's existentialist writings, and they will be rewarded later when Horner's black therapist orders him to read Sartre, and snorts at the idea of sincerity: "If you sometimes have the feeling that your mask is *insincere*—impossible word!—it's only because one of your masks is incompatible with another" (85). The discourse of "sincerity" is borrowed directly from Sartre's writings, in which the impossibility of sincerity follows logically from his conception of the "pre-reflective cogito," set forth in "The Transcendence of the Ego" (1936–37) and *Being and Nothingness* (1943). The black doctor's expostulation neatly reproduces the conflict in Sartre's thought between the structure of consciousness and the idea of sincerity: "the original structure of 'not being what one is' renders impossible in advance all movement toward being in itself or 'being what one is.' . . . How then can we blame another for not being sincere or rejoice in our own sincerity since this sincerity appears to us at the same time to be impossible?" This is also, for Sartre, the source of "ethical anguish"—for the self founded in the freedom of nothingness can never have any foundation which doesn't at once call into question both itself and any values the self might seek to establish upon it (*Being* 62, 37–39).

Horner enacts, to a farcical extreme, the dialectical contradictions of Sartre's thought. We should note, for example, that Horner, by admitting the absence of sincere feeling, implicitly claims the virtue of candor—of being sincere. With a special kind of existential integrity, Horner loyally adheres to the processes and conditions of consciousness, as he does in the opening words of his confession: "In a sense, I am Jacob Horner." Faithfully Sartrean, the statement of identity presupposes an "I" prior to and other than the one predicated. The very act of self-identification objectifies the self (the "I" or "transcendental ego") as distinct from consciousness. No degree of exactitude or phraseological qualification ("in a sense") can ever succeed in closing this gap between the "I" and the consciousness of the "I." The empty consciousness constantly recedes, back-peddling from the objects of its attention, from every effort to fill itself or become. The "self," Sartre asserts in *The Transcendence of the Ego*, is "sheer performance" (94).

The echoes of *Moby-Dick* are tightly woven into this Sartreanism, for Barth has translated the contrast between Ahab's assumptions of "depth" and "cause" (Ahab's maniacal determination to "strike through the mask") and Ishmael's persistent reminder that "surface" only gives way to more surface into the contemporary idiom of existential psychoanalysis, which repudiates the priority of essence. In Barth's scene, the popular idioms of the passage ("a thing I found myself doing" and "when walking alone I would find myself repeating") reproduce the conflict between Ahab's obsession and Ishmael's mild-mannered nihilism, for the popular idiom is at once the speech pattern of the everyday (Cartesian) assumption that consciousness is a reflective interiority (as the passerby here assumes) and Sartre's refutation of that concept. This internal dissonance reinforces the oscillation in the passage between references to an Ahab figure ("inscrutable" with "wrinkled brow") and an Ishmael figure (who comes upon Ahab, "finds himself") who survives to tell the story, the alienated outcast who begins his confession as Ishmael does through an act of self-naming ("In a sense, I am Jacob Horner"). Melville's two characters are here reproduced in postwar America as the schizophrenic dialectic of Horner's Sartrean consciousness.

All of this is part of the same existential monologue one can find metastasized throughout the period's semiotic tissues. In part to offer the reason for this spreading influence, Lukács noted that *Being and Nothingness* appeared in 1943, "when liberation from fascism was already in sight and when, just because of the decade-long rule of fascism, the longing for freedom was the deepest feeling of the intellectuals of all Europe." In this context, Sartre's existentialism "kept its popularity" because it gave "the notion of freedom a central place in its philosophy" (258–59; for Sartre's reply, *Search* 21f.).

In Sartre's concept, human freedom—though predicated upon a transcendent structure of consciousness—was also inevitably a form of aggression against the Other; and within *The End of the Road*, its dialectical difficulties help to reinforce Horner's rationalizations—his excuse for his role in Rennie's death and the destruction of her marriage with Joe Morgan. The circular binary that ties being and nothingness, interiority and surface together in a hamster wheel of futility continues to proliferate with self-confirming naturalness in the major dramatic opposition of the novel. Contrary to the exhausted Horner, who has a "vacuum" for a self (80), Joe is "terribly energetic" (14) and self-consistent. Rennie contrasts the two men: "You're not *real* like Joe is! He's the same man today he was yesterday, all the way through. He's genuine!" (64). The ghosts of Sartrean and Melvillean speculation lurk in these characterizations: in the enforced, rational adherence to his chosen values, Joe embodies Sartre's "*spirit of seriousness*" (*Being* 626) and is a caricature of "being-in-itself." Though "nothing is ultimately defensible," Joe tells Jake, "a man can act coherently; he can act in ways that he can explain, if he wants to" (43). The impossibility of sincerity is presented as the canker of this ingenuous position—that "nothingness" which "lies coiled in the heart of being" (21)—and the source of all the violence and destruction within the novel. Horner is the agent of that destruction because his identity is pure process, indifferent to the "bad faith" of the accumulated self: the inescapable nothingness or freedom of the for-itself erodes the stability of the Morgan marriage— not Jake Horner.

This marriage, moreover, is given a utopian resonance which eventually reminds us of Gulliver's journey to the land of the Houyhnhnms. The marriage of Rennie and Joe Morgan is a kind of Brook Farm experiment in husband-wife, male-female relations. "We'd stay together as long as each of us could respect everything about the other," Rennie tells Jake. Because Joe's idea of a marriage requires "the parties involved be able to take each other seriously," he likes Jake's needling Rennie: "in spite of your making fun of Rennie you seem willing to take her seriously. Almost no man is willing to take any woman's thinking seriously" (56, 42, 41). Joe's consistency, his sureness and lack of indecision, his rationality and absence of "craft or guile," (30) and the pervasive equine imagery of the novel are enough to suggest that the Morgan world may be an echo of Swift's Houyhnhnms, but the plausibility of that suggestion increases when we discover that a "Morgan" designates a specifically American breed of light horses, progeny of one prepotent Vermont stallion. As is true for the Houyhnhnms, the land of the Morgans is one in which all behavior is governed (or tries to be) by placid and self-assured reason. If in Swift's tale "houyhnhnm" means "perfection of nature," then in this one "Morgan"—meaning "horse"— subsumes within it all the smug confidence with which Swift's horses beg the question of their own reasoning's foundations and banish from existence all they do not understand as "the thing that was not," making its thought or representation impossible.

References to horses saturate the novel, not only because Rennie is an accomplished horsewoman, but because Joe consistently distinguishes between "horseshit" or "nonsense" on the one hand, and rational (horse) "sense" on the other.[3] Like horses, both Rennie and Jake have the habit of "whipping" their heads from side to side, and "Rennie" sounds a bit like "whinny." Additionally, the text underscores the Swiftean parallels by pointing to itself in ways that expose the fiction as a mask: "Whoa, now!" Jake says to Rennie; listening to Joe, Jake "gave the horse his head"; and driving to the abortion, Rennie speaks "hoarsely" (see David, and

3. Two essays have been written about the "horse" motif: the first by Jack David, "The Trojan Horse at the End of the Road," notes the presence of horse imagery that culminates in the reference, through Jake's statue of Laocoön, to the Trojan horse; the second, Robert V. Hoskins' "Swift, Dickens, and the Horses in *The End of the Road*," traces the sources of the horse imagery and is far more interpretive, suggesting, for example, that Gradgrind's insistence upon "facts" is "essentially what Jake Horner's Doctor offers as 'Informational Therapy' " (26). Hoskins does not notice that the conversation between Sissy Jupe and Gradgrind is reproduced in the debate between Blakesley and Jacob Horner. See below, 179–82.

Hoskins). The complex referentiality of the word "horse" achieves an admirable coherence in the novel's final example, when Horner compares man's reason to the Trojan horse by invoking the story of Laocoön: "It was no use: I could not remain simple-minded long enough to lay blame—on the Doctor, myself, or anyone. . . . [My] limbs were bound like Laocoön's— by the twin serpents of Knowledge and Imagination, which, grown great in the fullness of time, no longer tempt but annihilate" (187).

All of the above references can be aligned with the novel's unacknowledged quotation of Wittgenstein's *Tractatus Logico-Philosophicus*: "The world is all that is the case" (1.0). Horner's doctor uses this proposition as a pragmatic reminder to Horner (76), but it is part of a theory of language that excludes values and ethics from language: "It is clear that ethics cannot be put into words" (6.421); "The sense of the world must lie outside the world. In the world everything is as it is, and everything happens as it does happen; *in* it no value exists—and if it did exist, it would have no value" (6.41). This complex set of texts—those of Melville, Sartre, Swift, and Wittgenstein—may thus be subordinated within Barth's determination to bring "all non-mystical value thinking to the end of the road": Jake is set "loose" on Joe Morgan in order to show the unworkability of a value system based upon arbitrary acts of reason, and the narrative is constructed to show that experience—what happens—is too multiform and overwhelming to be apprehended or controlled by either reason or representation. Sartre's rationalism undoes itself in the struggle between Jake and Joe, and the body of the text, Rennie, is the morbid result.

As compelling as such a reading may be, this analysis is a form of paraphrase that obligingly follows in the tracks of the novel's evasive narrator and produces the ahistoricism typical of the novel and of cold war fiction generally. This was noted of fifties fiction by Irving Howe in different terms, when, at the end of the decade, he described recent output as "moral" but not "social" (*World* 93). Recall that John Higham described "The Cult of the 'American Consensus' " in postwar reappraisals of American history, as "a massive grading operation to smooth over America's social convulsions" (94). More recently, Carolyn Porter and Russell Reising have summarized the literary criticism of the period as being similarly indifferent to the historical or social constitution of the imagination.

Melville, Sartre, Swift, and Wittgenstein help establish the coherence of the novel, but from another perspective they stand exposed as elements within other discourses that constitute Barth's novel less coherently and which help isolate the dissonance within an art conceived as "good clean fun." The works of these writers are part of the characteristic complex of preoccupations and narratives produced by postwar literary-liberal culture: the book isn't about those subjects, but those subjects are sedimented within the rhetoric of the fiction, are mediating and tuning the novel at every point.

For example, we noted earlier that the name "Morgan" alludes to book 4 of *Gulliver's Travels*, but it was the mediating nudge of contemporary social history which made Swift's satire so appropriate to the story Barth set out to tell. Once we begin to historicize this reference, we see it as generated by the social and political discourses of the fifties, in which the "goodness" of human nature and the likelihood of social rationality were reappraised. Within that narrative, Swift's satiric portrait of human irrationality served to confirm and reinforce contemporary assessments of recent history and politics. This is part of a social text that includes the discourses of totalitarianism, the anxiety of freedom, rebellion and conformity, mass society, irrational man, and other tropes familiar to students of cold war culture. The discourses of the "new" or "tough-minded realism" that arose in response and which one finds informing foreign policy as well as theology and literary criticism are a fifties Toryism in which the Augustan reminders of human limitation gain renewed force.

Once we see Barth's intention mediated by this new conservatism, our understanding of the novel's major characters is transformed. We give new emphasis to the specifically American character of the "Morgan" as a Vermont horse, and Joe appears now clearly as a vestigial offspring of Emersonian self-reliance. That Joe has degrees in literature, philosophy, and history, and is writing a dissertation on "the saving roles of innocence and energy in American political and economic history" (61), marks him as a utopian humanist, the upbeat American version of the European Enlightenment and typical target of cold war admonitions from Schlesinger, Hartz, Vann Woodward, Niebuhr, and Kennan. Finally, within the anti-ideology discourse of the fifties, Morgan emerges as the scapegoat of contemporary politics, a figure of naive radicalism and liberal reason, attacked from the right and the "vital center" alike. Jacob Horner, on the other hand, now reappears as the Europeanization of American literature, a figure of weary sophistication and neurasthenia, introduced into Morgan's "ingenuous" (the word is Horner's) realm, much as Humbert Humbert takes a room in the American home of Dolores Haze. This reconceptualizing of what the two men represent coincides with the privileging of European "experience" over American "innocence" so typical of "new liberal" and "realist" rhetoric in the postwar. In Barth's novel that rhetorical opposition is reproduced in the contrast between Jake and Joe, and subsumed (as narrative) beneath the mask of Satire, rewritten in contemporary existential idiom as the smirk of nothingness.

This quite different perspective brings other elements of the novel into sharp relief. In the passage with which we began, for example, we find sandwiched between the two Ahab markers—between "inscrutable" and "wrinkled brow"—and their modernist (belletristic) twist the idiom of commerce itself, the allegorical specter of Mass Culture at its most seductive (which is to say, at its least expensive) that fills Horner's empty consciousness: "*Pepsi-Cola hits the spot; twelve full ounces: that's a lot.*"

The Pepsi jingle was one of the very first commercials to operate on the principle of repetition or "product recognition" so familiar to us now. In *No Time Lost*, former president of Pepsi-Cola Walter Mack tells the story of the moment when two unknown free-lance writers approached him with lyrics they had set to the melody of "John Peel," a traditional English hunting song:

> Pepsi-Cola hits the spot,
> Twelve full ounces, that's a lot,
> Twice as much for a nickel, too,
> Pepsi-Cola is the drink for you.

According to Mack, he bought the song for two thousand dollars, but none of the national radio stations would sell him time for the jingle because "nobody at any of the big networks would consider anything less than five minutes. . . . Even my own advertising agency argued against it, maintaining the public wouldn't pay any attention to a little ditty unsupported by hard sell" (134–36). Mack then turned to small radio stations in New Jersey, and the success of this new technique was quickly established.

In *The Cola Wars*, J. C. Louis and Harvey Z. Yazijian confirm Mack's account that Pepsi's fifteen-second jingle, without accompanying pitch, was the first of its kind. They point out that the advertising novelty was "phenomenally successful" and came to be called "the most famous oral trademark of all time." This commercial, they conclude,

> was played an estimated six million times. In 1941 alone, the ad was broadcast in one form or another over 469 radio stations in all variations and tempos and for all occasions from concerts and theatre to the World Series. By popular demand, copies were sent to the owners of fifty thousand juke boxes. A survey conducted in 1942 revealed that the jingle was the best-known tune in America. (68–69)

The popular intertext, upon which the entire ad campaign depended, was the marketing of Pepsi's competitor, Coca-Cola, which sold six ounces of its elixir for the same nickel that bought "twelve full ounces" of Pepsi. The jingle calls attention to how full and large the bottle is, but within novelistic discourse this advertisement is transformed by irony and becomes the sign of Horner's empty consciousness. At the same time, Horner's mannerisms give him the appearance of depth, of being—like Ahab at his chart—in deep thought ("a man lost in serious problems"), though he is thinking nothing.

By signifying emptiness while advertising fullness, the jingle thus reproduces the empty/full binary of the novel, most evident in the dramatic pairing of Jake (who has "run out of gas") and Joe (who is "terribly energetic"), and exposes its specifically historical basis in the American conflict between commercial promise and cultural product. Because the Pepsi jingle appears in Barth's novel at just those times when Jake Horner's consciousness is empty—but for the jingle—the jingle of fullness and value ("more bounce to the ounce"—Mack soon added more sugar to his drink than Coke had in its bottle) signifies the ability of mass market advertising to influence consumption by means other than direct appeals to reason or consciousness. An executive at the ad agency handling the Pepsi account remembered, "What made the jingle great . . . and what saved it from dying long ago, was Mack's decision to play the song alone" (Louis and Yazijian 68). The jingle's success in saturating the culture is demonstrated not only by its automatic appearance within Horner's consciousness, but also by Barth's use of it. The intrusion of the jingle seems like a perfect instance of Horkheimer and Adorno's assertion that "the might of industrial society is lodged in men's minds" (*Dialectic* 127), because the passerby's imitation of Horner's meaningless gestures reproduces modern advertising's indifference to reason or the hard sell. The mannerisms which signify deep thought propagate themselves, just as the jingle itself was propagated, surfacing unbidden in the mind of the consumer. With the Pepsi jingle, the correspondence between appearance and depth, the name and the thing, is translated into that between an advertisement and product.

Through the Pepsi jingle this endlessly variable binary is connected with capitalism and the culture of quantity, which, though there is no mention of this anywhere in the novel, seems to be equated with its reverse: quantity carries within itself "emptiness." Capital excavates the private consciousness and puts there in its place the public discourse, the robotlike directives and reflexes of consumerism—what Horkheimer and Adorno in 1944 called "cultural totality" (126), or C. Wright Mills, addressing the same threat, called the "cultural apparatus" (405–22).

But this characteristic theme or connection is surprisingly obscured in Barth's work, appearing here only as a subliminal fear of mass culture rather than constituting the dramatic engagements of characters in setting and plot. The threat of cultural totality is reinforced when Horner later describes the Pepsi ditty as "that test pattern of my consciousness" (69). Thus one mass medium's emptiness (the test pattern of the relatively new television) "reads" another's (the Pepsi commercial), both indicating a minimal consciousness that is plugged in, but on or in which nothing is playing save nothingness itself. This cultural intertext underlies the novel's metaphysical discourse (Sartrean "nothingness") and helps to reveal its material basis, here signaled to us openly as the enervation of mass culture: the thoughtless, the sold, the consumer, that on or through which capitalism plays its self-sustaining message. And this typical object of cold war criticism, which we see everywhere in the contempt for "mass culture" and in the fear of "populism" as the source of right-wing reaction, is revealed as part of the submerged dialogue producing and fissuring the novel.

Mass consciousness is thus equated with passivity, with the role of receiver, and with any thing or person that performs the signals broadcast by others. Not surprisingly, through such characters as Peggy Rankin and Rennie Morgan, this consciousness is sexually coded as a characteristic feminine susceptibility, but the gender marking isn't rigidly applied to particular characters by sex. Instead sexual relations are part of a struggle for power reproduced throughout the novel as a shifting relation between characters, as they occupy the position of master or slave. That is, we don't really have a simple struggle between Joe and Jake, but instead a power dynamic that plays itself out in every meeting of any two characters, in which one attempts to make the other awkward, emptying him or her of self through strength of personality. Thus Horner reports that it "is impossible to be at ease in the Progress and Advice Room" of the doctor, who makes one feel "as if you hadn't a personality of your own" (2). Rennie willingly accedes to her colonization by Joe: "I think I completely erased myself, Jake, right down to nothing, so I could start over" (57). The extremity of Rennie's rebirth lies coded within her name, for she was christened "Renee" from *renais* meaning "reborn," which underscores the conventional gender coding of the master-slave relation throughout the novel (see David). The two women, Peggy Rankin (piggy rank 'n' file?) and Rennie MacMahon ("reborn son of man"), are bred in the small town of Wicomico (what's so funny?), while the men are cerebral gods that descend upon them from the urban worlds of New York and Baltimore with all the force of modern advertising.

Horner's sexual status varies: when he is merely a TV screen, the passive receptor of popular ideology, he is filled or impregnated by culture, though at those moments he is not so much "female" as he is gelded, made impotent. On the other hand, Jake maintains a virulent machismo in his relations with Peggy Rankin, a local schoolteacher he picks up at the beach (a "bird who perches on the muzzle of [his] gun" [22]). With Rennie, he is less stable, keeping the upper hand so long as they debate abstractly, but occupying a more passive role when she teaches him to ride horses. In their first adultery, in fact, Rennie is "on top." Rennie, though unsure with the men in her life, shows no restraint in dictating to her horse, when she topples him over backward to teach him a lesson: " 'That'll fix him,' she grinned" (49). The alternating character of the master-slave relation is reinforced because this episode follows only a few pages after Joe's account of knocking Rennie out with a blow to her head: "I suppose it was rough, slugging Rennie," he tells Jake, "but I saw the moment as a kind of crisis. Anyhow, she stopped apologizing after that" (44).

In scenes such as these the postwar association of ideology with violence reappears. These power relations are maintained through violence, even though the characters think they are winning or acceding because of the strength of logic, articulation, or representation. When Jake is paralyzed again by the doctor's bullying "therapy," and is unable to respond, the doctor leaps on him, pounding him roughly. Rennie, too, labors under an illusion: "he'll always be able to explain his positions better than I can" (57), she says of her husband. This isn't to say that articulation itself is negligible, but to reveal (on the contrary) this novel's insistence that articulation—to unite, or join—is a form of violence within civilization, masking what is at root a struggle for power, for being itself at the expense of the other's self-possession.

In dramatizing such a belief, Barth's novel was only reproducing a contemporary view of liberalism's complicity with the horrors of Nazism and Stalinism. In the postwar, this view was pervasive, but Sartre supplied a useful philosophical rationale, the language of which strikingly echoes Niebuhr's Christian realism and Trilling's moral realism: "Thus I am brought to that paradox," he writes in his discussion of relations with others, "which is the perilous reef of all liberal politics and which Rousseau has defined in a single word: I must 'force' the Other to be free" (*Being* 409). This is precisely the paradox illustrated by Joe's slugging Rennie, but one which comes into plausible relief only when situated within the discourse of revisionist liberalism. Joe's abuse might well be described, in Niebuhr's influential phrase, as the "irony of American innocence" or the failure to recognize the totalitarianism latent within the most liberal intentions. This point was made over and over by numerous writers, as in the admonitions of Trilling I have cited earlier: "Some paradox of our natures leads us, when once we have made our fellow men the objects of our enlightened interest, to go on to make them the objects of our pity, then of our wisdom, ultimately of our coercion." Representation in this book always involves violence imposed upon another, because any coherent position, identity, or narrative exercises an imperialism of form; and this wariness is the aesthetic version of what Bell coined as "the end of ideology." Such are the underlying social and sexual politics of the novel's most quoted passage: "To turn experience into speech . . . is always a betrayal of experience, a falsification of it; but only so betrayed can it be dealt with at all, and only in so dealing with it did I ever *feel a man,* alive and kicking." To "the connoisseur," he adds later, "it's good clean fun" (119, emphasis mine, 135).

Of course with this development we begin to see how operations within the narrative raise issues about the ideological form of the narrative itself. Set against Pepsi consciousness (passive, without reason, pure receptivity, emptiness open to the rhetoric of fullness) is articulation, authorship, and fiction making, but within this opposition the storyteller emerges unencumbered, as a free-floating masculine god, his articulation a form of divine violation or rape. When Horner's mind is active, inventive, combative and full of wit, he is lifted out of the realm of the passive consumer, the inarticulate masses who are prey to the thought control of cultural totality.

Representation is thus shown by this novel to be caught in a double bind: on the one hand, all representation implicates the artist in betrayal and violence; on the other, failure to exercise the power of representation condemns one to colonization by the Other, specifically coded in this novel as mass culture (Pepsi commercials) and feminine passivity (Rennie's self-erasure). Buried within the Pepsi reference is the fifties discourse of those who thought, as Philip Rahv did, that the most radical act of the artist might lie in remaining aloof from the incursions of mass culture. Barth's novel represents that historically produced conclusion as an ahistorical consequence of representation, but the novel itself is equally a creation and part of that social text, insofar as it presents itself as the active counter to the passivity of advertising consciousness. The novel exists as wit and invention, the entire narrative testifying to the private consciousness as a source of cleverness rising above the enervations of mass culture. The two terms—Pepsi/novel—comprise a single combative unity, through which the conflict in liberal culture between a desire for action and a new suspicion of the masses is played out in literary culture as a battle between High Art and Mass Culture. Art, as self-negation, arises as an alternative to both the passivity of the masses (Rennie) and the naiveté of radical action (Joe).

This divorce of art and politics remains a motive buried within the novel and comes to the fore only indirectly, in an argument between Horner and one of his students, a boy named Blakesley. Horner is in the midst of giving a lesson in Prescriptive Grammar, when Blakesley interrupts to ask why the rules of grammar need be slavishly memorized if no one follows them. "English was invented before grammar books," he argues. This is the ideological center of the novel, the passage through which leak the most obvious social concerns (and consequences) of the narrative. For the student has based his objections to prescriptive law upon democratic cliché: "this is supposed to be a democracy, so if nobody but a few profs ever say, 'To whom were you just now speaking?', why go on pretending we're all out of step but you?" (128). The exchange between Horner and Blakesley is a set piece of classroom discourse, in which the brash populist sneers, he thinks, at the custodian of tradition and convention, and it brings to the fore the political importance of the sign as a battleground of class conflict.

Blakesley, it's clear at this point, is a substitute for Joe Morgan—a man of independence and ideas questioning the forms and conventions which maintain social stability. "A Joe Morgan type, this lad: paths should be laid where people walk," Horner thinks. "I hated his guts" (128). The figure of Blakesley reinforces our view of Morgan as an ingenuous liberal, and establishes the underlying motive for the novel's extraordinary and gratuitous hostility to the Morgan world. Through "Blakesley," Joe Morgan's energetic innocence is associated with the dead end of romantic rebellion and liberal hopes for the masses. Although Morgan is portrayed throughout—as Blakesley is here—as an American nonconformist, through Blakesley his individualism is conflated with democracy (the way people really speak), further situating Morgan within the contradictions of liberalism and the postwar discourse of "mass society."

Horner's defense deftly sidesteps the problems of majority power by an appeal to the arbitrary, contractual character of language. While Horner drives his point home, however, the textuality of the passage betrays the somewhat different set of concerns I have been developing. "Mr. Blakesley," Horner asks, "what does the word *horse* refer to?" (128). Horner's question suddenly invokes that moment in the second chapter of *Hard Times* (titled "Murdering the Innocents"), when Gradgrind asks the circus girl Sissy Jupe, "Give me your definition of a horse." Dickens invented the dialogue between Gradgrind and Sissy Jupe as a confrontation between Utility and Imagination, in order to expose the inhuman, mechanical forces of laissez-faire capitialism. In part, Dickens was moved to write *Hard Times* as a result of having witnessed the labor conditions and unrest in the manufacturing town of Preston.

Thus we have at least three levels of meaning operating simultaneously in Horner's dialogue with Blakesley: (1) the discourse on language, Horner's ostensible subject; (2) the allusion to *Hard Times* invoking Dickens' critique of utilitarianism; and (3) the postwar relations of art and politics which serve as the intertext to the Dickens allusion. That is, Barth's allusive "intertext" conjures up not only a prior text that reinforces the overt rhetoric of his fiction, but also a prior relation of artist and society that contradicts the elitist aesthetic of *The End of the Road*. But it was just this contradiction which postwar literary culture disarmed by designating "contradiction," "paradox," and "irony" as admirable qualities of both writers and their work. Indeed, it was the failure of liberals to recognize such paradox within their own project which led to the disasters of recent history.

Something of the contemporary currency of Dickens' novel appears in Trilling's appropriation of *Hard Times* in the preface to *The Liberal Imagination*:

> The paradox is that liberalism is concerned with the emotions above all else, as proof of which the word happiness stands at the very center of its thought, but in its effort to establish the emotions, or certain among them, in some sort of freedom, liberalism somehow tends to deny them in their full possibility. Dickens' *Hard Times* serves to remind us that the liberal principles upon which Mill was brought up, although extreme, were not isolated and unique, and the principles of Mill's rearing very nearly destroyed him, as in fact they did destroy the Louisa Gradgrind of Dickens' novel. (xii–xiii)

Within the aim to engage liberal thought with conservative ideas, Trilling employed Dickens' narrative as a cautionary tale, its target not utilitarianism but liberalism generally, despite the self-evidently liberal values of the novel; and he emphasized the novel's focus upon imagination and feeling, to the exclusion of Dickens' sympathies with the laborers of Coketown.

The intertextual presence of *Hard Times* thus further reveals *The End of the Road* as a subliminal meditation upon the relations of representation to the social and political conflicts of society, despite the novel's insistence that these conflicts have their source not in social and political history, but within the character of language itself. The word "horse," Horner reminds Blakesley, "is just a symbol . . . a noise that we make in our throats or some scratches on the blackboard. . . . the significances of words are arbitrary conventions, mostly; historical accidents." Horner concludes with the inherent conservatism of the intertextual point of view: "You're free to break the rules, but not if you're after intelligibility. If you *do* want intelligibility, then the only way to get 'free' of the rules is to master them so thoroughly that they're second nature to you" (129).

Barth's allusion to Dickens' *Hard Times* transforms the issues of Dickens' dialogue into those of the "affluent society" and its discourses, in which the hard times of the depression decade have been left behind, replaced by the threat of totalitarianism lurking within the manifestations of mass society. Barth's allusion stands bracketed as a nostalgic reference to a time when the artist felt the urgencies of political involvement. Now, the novel seems to say, the long effort to unite the artist with progressive politics has come to an end of the road.

Typically, readers have ignored the political struggle which lies beneath Horner's rationalizations about the problematics of representation, and have pretty much taken Barth/Horner at his word: some kind of syntax—inherently reductive and distorting—is necessary to the intelligibility of oneself, others, history, and the stories or fictions one tells if these are to be "social" phenomena. But the theoretical or abstract nature of the debate, which has been the primary focus of Barth criticism, is inseparable from the social practice which the novel enacts. Horner's position actually removes the possibility of change from the world of social history or politics and isolates it within the world of "articulation," within a narrative art imagined to be separable from social reality. This displacement is manifest within several givens of the novel's plot: the apparent blind alley into which this ménage à trois has taken the characters is a historical illusion, after all, dependent upon the imperfect development of prophylaxis and laws prohibiting abortion. Further, legalized segregation prevents the black doctor from writing Rennie a prescription or performing the abortion in the comparative safety of a hospital. And these legal conventions, of course, are sustained by the social conventions of the culture.

Set in the period from 1951 to 1953, and written in the fall of 1955, a year after desegregation of the schools (May 1954), the novel might be read as calling attention to the arbitrary, historical nature of these conventions. After all, such is Horner's argument to Blakesley, though he uses it to defend the status quo. One imagines that for many readers in 1958 (when the novel was eventually published), the black doctor's inability to buy himself a cup of coffee in the bus station where he finds the immobilized Horner would have been a pointed anachronism, for which not only *Brown v. Board of Education* but also the Montgomery boycott and the growing civil rights unrest would serve as intertexts. Though Horner notes the time he begins to write his story as October 4, 1955, there is no indication in the story that this date marks a year and five months after Chief Justice Earl Warren read the opinion overturning *Plessy v. Ferguson*. It may be of some relevance to note that the time he took to write his confession coincides exactly with the period in which Barth wrote the story Horner tells (Morrell 13).

In fact, however, though several readers have questioned the book's "ethical implications" (Harris 44–49), the social dimension of *The End of the Road* is never mentioned, in either reviews or criticism. Surely this is the result of readers following the markers of allusion and intentionality, all of which point to the inherent problematics of representation as the source of social conflict rather than the other way around. The aesthetics of the novel reinforce this repression of the plot's historicity because despite the graphic description of Rennie's botched abortion, which seems to remind readers of a world of feeling and value beyond language, that world exists only in and through the textual surface of the fiction. By representing the immobilization of the radical thinker as the natural consequence of thought itself, the novel represses the historicity of the plot's circumstances, and mystifies such politically malleable factors as segregation and anti-abortion laws. Although readers have generally grown impatient with Horner's self-interested rationalizing well before the abortion scene, the novel cannot disentangle itself from his love of articulation and the art of betrayal upon which its narrative intelligibility depends.

Jake's discontent with himself, then, may be the shadow of Barth's discomfort, as both withdraw into an ahistorical aestheticism, founded upon the ineradicable limits of representation: "given my own special kind of integrity, if I was to have [friends] at all I must remain uninvolved—I must leave them alone" (176). In his room after Rennie's death, Horner reads the bust of Laocoön as an allegory of the times: "my limbs were bound like Laocoön's—by the serpents Knowledge and Imagination, which, grown great in the fullness of time, no longer tempt but annihilate" (187). Because we know too much and imagine too well, he suggests the continuity of human society is breached from within, by the Trojan horse of reason itself.

Such conclusions were common enough within the literary-intellectual community of the postwar years. When R. W. B. Lewis published *The American Adam* in 1955, he concluded his study with a comment upon "the contemporary situation":

> The picture of man sketched by the dominant contemporary philosophies and ologies shows us a figure struggling to stand upright amid the most violent cross-currents: the American as Adam has been replaced by the American as Laocoön; the Emersonian figure—"the plain old Adam, the simple genuine self"—has been frowned quite out of existence.

This picture, he adds, is "clearly warranted" (195). Barth's novel describes the end of an idea held by Schiller and Lessing, in which art is the embodiment of freedom in beauty—Horner refers to Lessing's treatise once, noting of his "friend Laocoön" that his "grimace was his beauty"—for the form of freedom in postwar discourse, as Sartre insisted, is not beauty but "anguish" (*Being* 62).

We may think of *The End of the Road* as the effort to overcome Lessing's distinction between stone and poetry: as narrative sculpture, the novel exposes the statue's latent pain and torment, which Lessing thought sculpture could not afford to acknowledge. As this sculptural, plastic aspiration came to dominate Barth's experiments with narrative, from *Lost in the Funhouse* (1968) through *Letters* (1979), critics have seen in it the persistence of modernism, but have overlooked the cultural and political resonance of modernism in the postwar. Once recalled, however, this social text of *The End of the Road* begins to emerge like a photograph coming up beneath developer.

At the close of the novel, Horner appeals to the story of Laocoön and through that story to the literary authority of epic itself as a timeless warning, admonishing the artist of the futility of prophecy and political commitment; in fact, Horner leaves the statue behind him when he joins the black doctor at his Remobilization Farm. Horner's confession, one gathers, is a form of therapy through which the paralyzing difficulties of historical engagement are circumvented by the power of the printed word—of art itself—to give order and understanding without imposing either of them upon the world. But this evasion is unsuccessful: though the novel pretends that it comes to us from some place outside of town, beyond the human community, its textual constitution is a social mosaic of the very discourses it seeks to escape.

Afterword

Contemplative Fiction and American Postmodernism

> The being of human reality is suffering because it rises in being as perpetu-
> ally haunted by a totality which it is without being able to be it, precisely
> because it could not attain the in-itself without losing itself as for-itself.
> Human reality therefore is by nature an unhappy consciousness with no
> possibility of surpassing its unhappy state.
>
> Jean-Paul Sartre, *Being and Nothingness*, 1943

> The nothingness which fascinates recent philosophers is a myth of declin-
> ing capitalist society.
>
> Georg Lukács, "Existentialism," 1947

In an essay on the political radicalism of science fiction, Thomas Pynchon wrote that "mainstream fiction" in "the decade after Hiroshima" was
for the most part "paralyzed by the political climate of the cold war and
McCarthy years" ("Is It O.K.," 41). The statue of Laocoön may stand as
the central image of this paralysis, for its representation of tortured stasis is
a fitting symbol for the art of paradox and contradiction which dominated
literary discourse in the postwar years. Embodying desire within constraint
and freedom within necessity, the sculpture's universalism develops in the
postwar context a more particular relevance to the uneasy equilibrium which
Lionel Trilling described as the necessary contortion of the liberal imagination and its transcendent awareness. Laocoön is a widely disseminated
artist figure in literary criticism of this period, but it is given its influential
formulation by Trilling: "in any culture there are likely to be certain artists
who contain a large part of the dialectic within themselves, their meaning
and power lying in their contradictions; they contain within themselves, it
may be said, the very essence of the culture" (*Liberal* 9).

This paralysis was so often figured within a metaphysical frame—as in
the example of Jake Horner's eyes fixed on "ultimacy"—that one might
well conclude that fiction of the postwar sought its ground in forms of noth-

185

ingness: in the "chaos" that Invisible Man discovers through Rinehart; in the evangelical nihilism of the Misfit; in the vitality the hipster earns in the face of death; in the nothingness that undoes all social conventions in *The End of the Road*. This recourse to a metaphysical limit is one of the most recurrent characteristics of the fiction of this time. In O'Connor, this limit occurs as a moment of violence that reminds her characters of their religious needs. But in effect all of this writing is seeking a new ground or premise upon which to build. For Ellison, the ground of "chaos" offered a more level or democratic playing field than the current order, and so his character must not only confront the social duplicity in the central institutions of United States society, but also recognize all social forms as exigent fictions. Mailer's radicalism, too, appeals to nothingness as the ground out of which may emerge a new revolutionary consciousness.

This metaphysical appeal or grounding in discourse of absolutes is an expression of the impasse felt within the liberal community after World War II. Lukács called such appeals the "contemplative" rendering of an essentially political view obscured by the "myth of nothingness" (*Marxism* 251f.). To such observers as Lukács and Barthes, the "end of ideology" discourse inscribed within Barth's novel was so much mystification. The "definition of myth in a bourgeois society," Roland Barthes wrote in *Mythologies* (1957), "is depoliticized speech." It has the purpose, Barthes argued, "of giving an historical intention a natural justification, and making contingency appear eternal. Now this process is exactly that of bourgeois ideology." The essential function of such myths, he continues, "is to immobilize the world" and discourage "man against inventing himself" (142, 155). Similarly, Lukács' essay on Sartre situated the existential ideas of freedom directly within the contingencies of recent history and would not have credited such views as Schlesinger's that "ancient truths" about human nature had been rediscovered.

Sartre's meditations upon human freedom bear a family resemblance to similar meditations taking place within other contexts, especially in commentary current in the United States during the postwar period. Certainly Sartre's analysis of human freedom was easily integrated with such essays as Fromm's *Escape from Freedom*, and deployed in the service of cold war politics. Fromm argued that the freedom won in recent centuries from systems of hierarchy and oppression—the victory of liberalism—produced an individual with little idea of a "positive freedom" and thus burdened with the anxiety of an ungrounded liberation. Fromm's thesis, therefore, wasn't far from Sartre's description of freedom's "anguish."

Many prominent essayists of the period drew upon the theories of Sartre and Fromm, using them in their own contexts, both political and religious.

In *The Vital Center*, for example, Schlesinger declared that the uncertainties of freedom have "brought with it frustration rather than fulfillment" and cited in quick succession both Sartre's popular aphorism "Man is condemned to be free," and the title of Fromm's book: "The 'escape from freedom,' as Erich Fromm has called it, is a characteristic pattern of our age" (52). Schlesinger martialed these quotations and many others as part of his contrasting of American democracy with the Soviet system: "The totalitarian state . . . has risen in specific response to this fear of freedom" (53). Paul Tillich's book *The Courage to Be* was published as a book of existential theology, but in many respects it simply articulated the same pride in the difficulty of freedom that Schlesinger had defined in *The Vital Center*. Tillich distinguished between the "courage to be with," associated with Soviet collectivism, and the "courage to be" which he associated with individualist democracy. The danger, he told his Yale audience, is that "conformity" will turn into totalitarianism: "Conformity is growing, but it has not yet become collectivism" (104).

Within this discourse such passages as the following from Schlesinger, Barth, and Ellison can be set beside one another as variant expressions of a common system. "The eternal awareness of choice can drive the weak to the point where the simplest decision becomes a nightmare. Most men prefer to flee choice, to flee anxiety, to flee freedom" (*Vital* 52). It is just this threat of possibility that paralyzes Jake Horner in the Ohio bus station, "immobilized" by the "inability to choose." Similarly, Invisible Man reaches the underground space he describes as "a state neither of dreaming nor of waking, but somewhere in between, in which I was caught like Trueblood's jaybird that yellow jackets had paralyzed in every part but his eyes" (556).

Typically, within liberal aesthetics this mental paralysis is overcome in art, which transcends contraries by embodying them in a sculpted vision. As Trilling wrote of Hyacinth Robinson's death in *The Princess Casamassima*, "embodying two ideals at once, he takes upon himself, in full consciousness, the guilt of each. . . . By his death he instructs us in the nature of civilized life and by his consciousness he transcends it" (*Liberal* 86). Invisible Man thus emerges from his liminal state through the "attempt to write it down" (562) and concludes his story by asserting a very different point of view from the one which ends the interior narrative: "my world has become one of infinite possibilities. . . . Until some gang succeeds in putting the world in a strait jacket, its definition is possibility. Step outside the narrow borders of what men call reality and you step into chaos—ask Rinehart, he's a master of it—or imagination" (563). Invisible Man's decision to leave his underground hibernation and assume a social role enacts Ellison's idea of the artist's "tragic responsibility" (*Shadow* 33) to "transcend the limitations of pragmatic reality," by "the quality of moral imagination—the fountainhead of great art" (*Shadow* 37).

The ideological character of these assumptions—ultimacy, nothingness, metaphysics, transcendence—is manifest in their being understood as universal and natural, as the unalterable features of human existence and consciousness, laid bare by the lessons (or "reality") of recent history. The writings of both critic and writer were mediated by these discourses, which operated as a fifth column within the variety of their intention and aspiration, shaping and disturbing, in my examples, the writing of Ellison, O'Connor, Mailer, and Barth.

Although there is no natural limit to the number or kind of examples that might be adduced to show the aesthetic effects of political discourse that is absorbed and transformed by the literary imagination, one might note Peter Matthiessen's early novel *Partisans* (1955) as one further instance, because it recapitulates the liberal narrative in such stark outline. The central figure of this novel is Edwin Sand, an expatriate American in Paris, earning his living as a journalist. Early in the novel we learn that "hard on the heels of puberty, [Sand] had suffered a first attack of liberalism" (27) and that it was during this adolescence—fleeing Spain with his father, as the Loyalist armies were falling—that his father had given a ride across the border to a communist named Jacobi. Jacobi left an impression of high principle upon Sand, then fourteen, for he managed to convey the beginnings of an international perspective: "the real world is changing," he tells the boy. "In the past thirty years, in Russia and China and now in Spain, we've fought only the first battles. The true war, the Great Twentieth-Century War, will go on and on until it's won, even though few people recognize it exists" (25). In Paris fifteen years later, Sand is a burned-out journalist who has rejected the privilege his family might have provided, and who is impatient with the moral compromises of the postwar. His search for Jacobi is thus a search for political meaning, for the incarnation of ideals in political action that postwar discourse declared to be the fatal naiveté of the old liberal. When Sand learns Jacobi may be sequestered by the Party in Paris he goes looking, despite his editor's warning: "I'm a liberal myself . . . but we're fighting for survival these days, we can't fuss over our methods! Face the facts! Except for public consumption, at home and abroad, your kind of honor is out of date!" (33).

Not surprisingly, Edwin's pursuit of a prewar idealism—his youth embodied in his memory of a man he met only briefly years ago—concludes with a new realism. A woman he meets in the Paris underworld tells him, "the Party has changed, you know, it is purely political now. It is like a young idealistic boy who has learned to compromise, to put ambition above the ideal" (75). When Sand finally contacts Jacobi, the man retains his strength and dignity in Sand's eyes, but the words Jacobi speaks to him could have been spoken by Schlesinger or Niebuhr or Trilling: "This world awakening is the great historical force of our time. The Party grew out of it, and even exploited it, but one day will find that it can no longer be controlled. Humanity, like Marat, is too perverse to be controlled. . . . We wanted to believe that human beings would rise to the high principles of a cause, and they do, as long as the cause is not in power" (156).

In the example of Barth, this transition from Spanish Loyalism to moral ambiguity has the appearance of advancing or perpetuating modernist conundrums and preoccupations, and culminates in the sixties in "experimental," "metafictional," or "postmodern" writing, seemingly free of any relation to the cultural and political dilemmas of the artist in the forties and fifties. Certainly the term "postmodern" has its origin in historical conditions rather than in the evolution of form, and became necessary to the politics of culture as the antithesis of and contemporary formation that seals off and canonizes the work of modernism, now finished or exhausted, and in need of preservation against the incursions and depredations of mass culture. In essays by Harry Levin, Lionel Trilling, Daniel Bell, and Irving Howe, the term "postmodern" thus carries with it interpretations of culture which include the erosion of classes and of "class conflict" as meaningful concepts for understanding culture.

Thus the decline of labor as the agency of revolution has a specific relevance to the term "postmodern" in the United States, because it signifies a reformulation of the work of fiction and a transformation of ideas about political change. The possibilities and sources for such change seemed to have altered radically in the years following the war. Daniel Bell specifies the Truman election of 1948, and the defeat of Henry Wallace, as the watershed event signaling organized labor's willingness to cooperate with ownership. In 1949 Bell wrote that "whereas the fundamental outlook of nineteenth century utopian unionism . . . was to change capitalist society, the fundamental drive of twentieth century unionism is to assure a place and some weight in that social order" ("American Socialists," quoted in Brick 187). C. Wright Mills repeated this view in 1961 when he said the working class "doesn't seem to be at once available and effective as *our* agency any more" (254–55). Because these statements respond directly to the political realities of the fifties, they provide a historical sense for Fredric Jameson's statement thirty-five years later in the foreword to François Lyotard's *The Postmodern Condition* (1984): it has been necessary "to abandon the traditional Marxian vision of revolution and socialism, mainly out of a conviction that the industrial working class . . . no longer occupies the strategic position of power in this social formation" (xiii–xiv). These views of what was taking place in the years from, say, 1936 to 1950 also serve as background to the sense of displacement and alienation felt by so many, and recorded in such essays as Mills's "The Social Role of the Intellectual" and Bell's "The End of Ideology" in which both writers describe the "disenchanted and reflective" intellectual, for whom the "key terms" are "irony, paradox, ambiguity, and complexity" (Bell, *End* 300).

Postmodern fiction arises in response to this impasse—in some cases not by reestablishing a relationship between art and social history, but by treating the dilemmas of that engagement in purely formal terms. In "The Literature of Exhaustion," for example, Barth describes his subject as "how an artist may paradoxically turn the felt ultimacies of our time into material and means for his work—*paradoxically* because by so doing he transcends what had appeared to be his refutation, in the same way that the mystic who transcends finitude is said to be enabled to live, spiritually and physically, in the finite world" (32).

Those who locate the origins of American postmodernism in the mid-sixties and after must take into account a more historical foundation, for considered merely formally, the metafictions—or "stained glass"—of such writers as Barth, Hawkes, Gass, Coover, Sukenick, and Sorrentino appear to be only an exhausted modernism. And those, such as François Lyotard, who define postmodernism as "incredulity toward metanarratives" (xxiv) should take into account the suspicion of narrative frames fostered in the conservative atmosphere of the new liberalism. In some degree, American postmodernism is not separable from the emergence of fiction from the politics of paralysis in the postwar period.

The paroxysms of liberal thought continued in the sixties. The story of Oedipa Maas, in *The Crying of Lot 49*, after all, is the story of a culture's contradictions finding their way into the consciousness of an American housewife; or, more positively, of her coming into consciousness of those contradictions as the price for her escape from the numbing narcissism of her suburban life. Pynchon's description of McCarthyite mainstream fiction in "Is It O.K. to Be a Luddite?" helps to refocus the importance of that scene in which Oedipa, schooled in the era of Eisenhower and Foster Dulles, walks across Sproul Plaza during the heyday of the Free Speech movement:

> She moved through it carrying her fat book, attracted, unsure, a stranger, wanting to feel relevant but knowing how much of a search among alternate universes it would take. For she had undergone her own educating at a time of nerves, blandness and retreat among not only her fellow students but also most

of the visible structure around and ahead of them, this having been a national reflex to certain pathologies in high places only death had the power to cure, and this Berkeley was no somnolent Siwash out of her own past at all, but more akin to those Far Eastern or Latin American universities you read about, those autonomous culture media where the most beloved of folklores may be brought into doubt, cataclysmic of dissents voiced, suicidal of commitments chosen—the sort that bring governments down. (103–4)

The fiction of the Vietnam era bears upon the ways in which liberal thought found release in a different kind of politics and literature. Still it may be relevant to our interest in the liberal narrative to point out that Oedipa does not discover an "autonomous culture" threatening the dominant system, but instead develops a mode of consciousness that recognizes a world "congruent" to and inseparable from the "cheered land"—that is, she discovers the culture's tragic contradictions and develops a new compassion for them.

Thus Pynchon's writing is not without its "mystical" undertow, which may be felt as the continuing force of the liberal narrative in recent fiction. Certainly, such books as Mailer's *Armies of the Night* and Pynchon's *The Crying of Lot 49* are as much in dialogue with an enervated liberalism— though perhaps more discontented with it—as was *Invisible Man* and *The End of the Road*. The true labor of fiction throughout this period continues to be the struggle to develop a new relation between art and politics. At the very least, the fiction of our time is everywhere modified from within by discourses that have their origin in the politics and culture of the forties and fifties.

Works Consulted

Index

Works Consulted

Aaron, Daniel. *Writers on the Left: Episodes in American Literary Communism.* New York: Harcourt, 1961.

Abrams, Richard M., and Lawrence W. Levine, eds. *The Shaping of Twentieth-Century America: Interpretive Essays.* 2d ed. Boston: Little, Brown, 1971.

Adorno, Theodor. *Aesthetic Theory.* Trans. C. Lendhardt. New York: Routledge, 1984.

Aldridge, John. *After the Lost Generation: A Critical Study of the Writers of Two Wars.* New York: McGraw-Hill, 1951.

Alpert, Barry. "Gilbert Sorrentino—An Interview." *VORT* 6 (Fall 1974): 3–30.

Arendt, Hannah. *The Origins of Totalitarianism.* 1951. New York: Harcourt, 1973.

Asals, Frederick. *Flannery O'Connor: The Imagination of Extremity.* Athens: U of Georgia P, 1982.

Baker, Houston A., Jr. *Afro-American Poetics: Revisions of Harlem and the Black Aesthetic.* Madison: U of Wisconsin P, 1988.

Baker, Houston A., Jr. "To Move without Moving: An Analysis of Creativity and Commerce in Ralph Ellison's Trueblood Episode." *PMLA* 98 (October 1983): 828–45.

Bakhtin, M. M. *The Dialogic Imagination: Four Essays.* Austin: U of Texas P, 1981.

Barker, Lucius J., and Twiley W. Barker, Jr. *Freedoms, Courts, Politics: Studies in Civil Liberties.* Englewood Cliffs, N.J.: Prentice-Hall, 1972.

Barone, Dennis. "An Interview with Gilbert Sorrentino." *Partisan Review* 2 (1981): 236–46.

Barrett, William. *Irrational Man: A Study in Existential Philosophy.* New York: Doubleday Anchor, 1958.

Barth, John. *Chimera.* New York: Fawcett Crest, 1972.

Barth, John. *The Floating Opera.* 1956. New York: Avon, 1969.

Barth, John. *The Floating Opera and The End of the Road.* New York: Anchor, 1988.

Barth, John. *Letters.* New York: Putnam, 1979.

Barth, John. "The Literature of Exhaustion." *Atlantic Monthly,* August 1967, 29–34.

Barth, John. *Lost in the Funhouse.* 1968. New York: Anchor, 1988.

Barth, John. *The Sot-Weed Factor.* New York: Grosset & Dunlap, 1966.

Barthelme, Donald. "After Joyce." *Location* 1 (Summer 1964): 13–16.

Barthes, Roland. *Mythologies.* 1957. Selected and translated by Annette Lavers. New York: Hill and Wang, 1972.

Bell, Daniel. "American Socialists: What Now?" *Modern Review* 2 (January 1949): 345–53.

Bell, Daniel. *The End of Ideology: On the Exhaustion of Political Ideas in the Fifties.* New York: Collier, 1961.

Bellamy, Joe David. "Having It Both Ways." *New American Review* 15 (1972): 134–50.

Bellow, Saul. *The Adventures of Augie March*. 1953. New York: Viking, 1960.

Bellow, Saul. *Dangling Man*. 1944. New York: Signet, 1965.

Bellow, Saul. "Distractions of a Fiction Writer." In Hicks.

Bellow, Saul. "Man Underground." In *Ralph Ellison: A Collection of Critical Essays*, ed. John Hersey. Englewood Cliffs: Prentice-Hall, 1974. Orig. pub. *Commentary* 13 (June 1952): 608–10.

Bellow, Saul. *The Victim*. 1947. New York: Viking Compass, 1962.

Bendiner, Robert. "The Liberals' Political Road Back." *Commentary* 15 (January–June 1953): 431–37.

Berkhofer, Robert F., Jr. "Clio and the Culture Concept: Some Impressions of a Changing Relationship in American Historiography." *Social Science Quarterly* 55 (September 1972): 297–320.

Bernstein, Barton J. "The Ambiguous Legacy: The Truman Administration and Civil Rights." In Abrams and Levine 537–70. Also in *Politics and Policies of the Truman Administration*, ed. Barton J. Bernstein. New York: Quadrangle Books, 1970.

Bird, Caroline. "The Unlost Generation." *Harper's Bazaar*, February 1957, 104–7, 174–75.

Biskind, Peter. *Seeing Is Believing: How Hollywood Taught Us to Stop Worrying and Love the Fifties*. New York: Pantheon, 1983.

Blackmur, R. P. *The Art of the Novel*. New York: Scribners, 1934.

Blackmur, R. P. "For a Second Look." *Kenyon Review* 11 (Winter 1949): 7–10.

Bloom, Alexander. *Prodigal Sons: The New York Intellectuals and Their World*. New York: Oxford, 1986.

Bluestone, George. "John Wain and John Barth: The Angry and the Accurate." *Massachusetts Review* 1 (1960): 528–89.

Booklist 51: 248.

Boorstin, Daniel J. *The Genius of American Politics*. Chicago: U of Chicago P, 1953.

Bottomore, Tom. *The Frankfurt School*. New York: Tavistock, 1984.

Breslin, James E. B. *From Modern to Contemporary: American Poetry, 1945–1965*. Chicago: U of Chicago P, 1984.

Brick, Howard. *Daniel Bell and the Decline of Intellectual Radicalism: Social Theory and Political Reconciliation in the 1940s*. Madison: U of Wisconsin P, 1986.

Brooks, Cleanth. *The Well-Wrought Urn: Studies in the Structure of Poetry*. 1947. New York: Harvest, 1975.

Brown, Norman O. *Life against Death: The Psychoanalytic Meaning of History*. New York: Vintage, 1959.

Burroughs, William. *Junky*. 1953. New York: Penguin, 1977.

Burroughs, William. *Naked Lunch*. New York: Grove Black Cat, 1966.

Burroughs, William, and Brion Gysin. *The Third Mind*. New York: Viking, 1978.

Cain, William E. *F. O. Matthiessen and the Politics of Criticism*. Madison: U of Wisconsin P, 1988.

Callahan, John F. "Frequencies of Eloquence." In O'Meally, *New Essays on Invisible Man*.

Cantor, Milton. *The Divided Left: American Radicalism, 1900–1975*. New York: Hill and Wang, 1978.

Caute, David. *The Great Fear: The Anti-Communist Purge under Truman and Eisenhower*. New York: Simon and Schuster, 1978.

Chafe, William H. *The Unfinished Journey: America since World War II*. New York: Oxford, 1986.

Chase, Richard. *The American Novel and Its Tradition*. 1957. Baltimore: Hopkins, 1980.

Chase, Richard. "Art, Nature, Politics." *Partisan Review* 12 (1950): 580–94.

Chase, Richard. "The Fate of the Avant-Garde." In Howe, *Idea of the Modern*. Originally published in *Partisan Review* 24 (1957): 363–75.

Chase, Richard. *Herman Melville: A Critical Study*. 1949. New York: Hafner, 1971.

Chase, Richard. "A Novel Is a Novel." *Kenyon Review* 14 (Autumn 1952): 678–84.

Cooney, Terry A. *The Rise of the New York Intellectuals: Partisan Review and Its Circle, 1934–1945*. Madison: U of Wisconsin P, 1986.

Cowley, Malcolm. *The Literary Situation*. 1954. New York: Viking, 1958.

Creeley, Robert. *A Quick Graph: Collected Notes and Essays*. Ed. Donald Allen. San Francisco: Four Seasons Foundation, 1970.

Crossman, Richard, ed. *The God That Failed: Six Studies in Communism*. New York: Harper, 1949.

Cruse, Harold. *The Crisis of the Negro Intellectual*. New York: William Morrow, 1967.

Dalfiume, Richard M. "The 'Forgotten Years' of the Negro Revolution." In Abrams and Levine 518–34. Orig. pub. *Journal of American History* 55 (June 1968): 90–106.

David, Jack. "The Trojan Horse at the End of the Road." *College Literature* 4 (Spring 1977): 159–64.

Dewey, John. "Anti-Naturalism in Extremis." *Partisan Review* 10 (1943): 24–39.

Dewey, John. *Freedom and Culture*. New York: Putnam, 1939.

Dewey, John. *Liberalism and Social Action*. New York: Putnam, 1935.

Dickstein, Morris. *Gates of Eden: American Culture in the Sixties*. New York: Basic Books, 1977.

Diggins, John P. "Consciousness and Ideology in American History: The Burden of Daniel J. Boorstin." *American Historical Review* 76 (February 1971): 99–118.

Donald, James and Stuart Hall, eds. *Politics and Ideology*. Philadelphia: Open UP, 1986.

Du Bois, W. E. Burghardt. *The Souls of Black Folk*. 1903. New York: Fawcett, 1961.

Ehrenreich, Barbara. *The Hearts of Men: American Dreams and the Flight from Commitment*. New York: Doubleday, 1983.

Ekirch, Arthur A., Jr. *The Decline of American Liberalism*. New York: Longman's, 1955.

Ellison, Ralph. "Anti-War Novel." *New Masses* 35 (June 18, 1940): 29–30.

Ellison, Ralph. "Big White Fog." *New Masses* 37 (November 12, 1940): 22–23.

Ellison, Ralph. "Creative and Cultural Lag." *New Challenge* 2 (Fall 1937): 90–91.

Ellison, Ralph. *Going to the Territory*. 1986. New York: Vintage, 1987.

Ellison, Ralph. *Invisible Man*. 1952. New York: Vintage, 1972.

Ellison, Ralph. "Negro Prize Fighter." *New Masses* 37 (December 17, 1940): 26–27.

Ellison, Ralph. "Ruling Class Southerner." *New Masses* 30 (December 5, 1939): 27.

Ellison, Ralph. *Shadow and Act*. 1964. New York: Vintage, 1972.

Ellison, Ralph. "Society, Morality, and the Novel." In Hicks.

Ellison, Ralph. "Stormy Weather." *New Masses* 37 (September 24, 1940): 20–21.

Enck, John. "John Barth: An Interview." *Wisconsin Studies in Contemporary Literature* 6 (Winter-Spring 1965): 3–14.

Enck, John. "John Hawkes: An Interview." *Wisconsin Studies in Contemporary Literature* 6 (Summer 1965): 141–55.

Erikson, Erik H. *Childhood and Society*. 1950. New York: W. W. Norton, 1963.

Fiedler, Leslie. *An End to Innocence: Essays on Culture and Politics*. Boston: Beacon, 1955.

Fiedler, Leslie. *Love and Death in the American Novel*. 1960. New York: Stein and Day, 1975.

Filler, Louis. "The Dilemma, So-Called, of the American Liberal." *Antioch Review* 8 (June 1948): 131–51.

"Flannery O'Connor: A New Shining Talent among Our Storytellers." *New York Herald Tribune Book Review*, June 5, 1955, 1.

Frank, Joseph. "Lionel Trilling and the Conservative Imagination." *The Widening Gyre: Crisis and Mastery in Modern Literature*. 1963. Bloomington: U of Indiana P, 1968.

Fromm, Erich. *Escape from Freedom*. 1941. New York: Avon, 1969.

Fromm, Erich. *The Sane Society*. New York: Rinehart, 1955.

Galbraith, John Kenneth. *The Affluent Society*. New York: NAL, 1958.

Gates, Henry Louis, Jr. *Figures in Black: Words, Signs, and the "Racial" Self*. New York: Oxford UP, 1987.

Gayle, Addison. *Richard Wright: Ordeal of a Native Son*. New York: Doubleday, 1980.

Gilbert, James Burkhart. *Writers and Partisans: A History of Literary Radicalism in America*. New York: John Wiley, 1968.

Girvetz, Harry K. *The Evolution of Liberalism*. Orig. *From Wealth to Welfare: The Evolution of Liberalism*. 1950. New York: Collier, 1963.

Goldman, Eric F. *The Crucial Decade—And After: America, 1945–1960*. New York: Vintage, 1960.

Goodman, Paul. *Utopian Essays and Practical Proposals*. New York: Vintage, 1964.

Goodman, Percival, and Paul Goodman. *Communitas: Means of Livelihood and Ways of Life*. 1947. New York: Vintage, 1960.

Graff, Gerald. *Literature against Itself: Literary Ideas in Modern Society*. Chicago: U of Chicago P, 1979.

Green, Eddie. "A Good Man Is Hard to Find." Copyright 1917 by Edwin H. Morris & Company, Inc., New York. Rpt. in Sandy King, *World's Greatest Hits from 1900–1919*. Miami Beach, Fla.: Charles Hansen Music Corp., 1973.

Greenberg, Clement. "Avant-Garde and Kitsch." *Partisan Review* 6 (1939): 34–39.

Greene, James. "The Comic and the Sad." *Commonweal* 62 (July 22, 1955): 404.

Guilbaut, Serge. *How New York Stole the Idea of Modern Art: Abstract Expressionism, Freedom, and the Cold War.* Trans. Arthur Goldhammer. Chicago: U of Chicago P, 1983.

Gutman, Stanley T. *Mankind in Barbary: The Individual and Society in the Novels of Norman Mailer.* Hanover, N.H.: U P of New England, 1975.

Hall, Stuart. "Variants of Liberalism." In Donald and Hall.

Harnoncourt, René d'. "Challenge and Promise: Modern Art and Society." *Art News,* November 1949.

Harris, Charles. *Passionate Virtuosity: The Fiction of John Barth.* Urbana: U of Illinois P, 1983.

Hartz, Louis. *The Liberal Tradition in America: An Interpretation of American Political Thought Since the Revolution.* New York: Harcourt, 1955.

Hicks, Granville, ed. *The Living Novel.* New York: Macmillan, 1957.

Higham, John. "Beyond Consensus: The Historian as Moral Critic." *American Historical Review* 67 (April 1962): 609–25.

Higham, John. "The Cult of the 'American Consensus.' " *Commentary* 27 (February 1959): 93–100.

Hirsch, David H. *Reality and Idea in the Early American Novel.* Paris: Mouton, 1971.

Hobhouse, L. T. *Liberalism.* 1911. New York: Oxford, 1964.

Hodgson, Godfrey. *America in Our Time.* 1976. New York: Vintage, 1978.

Hofstadter, Richard. *The Age of Reform: From Bryan to F.D.R.* New York: Vintage, 1955.

Hollingsworth, J. Rogers. "Consensus and Continuity in Recent American Historical Writing." *South Atlantic Quarterly* 61 (Winter 1962): 40–50.

Hook, Sidney. "The New Failure of Nerve." *Partisan Review* 10 (1943): 2–23.

Horkheimer, Max, and Theodor Adorno. *Dialectic of Enlightenment.* Trans. John Cumming. Orig. German edition, 1944. New York: Continuum, 1987.

Horowitz, Irving Louis, ed. *Power, Politics, and People: The Collected Essays of C. Wright Mills.* New York: Ballantine, 1963.

Hoskins, Robert V., III. "Swift, Dickens, and the Horses in *The End of the Road.*" *James Madison Journal* 37 (1979): 18–32.

Howard, Daniel. "The New Criticism of the Novel." *Kenyon Review* 21 (1959): 309–20.

Howe, Irving. "Black Boys and Natives Sons." *Dissent* (Autumn 1963): 353–68.

Howe, Irving. *A Margin of Hope: An Intellectual Autobiography.* New York: Harcourt, 1982.

Howe, Irving. "A Negro In America." *Nation* 174 (May 1952): 454.

Howe, Irving. *Politics and the Novel.* New York: Horizon, 1957.

Howe, Irving. *A World More Attractive: A View of Modern Literature and Politics.* New York: Horizon, 1963.

Howe, Irving, ed. *The Idea of the Modern in Literature and the Arts.* New York: Horizon, 1967.

Jack Kerouac, On the Road: Text and Criticism. New York: Penguin, 1979.

Jameson, Fredric. "Ideology of the Text." *Salmagundi*, nos. 31–32 (Fall 1975–Winter 1976): 204–46.

Jay, Gregory S. "Hegel and Trilling in America." *American Literary History* 1 (Fall 1989): 565–92.

Johnson, Joyce. *Minor Characters*. Boston: Houghton Mifflin, 1983.

Kael, Pauline. *I Lost It at the Movies*. Boston: Little, Brown, 1965.

Kaiser, Ernest. "A Critical Look at Ellison's Fiction and at Social and Literary Criticism by and about the Author." *Black World* 20 (December 1970): 53–97.

Kazin, Alfred. "Psychoanalysis and Literary Culture Today." In *Psychoanalysis and Literature*, ed. Hendrik M. Ruitenbeek. New York: E. P. Dutton, 1964.

Kazin, Alfred. *Starting Out in the Thirties*. Boston: Little, Brown, 1965.

Kegley, Jacquelyn. "*The End of the Road*: The Death of Individualism." In *Philosophy and Literature*, ed. A. Phillips Griffith. Cambridge: Cambridge UP, 1984.

Kempton, Murray. "The Literature of Crisis." *Part of Our Time*. New York: Simon and Schuster, 1955.

Kennan, George F. *American Diplomacy, 1900–1950*. New York: NAL, 1951.

Kerner, David. "Psychodrama in Eden." *Chicago Review* 13 (Winter–Spring 1959): 59–67.

Kerouac, Jack. *On the Road*. New York: Signet, 1957.

Kerouac, Jack. *The Town and the City*. New York: Harcourt, 1948.

Koch, Kenneth. "Fresh Air." In *The New American Poetry*, ed. Donald Allen. New York: Grove, 1960.

Kreidl, John. *Nicholas Ray*. Boston: G. K. Hall, 1977.

Krim, Seymour. "The Fiction of Fiction: A Critical Nudger." *Partisan Review* 19 (May–June 1952): 351–53.

Krupnick, Mark. *Lionel Trilling and the Fate of Cultural Criticism*. Evanston: Northwestern UP, 1986.

Lasch, Christopher. *The Agony of the American Left*. New York: Knopf, 1969.

Lasch, Christopher. *The New Radicalism in America, 1889–1963: The Intellectual as a Social Type*. New York: Knopf, 1965.

Laski, Harold J. *The Rise of Liberalism: The Philosophy of a Business Civilization*. New York: Harper, 1936.

LeClair, Thomas, and Larry McCaffery, eds. *Anything Can Happen: Interviews with Contemporary American Novelists*. Urbana: U of Illinois P, 1983.

Lewis, R. W. B. *The American Adam: Innocence, Tragedy, and Tradition in the Nineteenth Century*. Chicago: U of Chicago P, 1955.

Lewis, R. W. B. "Eccentrics' Pilgrimage." *Hudson Review* 6 (Spring 1953): 144–50.

Lindner, Robert. *Must You Conform?* 1952. New York: Rinehart, 1956.

Lindner, Robert. *Prescription for Rebellion*. 1952. New York: Grove, 1962.

Lindner, Robert. *Rebel without a Cause: The Story of a Criminal Psychopath*. Introduction by Sheldon and Eleanor Glueck. New York: Grove Black Cat, 1944.

Louis, J. C., and Harvey Z. Yazijian. *The Cola Wars*. New York: Everest House, 1980.

Lucid, Robert F. *Norman Mailer: The Man and His Work*. Boston: Little, Brown, 1971.

Lukács, Georg. *Marxism and Human Liberation*. Ed. E. San Juan. New York: Delta, 1973.

Lyotard, Jean-François. *The Postmodern Condition: A Report on Knowledge*. Foreward by Fredric Jameson. Trans. Geoff Bennington and Brian Massumi. Minneapolis: U of Minnesota P, 1984.

Macdonald, Dwight. *Against the American Grain*. New York: Vintage, 1962.

Macdonald, Dwight. "A Theory of Mass Culture." *Diogenes* (Summer 1953): 1–17.

Mack, Walter. *No Time Lost*. New York: Atheneum, 1982.

Mailer, Norman. *Advertisements for Myself*. 1959. New York: Berkeley Medallion, 1966.

Mailer, Norman. *The Armies of the Night: History as a Novel, the Novel as History*. New York: Signet, 1968.

Mailer, Norman. *Barbary Shore*. New York: Signet, 1951.

Mailer, Norman. *Cannibals and Christians*. New York: Dell, 1966.

Mailer, Norman. *Executioner's Song*. New York: Warner, 1979.

Mailer, Norman. *The Naked and the Dead*. New York: Signet, 1948.

Mailer, Norman. *The Presidential Papers*. London: Transworld, 1965.

Mailer, Norman. *Why Are We in Vietnam?* New York: Berkeley Medallion, 1968.

Manso, Peter, ed. *Mailer: His Life and Times*. New York: Simon and Schuster, 1985.

Marcuse, Herbert. *Eros and Civilization: A Philosophical Inquiry into Freud*. New York: Vintage, 1962.

Matthiessen, Peter. *Partisans*. New York: Viking, 1955.

McAuliffe, Mary Sperling. *Crisis on the Left: Cold War Politics and American Liberals, 1947–1954*. Amherst: U of Massachusetts P, 1978.

McCarthy, Mary. "The Fact in the Fiction." *Partisan Review* 27 (Summer 1960): 438–58.

McNally, Dennis. *Desolate Angel: Jack Kerouac, the Beat Generation, and America*. New York: McGraw-Hill, 1980.

Miller, Douglas T., and Marion Nowak. *The Fifties: The Way We Really Were*. New York: Doubleday, 1977.

Miller, Richard H. *The Evolution of the Cold War: From Confrontation to Containment*. New York: Holt, Rinehart, 1972.

Mills, C. Wright. *Power, Politics, and People: The Collected Essays of C. Wright Mills*. Ed. Irving Louis Horowitz. New York: Ballantine, 1963.

Mills, Hilary. *Mailer: A Biography*. New York: Empire Books, 1982.

Mills, Nicolaus. *American and English Fiction in the Nineteenth Century: An Antigenre Critique and Comparison*. Bloomington: Indiana UP, 1973.

Mizener, Arthur. "The Novel of Manners in America." *Kenyon Review* 12 (Winter 1950): 1–19.

Morrell, David. *John Barth: An Introduction*. University Park: Pennsylvania State UP, 1976.

Murphy, Geraldine. "The Politics of Reading *Billy Budd*." *ALH* 1 (Summer 1989): 361–82.

Neal, Larry. "Ellison's Zoot Suit." *Black World* 20 (December 1970): 31–52.

Negro Quarterly: A Review of Negro Life and Culture: Numbers 1–4. New York: Negro Universities P, 1969.

Niebuhr, Reinhold. *The Children of Light and the Children of Darkness: A Vindication of Democracy and a Critique of Its Traditional Defense.* New York: Scribners, 1944.

Niebuhr, Reinhold. *The Irony of American History.* New York: Scribners, 1952.

O'Connor, Flannery. *The Complete Stories.* Edited and introduced by Robert Giroux. New York: Farrar, 1971.

O'Connor, Flannery. *A Good Man Is Hard to Find and Other Stories.* 1955. New York: Harcourt, 1976.

O'Connor, Flannery. *The Habit of Being.* Edited and introduced by Sally Fitzgerald. New York: Farrar, 1979.

O'Connor, Flannery. *Mystery and Manners: Occasional Prose.* Ed. Sally Fitzgerald and Robert Fitzgerald. New York: Farrar, 1961.

O'Connor, Flannery. *Three.* New York: NAL, n.d.

O'Connor, William Van. "The Grotesque in Modern American Fiction." *College English* 20 (1958–59): 342–46.

O'Meally, Robert. *The Craft of Ralph Ellison.* Cambridge: Harvard UP, 1980.

O'Meally, Robert, ed. *New Essays on Invisible Man.* Cambridge, England: Cambridge UP, 1988.

Ortega y Gasset, José. *The Revolt of the Masses.* 1930. London: Unwin, 1961.

Orwell, George. "In the Whale." *A Collection of Essays.* New York: Harcourt, 1953.

"Our Country and Our Culture." *Partisan Review* 19 (May–June 1952): 283–326.

Paul, Sherman. *Olson's Push: Origin, Black Mountain, and Recent American Poetry.* Baton Rouge: Louisiana State UP, 1978.

Pearson, Norman Holmes. "The Nazi-Soviet Pact and the End of a Dream." In Abrams and Levine 438–454. Also in *America in Crisis: Fourteen Crucial Episodes in American History,* ed. Daniel Aaron. New York: Knopf, 1952.

Pease, Donald E. "*Moby Dick* and the Cold War." In *The American Renaissance Reconsidered,* ed. Walter Benn Michaels and Donald E. Pease. Baltimore: Johns Hopkins UP, 1985.

Pease, Donald E. *Visionary Compacts: American Renaissance Writings in Cultural Context.* Madison: U of Wisconsin P, 1987.

Pells, Richard. *The Liberal Mind in a Conservative Age: American Intellectuals in the 1940s and 1950s.* New York: Harper, 1985.

Pells, Richard. *Radical Visions and American Dreams: Culture and Social Thought in the Depression Years.* Middletown: Wesleyan UP, 1973.

Percy, Walker. *The Moviegoer.* 1961. New York: Avon, 1980.

Podhoretz, Norman. *Breaking Ranks: A Political Memoir.* New York: Harper, 1979.

Porter, Carolyn. *Seeing and Being: The Plight of the Participant Observer in Emerson, James, Adams, and Faulkner.* Middletown: Wesleyan UP, 1981.

Prince, Alan. "An Interview with John Barth." *Prism,* Spring 1968, 42–62.

Pynchon, Thomas. *The Crying of Lot 49.* New York: J. B. Lippincott, 1966.

Pynchon, Thomas. "Is It O.K. to Be a Luddite?" *New York Times Book Review,* October 28, 1984, 1, 40–41.

Pynchon, Thomas. *Slow Learner: Early Stories.* Boston: Little, Brown, 1984.

Rahv, Philip. *Image and Idea.* Norfolk, CT: New Directions, 1949.

Rahv, Philip. *The Myth and the Powerhouse.* New York: Farrar, 1965.

Ransom, John Crowe. "The Understanding of Fiction." *Kenyon Review* 12 (Spring 1950): 189–218.

Reich, Wilhelm. *The Mass Psychology of Fascism.* 1933. Trans. Vincent R. Carfagno. New York: Simon and Schuster, 1970.

Reising, Russell. *The Unusable Past: Theory and the Study of American Literature.* New York: Methuen, 1986.

Rideout, Walter B. *The Radical Novel in the United States 1900–1954: Some Interrelations of Literature and Society.* 1956. New York: Hill and Wang, 1966.

Riesman, David, with Nathan Glazer and Reuel Denney. *The Lonely Crowd: A Study of the Changing American Character.* 1950. New Haven: Yale UP, 1961.

Rogin, Michael. *The Intellectuals and McCarthy: The Radical Specter.* Cambridge: M.I.T. Press, 1967.

Rogin, Michael. "Kiss Me Deadly: Communism, Motherhood, and Cold War Movies." *Representations* 6 (Spring 1984): 1–36.

Roth, Philip. "Writing American Fiction." *Reading Myself and Others.* New York: Farrar, 1975.

Sandeen, Eric J. "*The Family of Man* at the Museum of Modern Art: The Power of the Image in 1950s America." *Prospects* 11 (1987): 367–91.

Sartre, Jean-Paul. *Being and Nothingness: An Essay on Phenomenological Ontology.* Introduction and translation by Hazel Barnes. New York: Philosophical Library, 1956.

Sartre, Jean-Paul. *Search for a Method* 1963. Trans. and with an Introduction by Hazel E. Barnes. New York: Knopf, 1967.

Sartre, Jean-Paul. *The Transcendence of the Ego: An Existential Theory of Consciousness.* Translated and with an Introduction by Forrest Williams and Robert Kirkpatrick. New York: Farrar, 1957.

Schaub, Thomas H. "Ellison's Masks and the Novel of Reality." In O'Meally, *New Essays on Invisible Man.*

Schlesinger, Arthur, Jr. "Not Left, Not Right, but a Vital Center." *New York Times Magazine*, April 4, 1948, 7, 44–47.

Schlesinger, Arthur, Jr. *The Vital Center: The Politics of Freedom.* Boston: Houghton Mifflin, 1949.

Schorer, Mark. "Technique as Discovery." *Hudson Review* 1 (September 1948): 67–87.

Singleton, M. K. "Leadership Mirages as Antagonists in *Invisible Man.*" In *Twentieth Century Interpretations of Invisible Man*, ed. John M. Reilly. Englewood Cliffs, N.J.: Prentice-Hall, 1970.

"The Situation in American Writing: Seven Questions." *Partisan Review* (1939). Rpt. in *The Partisan Reader.* New York: Dial, 1946.

Skotheim, Robert A. *Totalitarianism and American Social Thought.* New York: Holt Rinehart, and Winston, 1971.

Smith, Valerie. "The Meaning of Narration in *Invisible Man.*" In O'Meally, *New Essays on Invisible Man.*

Sorrentino, Gilbert. "Remembrances of Bop in New York, 1945–50." *Kulchur* 3, no. 10 (Summer 1963): 70–82.

Spender, Stephen. "New Novels." *Listener* 49 (January 15, 1953): 115.

"The State of American Writing, 1948." *Partisan Review* 15 (August 1948): 855–94.

Stepto, Robert B. *From Behind the Veil: A Study of Afro-American Narrative*. Urbana: U of Illinois P, 1979.

Stepto, Robert B. "Literacy and Hibernation: Ralph Ellison's *Invisible Man*." *Carleton Miscellany* 18 (Winter 1980): 112–41.

Styron, William. "Letter to an Editor." *Paris Review* 1 (Spring 1953): 9–13.

"Such Nice People." *Time* 65 (June 6, 1955): 114.

Tanner, Tony. *City of Words: American Fiction, 1950–1970*. New York: Harper, 1971.

Tate, Allen. *The Man of Letters in the Modern World*. New York: Meridian, 1955.

Tate, Allen. *Reason in Madness: Critical Essays*. New York: Putnam, 1941.

Tatham, Campbell. "Message [Concerning the *Felt* Ultimacies of One John Barth]." *Boundary 2* 3 (1975): 259–87.

Tillich, Paul. *The Courage to Be*. New Haven: Yale UP, 1955.

Trilling, Diana. "The Other Night at Columbia." *Partisan Review* 26 (Spring 1959): 214–30.

Trilling, Lionel. *Beyond Culture: Essays on Literature and Learning*. New York: Viking, 1965.

Trilling, Lionel. *Freud and the Crisis of Our Culture*. Boston: Beacon, 1955.

Trilling, Lionel. *A Gathering of Fugitives*. Boston: Beacon, 1956.

Trilling, Lionel. "George Orwell and the Politics of Truth." In *George Orwell: A Collection of Critical Essays.*, ed. Raymond Williams. Englewood Cliffs: Prentice, 1974.

Trilling, Lionel. *The Middle of the Journey*. 1947. New York: Harcourt, 1975.

Trilling, Lionel. *The Liberal Imagination*. 1950. New York: Scribners, 1976.

Trilling, Lionel. *The Opposing Self: Nine Essays in Criticism*. New York: Viking, 1955.

Trotsky, Leon. *The History of the Russian Revolution*. Vol. 1. New York: Simon and Schuster, 1932.

"The Unbeautiful & Damned." *Time* 58 (September 10, 1951): 106.

Viereck, Peter. *The Unadjusted Man: A New Hero for Americans*. Boston: Beacon, 1956.

Volosinov, V. N. *Marxism and the Philosophy of Language*. Trans. Ladislav Matejka and I. R. Titunik. Cambridge: Harvard UP, 1986.

Wald, Alan M. *The New York Intellectuals: The Rise and Decline of the Anti-Stalinist Left from the 1930s to the 1980s*. Chapel Hill: U of North Carolina P, 1987.

Walhout, Mark. "The New Criticism and the Crisis of American Liberalism: The Poetics of the Cold War." *College English* 49 (December 1987): 861–71.

"WANTED: AN AMERICAN NOVEL." *Life* 39 (September 12, 1955): 48.

Warren, Austin. *Rage for Order: Essays in Criticism*. Chicago: U of Chicago P, 1948.

Warshow, Robert. "The Liberal Conscience in 'The Crucible.'" *Commentary* 15 (March 1953): 265–71.

Washington, Booker T. *Up from Slavery*. 1901. New York: Bantam, 1959.

Webster, Grant. *The Republic of Letters: A History of Postwar American Literary Opinion*. Baltimore: Johns Hopkins UP, 1979.

Wechsler, James. *Reflections of an Angry Middle-Aged Editor*. New York: Random, 1960.

Wellek, René, and Austin Warren. *Theory of Literature*. 1949. 3d ed. New York: Harcourt, 1956.

"What's Wrong with the American Novel?" *American Scholar* 24 (Autumn 1955): 464–503.

Wilson, Edmund. *Classics and Commercials: A Literary Chronicle of the Forties*. 1950. New York: Farrar, 1967.

Wilson, Edmund. *The Triple Thinkers: Twelve Essays on Literary Subjects*. New York: Farrar, 1948.

Winters, Yvor. *In Defense of Reason*. New York: Swallow Press and William Morrow, 1947.

Wise, Gene. *American Historical Explanations: A Strategy for Grounded Inquiry*. Homewood, Ill.: Dorsey, 1973.

Wittgenstein, Ludwig. *Tractatus Logico-Philosophicus*. 1921. Introduction by Bertrand Russell. Trans. D. F. Pears and B. F. McGuinness. London: Kegan Paul, 1961.

Woodward, C. Vann. *The Burden of Southern History*. Baton Rouge: LSU P, 1960.

Wright, John S. "The Conscious Hero and the Rites of Man: Ellison's War." In O'Meally, *New Essays on Invisible Man*.

Wright, Richard. "How 'Bigger' Was Born." *Native Son*. 1940. New York: Harper & Row, 1966.

Writers at Work. Introduction by Van Wyck Brooks. 2d ser. New York: Viking, 1963.

Writers at Work. Introduction by Alfred Kazin. 3d ser. New York: Viking, 1967.

Writers at Work. Ed. George Plimpton. 4th ser. New York: Viking, 1976.

Wylie, Philip. *Generation of Vipers*. New York: Farrar & Rinehart, 1942.

Index